MORE GOD, LESS CRIME

More God, Less Crime

Why Faith Matters and How It Could Matter More

Byron R. Johnson

TEMPLETON PRESS

Templeton Press
300 Conshohocken State Road, Suite 550
West Conshohocken, PA 19428
www.templetonpress.org

Typeset and designed by Gopa & Ted2, Inc.

The Library of Congress has cataloged the hardcover edition
as follows:

Johnson, Byron R.
  More God, less crime : why faith matters and how it could
matter more / Byron R. Johnson.
    p. cm.
  Includes bibliographical references and index.
  Includes bibliographical references.
  ISBN-13: 978-1-59947-373-4 (hardback : alk. paper)
  ISBN-10: 1-59947-373-9 (hardback : alk. paper) 1. Christianity
and justice. 2. Criminology—Religious aspects—Christianity.
3. Crime—Religious aspects—Christianity. 4. Crime prevention.
5. Church work with criminals. I. Title. II. Title: Why faith
matters and how it could matter more.
  BR115.J8J64 2011
  261.8'3360973—dc22

                                                    2010051915

Printed in the United States of America

20 21 22 23 24 25   10 9 8 7 6 5 4 3 2

Contents

Foreword

"MORE GOD, LESS CRIME." Many assume this cause-and-effect statement to be true. Others bridle against the idea, claiming that faith does not enhance virtue or attenuate vice. Byron Johnson masterfully moves us beyond ideology in this debate and shows us the evidence.

In *More God, Less Crime*, Johnson explains that faith-based organizations (FBOs) work, that their programs deliver better citizens. And then, carefully and systematically, he details how and why they do, citing decades of research on the links between religiosity and reductions in delinquent behavior and deviant activities. Without cutting methodological corners, he lays out the statistical impact of religion on crime—relying on, as he puts it, the "differences you can measure."

But he goes further, asking why people object to the patterns in these data. Opposition to embracing the benefits of faith is based, he maintains, on misguided concerns about political correctness, on misplaced fears about proselytism, and on misunderstanding the nature of separation between church and state. After teaching at a wide range of academic institutions for a quarter century, the author knows all too well the hostility toward people of faith and faith-based approaches that exists in large swaths of the academy. What he characterizes as that "last acceptable prejudice" can also be found in government circles, he claims, where bias toward FBOs continues to be an obstacle. "Hostility against faith-based approaches will always exist," he concludes. "But this bias should neither prevent people of faith from trying to confront these problems, or scholars from studying these efforts."

Resistance also exists on the church side of the church-state ledger. Johnson does not pull his punches here either. He rejects the purist views of those in the faith community who declare that they don't need to partner with government, that they shouldn't be "unequally yoked" with secular organizations. Now, he argues, is not a time for separatism or isolation. The stakes are too high, and the potential impact for good too great.

Documenting many examples of the impact of successful sacred-secular partnerships, Johnson introduces us to the Boston Miracle, in which collaboration between church congregations and the Boston Police Department decisively stemmed the tide of violence in that city. And the Amachi experiment in Philadelphia, which mentors the children of incarcerated parents. And the VFZ (Violence Free Zone) initiative in Milwaukee to revitalize public schools in troubled neighborhoods. And the collaboration between the Texas Department of Criminal Justice and Chuck Colson's Prison Fellowship in the Texas InnerChange Freedom Initiative.

These successes are not just isolated anecdotes, Johnson asserts, but rather they are scalable events, capable of replication elsewhere around the country.

Johnson's book outlines a societal win-win: more God, which he argues is good for individuals; less crime, which is obviously good for everybody else. In short, religion can transform the faithful themselves and the communities in which they live. Religion can reduce drug use, domestic violence, delinquency, gang activity, prison recidivism, and other forms of negative behavior. "Religion is a powerful antidote to crime," Johnson states, and religion can promote beneficial outcomes and patterns of behavior as well.

Johnson does not shy away from policy recommendations. He argues forcefully that government should not resist faith-based initiatives but rather embrace them, as the ultimate examples of American enterprise, ingenuity, problem-solving, and can-do. In America we should be able to look beyond ideology and endorse "what works"—a phrase Johnson comes back to repeatedly in this book.

Perhaps even more provocatively for many in the nonprofit world, Johnson argues that FBOs should not resist government, either: faith-based efforts are not sufficient in themselves. Effective as they are, FBOs need powerful partners to solve the problems that beset our communities. Such organizations must find ways of cooperating with others even more; public-private partnerships are his answer. These types of ventures can deliver real and lasting improvements in police-community relations, the raising of at-risk inner-city children, our public schools, gang-based crime, youth homicide, the state of the nation's prisons, prison recidivism, and the lives of the children of prisoners.

This book was written for believers and nonbelievers; for those both critical and sympathetic to his views; for both *nonprofitistas* and government employees. From start to finish, Johnson empirically demonstrates the impact of faith-based partnerships, making the proposition of "more God, less crime" less an act of faith, and more a matter of fact.

Arthur C. Brooks
President, American Enterprise Institute

Introduction

THE CENTRAL ARGUMENT of *More God, Less Crime* is that faith-motivated individuals, faith-based organizations, and the transformative power of faith itself are proven keys in reducing crime and improving the effectiveness of our criminal justice system. We now know that intentional partnerships between congregations and law enforcement can lead to dramatic improvement in police-community relations and reductions in crime, youth violence, and gang activity. We also know that faith-based programs can provide an antidote to the harmful culture that permeates so many of our correctional facilities. In this way, religion can help change prisons from an environment for learning even more deviant behavior to places where rehabilitation is a realistic possibility. Additionally, faith-motivated mentors and faith-based groups can provide both the support and supervision necessary to help not only prisoners but also those former prisoners stay crime-free by leading moral and productive lives.

More God, Less Crime presents empirical evidence in support of these claims and also provides examples of how faith-based approaches are successfully addressing some of the most difficult social problems facing our society. Exemplary programs and best practices suggest how and why faith-based groups should become central allies in comprehensive strategies to improve law enforcement, the courts, and our correctional system. Finally, the book describes how communities of faith are uniquely positioned to become the centerpiece of a new crime-fighting strategy to confront the biggest obstacle of all: the disadvantaged communities from which come the vast majority of those populating our criminal justice system.

Two hundred years ago, *More God, Less Crime* would have been a simple challenge to make to practitioners, decision makers, and the American public. Not so today. "Experts" will almost certainly reject my thesis over concerns about proselytizing, violating church-state separation, and the lack of sufficient evidence to support the notion that faith-based approaches really work. But the real reason that so many will reject *More God, Less Crime* has little to do with the concerns mentioned above. In an age of political correctness, perhaps the last acceptable prejudice is the one leveled against the involvement of highly religious people and their faith-based approaches to social problems—problems the government cannot fix without them.

Because of this prejudice, I expect a mixed response from practitioners and professionals working within the criminal justice field. Among those who attend religious services regularly and tend to be active in their faith, I expect a largely positive response to the argument this book puts forward. After all, the highly religious are largely responsible for the findings, programs, and practices highlighted in the book. Among those who do not attend religious services or who are largely inactive, I expect the findings presented here to do little to change their minds.

Though it is the primary culprit in hindering progress we could otherwise be making, the prejudice toward religion is by no means the only prejudice that prevents faith-based approaches from accelerating. Many faith-motivated individuals and groups hold biases against secular organizations and the government that have both discouraged and prevented the possibility of partnerships forming between the two. Many people within faith-based organizations have little, if any, trust of government programs and even question the state's motives. As a result, many faith-based organizations isolate themselves and become insular. For example, when I have approached leaders of faith-based organizations about the possibility of conducting research or evaluating their organization or programs, I have often been told, "We don't need academic research to validate our work. We answer to God, not to researchers." One of my favorite responses is, "We already know our programs are effective." It is not a surprise, therefore, that many faith-based organizations do not have a history for seeking partnerships with secular entities, even if the ultimate goal—such as crime reduction—is the same.

Book Overview

In section 1 I highlight three very different and yet highly successful faith-based approaches to crime prevention. These exemplary programs prove not only that faith-based strategies and approaches to crime reduction can be successful but also that these efforts can be replicated. Chapter 2 describes the unprecedented reduction of gang violence and youth homicides stemming from the efforts of an intentional partnership between clergy and police to stem the tide of violence in Boston. This chapter documents how congregations and governmental authorities were able to put aside their differences in order to work together and support each other in achieving the common objective of saving lives. The incredible story of the "Boston Miracle" is a remarkable reminder of the ability of faith-based groups to not only initiate but also sustain crime-fighting approaches in our most distressed communities.

Chapter 3 outlines how adult mentors can positively influence the most overlooked and at-risk group in America: children of prisoners. Drawing from inner-city houses of worship, I describe how the Philadelphia-based project called Amachi has changed the way we think and approach mentoring at-risk youth. In spite of the enormous obstacles hindering the replication of any successful intervention, the Amachi model in just ten years has spread to literally hundreds of diverse communities throughout the country. Thousands of children of prisoners are now the beneficiaries of this pathbreaking program.

Chapter 4 illustrates how inner-city schools plagued by gangs and violence can be positively influenced through the efforts of a program called the Violence-Free Zone, which is the brainchild of Robert Woodson, a highly regarded social entrepreneur with a track record for developing positive youth development programs in some of our cities' most disadvantaged communities. The cornerstone of the Violence Free Zone is the presence and mentoring role of Youth Advisors working within the public schools. These youth advisors are individuals from the very same communities and are motivated out of their faith commitments as well as their own personal journeys to assist and mentor youth in public schools and help them make positive and responsible choices, ultimately reducing violence and improving a host of other outcomes.

Section 2 of the book reports on the empirical evidence bolstering the book's premise—that more God leads to less crime. Chapter 5 provides a systematic review of all the studies that have examined the impact of religion on crime. This objective review covers 272 published studies over a sixty-five-year period and represents the largest review of this literature to date. The conclusions from this review provide overwhelming support for the notion that religion is a powerful antidote to crime.

Chapters 6 and 7 are based on an evaluation I completed on the Inner-Change Freedom Initiative (IFI), located outside of Houston, Texas. Operated by Prison Fellowship, IFI was the first faith-based prison program in America. Chapter 6 documents how inmates in IFI and a matched group (i.e., prisoners not participating in the faith-based program) compare when looking at the likelihood of being re-arrested or reincarcerated following release from prison. Chapter 7 describes how the evaluation yielded important insights to inmate behavior, the prison culture, and spiritual development. Furthermore, and most important, the chapter makes important connections between the role of spiritual development and the process of rehabilitation.

Chapter 8 addresses a common concern of religious and nonreligious observers, the sincerity or authentic nature of religious conversions that commonly take place behind bars. This chapter draws on observational work, prison research, and accounts of a number of prisoners who have, for example, become born-again Christians. The chapter provides insights into the potential for spiritual transformation to serve as an important turning point in the life course. In this way, spiritual transformations can be seen as strategic and compelling events that lead to and enhance long-term change.

Section 3 explains how the faith factor is central to the development of a comprehensive crime reduction strategy. I begin by explaining in chapter 9 why religion matters. Though this might seem obvious to highly active religious individuals, the chapter details the many ways in which faith communities are able to make a positive difference in lives impacted by crime. Beyond the transformative power of faith itself, the vast and diverse overlapping volunteer networks of support represent meaningful and essential tools in a holistic approach to combating crime.

Chapter 10 details how the current prisoner reentry crisis can only be confronted effectively through the combined efforts of sacred and secular partnerships. Biases and prejudices on both sides have largely prevented the flourishing of innovative and powerful public-private collaborations. Overcoming the misconceptions and stereotypes that commonly exist can open the possibility for intentionally addressing the many obstacles to prisoner reentry and aftercare. Chapter 11 extends this analysis by showing how intermediary organizations, both faith-based and secular, are the essential but often missing ingredient in coordinated responses to difficult social problems. We need faith, to be sure, but we also need the strategic oversight that only intermediaries can provide if we are to ever be successful in sustaining long-term solutions to the problems that crime poses.

MORE GOD, LESS CRIME

## CHAPTER 1

The Last Acceptable Prejudice

IN AN UNUSUAL but relevant twist, I want to begin this book by sharing in this first chapter a personal experience of mine as a college professor very early in my career. Though I have rarely discussed the experience, it is relevant and informs my predictions regarding the reception—negative and positive—I expect to receive for *More God, Less Crime.*

I come from a large, close-knit Christian family where faith was paramount and the role of education was highly valued. My father was a college professor, and my mother an elementary school teacher. As long as I can remember, the expectation in our home was that each of my siblings (four sisters and two brothers) and I would not only go to college but also to graduate school. And we did.

After graduating from college in three years with a degree in psychology, I immediately enrolled in graduate school and began working on a master's degree in psychology at Middle Tennessee State University (MTSU). After completing my first year of graduate studies, I took a job as a parole officer working for the Tennessee Department of Corrections. I enjoyed the work, and I quickly realized that I needed to shift my educational pursuits from psychology to criminology.

My newfound interest in criminal justice caused me to consider entering a second graduate program in criminology at the University of Tennessee–Chattanooga (UTC). I had to quit the probation job in order to enroll as a full-time student at UTC while completing my thesis at MTSU. I would graduate with a master's degree from MTSU and UTC on consecutive weekends in August 1980.

I moved to Tallahassee two weeks later to begin work on a PhD in criminology at Florida State University (FSU). The choice was an easy one for me. FSU is in the same region of the country as my hometown of Cleveland, Tennessee, and the School of Criminology was widely recognized as offering one of the top programs in the country. I quickly stood out among the cohort of graduate students entering the program as someone who was devoutly religious and had a clean-cut image. I got along well with my fellow graduate students and liked the professors whom I would study under for four years. Though I never felt discriminated against because of my faith, it's fair to say that a few faculty eyebrows raised when I selected religion as my substantive area of study within criminology. Why would anyone select religion as an area of research to pursue? No one had selected this area before, and research on the topic was virtually nonexistent. To his credit, my major professor, Dr. Marc Gertz, fully supported my interest in religion, and he agreed that the scarcity of research on religion and crime was reason enough to pursue the topic.

In 1984 I married, completed my dissertation, and received a tenure-track job appointment in criminal justice at the University of Dayton. I thoroughly enjoyed teaching at Dayton, but a heavy teaching load (four courses per semester) made it difficult to make research the priority I knew it needed to be. After teaching for two years I accepted a tenure-track job at Memphis State University (now the University of Memphis). When I told the dean of Dayton's College of Arts of Sciences, Frank Lazarus, of my job offer at Memphis, he asked if I would consider staying at Dayton, and that he was ready to counter the Memphis offer. I explained that the decision wasn't based on money, but a reduced teaching load and the opportunity to be in a department with a graduate program—factors I was certain would enhance my research productivity. Dean Lazarus indicated he was sad to lose me, stating that while I wasn't of their religious tradition (Dayton is Catholic), I affirmed their tradition and would be sorely missed.

I became a member of the Criminal Justice Department at Memphis in the fall of 1986, and was actively engaged in research, teaching, and service—the three criteria for determining tenure and promotion decisions. Although these three activities are theoretically equal, it is widely understood that far more weight is given to research than teaching or service. "Publish or perish" is an adage commonly accepted within the academic community, especially research universities. Indeed, very few people are denied tenure because they teach poorly or provide little service. Most research universities now instruct junior faculty to avoid service and regularly provide reduced teaching loads initially, making it easier for young faculty to get a quick start on publishing, and hopefully improving the likelihood they won't perish.

My wife and I fell in love with Memphis and planned to stay there. By all accounts I was doing well as an assistant professor. I had very high teaching evaluations, was publishing one or two articles per year in refereed journals, and, to my knowledge, received the first federal grant in the history of the Criminal Justice Department. I was involved in a number of departmental committees and got along with faculty colleagues in my department.

Though my progress seemed to be superior, the department chair's evaluations of me were only average. It became increasingly obvious that being an outspoken Christian agitated the department chair. Forming a Christian faculty fellowship accented his frustration, especially when it became a vibrant presence on the campus. My religious activities, coupled with my research on religion, became an increasing source of resentment for the chair. He told me emphatically that none of my publications appearing in sociology journals focusing on religion would count toward tenure. It did not matter that the journals were peer-reviewed or had excellent standing. As a result, for the next several years I only submitted articles for publication having nothing to do with religion. I changed my entire research agenda for two years—forgoing studies on religion and crime—in an effort not to jeopardize my case for tenure. Colleagues at other universities, some who were religious and others who clearly were not, uniformly expressed shock that a department chair would say an article published in a scholarly journal would not count toward tenure because the subject matter involved religion. They assured me it would be impossible not to have those publications considered during the tenure review process.

In early May 1990, after turning in final grades for the spring semester, the department chair walked into my office with a big smile on his face and handed me a letter from the university president. He stood there and watched me open and read the letter. He stayed in my office until I was finished reading the letter. It was a nonrenewal letter. I had been fired. With a victorious grin, he then turned and walked out of my office without saying anything. I was stunned and devastated. Though I had known the chairperson would not do me any favors when I applied for tenure in the fall—just three months away—I never remotely suspected something like this was possible. I immediately drove home to break the news to my wife. We were heartbroken. We had three kids (ages five, three, and twenty-two months) and had not planned on ever leaving Memphis, much less having to leave academics altogether. After all, how would I be able to get another academic appointment after being fired?

Reading the faculty policy manual I discovered that in the event of termination, there was still the opportunity to meet and discuss the non-renewal with one's respective dean as well as the university provost. I immediately scheduled an appointment with the dean of the College of Arts and Sciences. The meeting lasted every bit of two minutes. I simply asked why I was terminated considering that my student evaluations were high, I had been publishing journal articles in refereed journals, had been awarded a federal grant, was active in university and community service, and had received average evaluations from the department chair. He simply said, "I don't need to have a reason."

Bewildered, I responded, "You're not going to give me a reason?"

He answered, "I can let you go if I don't like the color of your eyes."

The department chair and dean had obviously talked at length about my situation, and I was certain my religious beliefs and activities had frustrated or embarrassed the dean as much as the chairperson.

I next scheduled an appointment with the provost, the second most powerful person on campus. I was optimistic about meeting with the provost because he had on occasion attended the Christian Faculty Fellowship I helped start, and I considered him a friend. As a result of our interaction through the Christian Faculty Fellowship, at his request I agreed to teach a Sunday school class at his church several years earlier. I was certain that meeting with the provost would clear any misunderstanding, and he would quickly realize my termination was a mistake and could not be supported since I had excelled in teaching, research, and service—the three criteria used for evaluating faculty.

I was heartened when he started the meeting by stating he felt bad about the termination and that he hadn't been sleeping well because of it. He indicated he had essentially signed off on a decision that the department chair and the dean of the College of Arts and Sciences supported. I reviewed my record with the provost and indicated I was confident of getting tenure if allowed to apply for it in three months. I also indicated that if he would agree to reverse the termination decision, I would even be willing to waive all rights to appeal, in the event I was turned down for tenure. He said he would consider the matter and get back to me. I left the provost's office feeling like my prospects had improved dramatically and that he was going to reverse his earlier decision.

I waited to hear from the provost and told colleagues, friends, and family I felt the decision would be reversed. As it turns out, I never did hear back from the provost. With the fall semester just days from starting, I scheduled an appointment to see him again. This meeting had a far different feel from the first. He started the meeting by saying he had considered the matter and his previous decision to terminate would stand. He then said, "Byron, I really like you. You're a very nice guy—an honorable person. But the reality is you simply don't fit in here." He then asked if he could give me some personal advice. "I think you need to consider getting a job teaching at some small Christian college, because that's where you'll really fit in."

I responded, "I don't want to teach in a small Christian college. I've done a good job here, and I'm qualified to teach here or another major university."

The provost then added, "Can I be honest with you? If you do end up at another state university, you are going to have the same problem you've had here."

I remember thinking to myself at that moment, *He's essentially saying the "problem" has nothing to with my research, teaching, or service. It was all about my visibility as a Christian.* The pivotal point of the conversation happened when I responded, "If I were a Marxist we wouldn't even be having this conversation, would we?"

The provost nodded in agreement and stated, "You simply run against the grain . . . and you need to end up at a place where your beliefs are a better fit than they are here."

Somehow I mustered up enough nerve to say, "I disagree completely. I am going to get hired at another state university, and I am going to be successful."

Looking back, I genuinely think he hoped I was right, but I knew he thought I was wrong. We shook hands, and the brief meeting was over. Following the meeting with the provost, I was already second-guessing my bold prediction about being able to land a job at another state university. I thought to myself, *Who would want to hire someone who got a terminal contract without even getting the opportunity to apply for tenure?*

Despite my fears I did go on to fulfill my promise to the provost. Within nine years I had helped to establish a major research center at the University of Pennsylvania to study the role of religion in urban society. Although my story took place twenty-one years ago, I tell it here because it exemplifies the kind of antipathy toward religion that unfortunately still pervades secular institutions and prevents them from acknowledging the positive role that religion can play in public life.

And even though my experiences at Penn were largely positive, I believe much of the research we produced made Penn colleagues and administrators uncomfortable. This was because the research we produced continued to find that religion mattered in important and beneficial ways. I believed then, as I do now, that if we could have at least produced some studies documenting religion to be associated with harmful outcomes, Penn would have more intentionally supported the work. As I show in chapter 5, scholars have a hard time documenting that religion is harmful. Thousands of published studies across a diverse range of disciplines find religion, no matter how it is measured, consistently related to positive and beneficial outcomes.

In 2004 I decided to come to Baylor, which was certainly the right choice. Having directed research centers at five different universities, and having interacted with colleagues at scores of other university research centers, I have come to understand that the only way to build and sustain a major research center is to have (1) significant core funding, (2) the unequivocal support of the university administration, and (3) direct and intentional access to donors. Baylor has enthusiastically provided all three, and as a result we continue to expand aggressively our research. With seven distinguished professors, postdocs, graduate students, and close to one hundred resident and nonresident research fellows, the Institute for Studies of Religion (ISR) has become, in less than seven years, the most muscular research center in the world dedicated to the scientific study of religion.

Though it may sound strange, I rarely think back to those days at Memphis State, and I have never been bitter about the experience. How could I? If I hadn't been fired, I might still be there! Writing this chapter has caused me to revisit some of these matters for the first time in twenty years. Looking back, I believe the provost at Memphis State was both spineless and correct in his advice to me. His counsel was essentially this: go teach in a small Christian college because any major university was going to discriminate against me in the same way Memphis State had. This was not only an admission of a very real religious hostility among administrators at Memphis State but, from his point of view, also an indictment of most other major universities.

My twenty-five years of experience within the academy at a wide range of schools confirms that the provost was actually right to suggest that hostility exists toward religion at many American universities. He was right to indicate that a professor who was outspoken about his or her faith would face discrimination. Although I'm no less committed in my faith today than when I received my termination letter in 1990, I am much more careful about how I communicate my faith.

My counsel to young assistant professors is to wait until they have tenure before they become very visible with their faith. Although professors have every right to carry their religious beliefs with them on the college campus, my advice is based on the fact that a distinct antireligious sentiment exists on many campuses, which is especially ironic since so many of our universities started out as religious institutions. The subject of religious discrimination within the academic community is a real one that goes well beyond the scope of this book. However, it is relevant because the hostility I have experienced and observed within the academy looks painfully similar to the discrimination I have witnessed for years against faith-motivated individuals, faith-based organizations, and their faith-infused approaches to any number of social ills.

As a young assistant professor I was making a positive contribution to my discipline and to the life of the university. In the end, it didn't matter because my faith made a few key people uncomfortable. After my departure from Memphis State, I went on to receive recognition for excellence in teaching; my scholarship became recognized within criminology. As evidence of this observation, I was recently asked to write a paper on religion and crime as part of the Presidential Panel series of the 2010 annual meeting of the American Society of Criminology.[1] Francis T. Cullen, a major figure within the field of criminology and former president of the American Society of Criminology as well as the Academy of Criminal Justice Sciences, offered a response to our paper. Cullen admits that despite the empirical evidence indicating religion is important, criminologists have had a blind spot with regard to religion. Cullen states, "The genius of Johnson and Jang's essay, however, is that they ask fellow criminologists to set aside any preexisting predilections and to consider religion in a very secular scientific way."

My research has also been taken seriously in public policy circles.[2] Along the way, I have been fortunate to generate more than $24 million in grant funding—more than a million dollars per year since leaving Memphis. People have asked me if I think those administrators at Memphis State responsible for my termination would have second thoughts if they knew my career would turn out this way. My response? Not likely.

SCALABLE SOLUTIONS

In a similar way, I fear it may not matter that we can prove faith to be a key part of the solution for the problems continuing to plague our criminal justice system. Nonetheless, my hope is that this book might yet provide the impetus for rallying even more "armies of compassion" in the fight against social problems. Hostility against faith-based approaches will always exist, but this bias should not prevent people of faith from trying to confront these problems or scholars from studying these efforts.

The criminal justice system has enormous problems that require effective and scalable solutions. The escalating costs of crime and justice are staggering. The total criminal justice system expenditures for 2006 exceeded $214 billion.[3] This figure does not include the social costs of crime or the costs associated with the fear of crime. Furthermore, these costs do not include the devastating impact of crime on victims or their families. Additionally, the dark side of crime, which refers to crime not reported to police, is another of the unknown costs of crime, not to mention the loss of revenue from having so many people incarcerated that might otherwise be contributing to rather than draining our tax base.

So what is the total cost of crime in America? Remarkably, criminologists have largely ignored this question over the years. According to Mark A. Cohen, an economist at Vanderbilt University who studies the costs of crime, "What I found was a dearth of information on the costs of crime and—more importantly—a serious misuse of the data that was available."[4] For example, Cohen points out a highly regarded study that analyzed an Illinois early-release prison program and its impact on recidivism and costs. The study, published in 1986, determined that reduced prison costs more than offset the cost associated with the slight increase in crimes committed by recidivists (repeat offenders) and concluded that the Illinois early-release program was effective and saved money.[5]

However, Cohen replicated the study and came to the opposite conclusion. Cohen argued that the "costs" of higher crime rates were simply calculated by the out-of-pocket costs such as medical expenses and damaged property. For example, the cost of a rape was estimated to be about $350. Thus, if a prisoner was let out early and committed a rape, the "cost" of that failure was estimated to be $350 plus some nominal fees for criminal justice processing. The study did not consider the pain and suffering of crime victims as a measure of the harm caused by crime. Cohen recalculated the benefit-cost ratios from the Illinois early-release study and found that letting prisoners out early actually cost more in terms of the impact on crime victims than it saved taxpayer dollars for the cost of prisons. In sum, Cohen found the early-release study had far underestimated the total cost of crime by failing to consider the pain and suffering that crime victims experienced.

When one calculates the total costs incurred through private security companies, you can add another $225.8 billion. When one adds the costs associated with time spent securing assets, as well as time spent on neighborhood watch programs, you can add another $90.3 billion. Therefore, the total cost of society's response to crime is $316.1 billion, which doesn't yet include the cost of crime experienced by victims. Sadly, until relatively recently scholars, practitioners, and policy makers have largely ignored crime victims. The Office for Victims of Crime (OVC) was established in 1984, as a result of Ronald Reagan fulfilling his campaign promise to bring attention to the plight of this largely overlooked group. Economists have helped to estimate the total cost per victimization by the number of victimizations in the United States. According to these figures, in 1993, the one-year cost of crime to victims totaled $450 billion,[6] approximately eighteen hundred dollars per year for every person in the United States.

According to Cohen, incorporating other social costs in the equation suggests that the annual cost of crime to society is as much as $1 trillion or more. Economists are helping us understand that the real costs of crime, which include the hidden cost to victims and society, are significantly higher than criminologists have understood. Economists are also correct to suggest that programs or interventions designed to reduce crime, if found to be effective, can save taxpayers a great deal of money.

Not only are faith-based approaches beginning to show promise when it comes to the issue of effectiveness, but they are also incredibly cost-efficient. Many faith-based programs are overwhelmingly staffed by volunteers. Indeed, a number of faith-based organizations are adopting programs that are completely or almost completely volunteer-staffed and -led. Congregations, more than any other institution in America, are volunteer-rich organizations that generate millions of capable and highly talented people that feed these faith-based approaches.[7] This book recognizes and documents how faith-based approaches are already making a difference in confronting key problems. In sum, if only considering costs and benefits from a purely economic perspective, we can no longer afford not to take seriously faith-based approaches to crime reduction. *More God, Less Crime* outlines the pivotal role yet to be played if we can overcome the last acceptable prejudice that continues to hinder partnerships and networks of support where sacred and secular efforts come together in addressing many of our current crime-related problems.

## CHAPTER 2

Preachers Partner with Police to Reduce Gang Violence: The Boston Miracle

The police and the ministers really do have a common goal—keeping kids from getting killed.[1]

IN 1990 VIOLENCE and especially youth violence connected to gang wars and drug-related crimes was escalating to unprecedented levels and was creating many serious problems for multiple neighborhoods within the city of Boston. A record 152 homicides and 1,000 aggravated assaults were reported in 1990. The increasing violence—especially gang violence—horrified Boston citizens and frustrated civic leaders and professionals working within the criminal justice system. The problem was simply too big for the Boston Police Department and other units of local government to handle singlehandedly. Faced with a struggling economy in the early 1990s, and an inability to address the rise in violence through conventional means, there was, by necessity, a need to consider new approaches. In an unprecedented series of partnerships and cooperative work on the part of the entire city, something very special happened that would become known as the Boston Miracle.[2]

Among the most publicized critics of the Boston Police Department at this time were members of the religious community, and especially a number of key African American clergy. A dramatic and shocking event in May 1992, however, would mark a turning point for a number of Boston's African American congregations, and would finally bring them together to address a common problem: out-of-control youth and gang violence.

Robert Odom, age twenty, was killed as the result of a drive-by shooting led by local gang members. As some three hundred people gathered for Odom's funeral on May 14, mourners were horrified when gang members violently disrupted the service by chasing another youth into the funeral service at Morning Star Baptist Church. While grieving over the senseless murder of one youth, they found themselves observing the beating and stabbing of another youth at the funeral service. The shootout at Morning Star Baptist Church represented an unimaginable and horrific act; the violent crime spree at Odom's funeral caused initial pandemonium, but it was quickly replaced by a new resolve to action. The unthinkable act served to galvanize and inspire a number of urban pastors and congregations not only to organize but also to respond in a far different way from their previous exchanges and interactions with Boston law enforcement.

Led by local ministers, a coalition made the decision to take on the responsibility of engaging the lives of young people who seemingly had little hope of escaping the violence and destructive behavior that had become so prevalent in many of the troubled neighborhoods and areas of greater Boston, including Dorchester and Mattapan. The Reverend Eugene Rivers, pastor of the Azusa Christian Community in Dorchester—one of the more visible leaders of the TenPoint Coalition, and a frequent as well as outspoken critic of Boston police—led the charge in replacing opposition with collaboration. Other prominent leaders included Rev. Ray Hammond, pastor of the Bethel AME Church in Dorchester, and Rev. Jeffrey Brown, pastor of the Union Baptist Church in Cambridge.[3] In order to better understand what actually happened, I interviewed Rev. Brown and asked him to reflect on the role of the church and faith-motivated people in reducing violence in Boston.

> I started in ministry at Union Baptist Church in Cambridge, Massachusetts, fresh out of seminary. I initially thought that good teaching and preaching would be the ticket for attracting young people to our church. It didn't take long in full-time ministry before I noticed several disturbing things: (1) young people in the neighborhood weren't connecting with our church, and (2) with increasing regularity I was officiating or attending funerals of teenagers from our community. Violence

and homicides were happening for trivial reasons. A wrong look, a comment about someone's clothes, or something so seemingly insignificant could lead to violence and even death.

This came to a head on January 21, 1990. I'll never forget that date, when two kids were killed next to my church. Jesse McKie and Roberto Carrion were residents of a local housing project and were running from members of a rival gang. They were running toward our church when they were killed. They were simply running for their lives and they were headed toward the church, but there was nothing going on at the church—no one was home. Jesse died within one hundred yards from my church. The closer I looked at the situation, the more difficult it was to reconcile these realities with my calling as a pastor.

I wrestled with this paradox for some time, and I came to realize the gulf between me and these kids was huge, even though I wasn't that much older than them. All the sermonizing I was delivering on building community was missing the mark. This struggle helped me realize the Lord was calling us to go outside the four walls of our church. I began to finally realize the need to redefine what community actually meant if I was going to successfully engage these kids with God's love. From that point on we didn't wait for the youth to come to us. We started going directly to them. In order to meet them where they were, we had to be intentional about the community we had been neglecting.[4]

These ministers intentionally reached out to at-risk youth in an effort to listen and learn and to begin building solid relationships. This was the beginning of the TenPoint Coalition, an alliance of inner-city ministers whose mission was and remains to mobilize the Christian community on behalf of black and Latino youth, especially those at risk for violence, drug abuse, and other destructive behaviors.[5] Unlike most social service organizations that simply react to social problems like crime and delinquency, faith-motivated leaders in Boston became intentional and proactively engaged gang leaders and at-risk youth. The police or other social-service providers could not have led or undertaken this strategy.

Because these ministers knew the community, as well as the troublemakers within their neighborhoods, and because local residents respected the ministers, this clergy-led movement was able to establish itself as a force that could be trusted. The Boston TenPoint Coalition would grow to become an ecumenical group comprising approximately forty-five to seventy churches, whose clergy and lay leaders work to transform the culture of violence in the Greater Boston community, one neighborhood at a time, and one young person at a time.[6]

To fully appreciate the magnitude of these developments, recognize that relations between African American community leaders and Boston police were deeply strained for many years prior to the events of May 1992. Rivers was known for his relentless complaining about the law enforcement community and had a well-deserved reputation as a cop basher. However, the TenPoint Coalition would be the organizational catalyst for a seismic shift in relations between the African American community and the Boston law enforcement community. In a dramatic reversal, partnership and teamwork would replace the antagonism between clergy and police.[7] The TenPoint Coalition and their Ten Point Plan for the 21st Century promote ten distinct action steps to help youth develop more positive and productive lifestyles:

1. Promote and campaign for a cultural shift to help reduce youth violence, both physically and verbally, within the Black community by initiating conversations, introspection, and reflection on the thoughts and actions that hold us back as a people individually and collectively.

2. Develop, as churches, a curriculum regarding Black and Latino history with an emphasis on the struggles of women of color to help young people understand that the God of history has been and remains active in all our lives.

3. Acknowledge and respond to the impact of trauma as a physical and emotional reality on the lives of our young people and their families as a direct result of violence.

4. Build meaningful relationships with high-risk youth by recognizing their reality on their terms and in their spaces.

5. Focus specially on connecting and rebuilding the lives of youth who have been incarcerated and stigmatized by mainstream society.

6. Provide youth advocacy and one-on-one mentoring for high-risk youth.

7. Provide gang mediation and intervention for high-risk youth with the goal of establishing cease-fires and building the foundation for active peace.

8. Establish accountable, community-based economic development projects that are organic visions of revenue generation and demystify the accumulation and power of money through financial literacy.

9. Build partnerships with the social/secular institutions of our city, with suburban and downtown communities of faith to help provide spiritual, human, and material support.

10. Provide ongoing training for individual churches along with a systematic program in leadership development to create, maintain, and sustain community mobilization.[8]

When referring to the state of the communities where their congregations were located, pastors agreed with Rivers's contention that "the black church is the last institution standing." Additionally, and perhaps most important, the ministers of the TenPoint Coalition have become an intermediary, if you will, between police and local residents.[9] In this intermediary role, these clergy are simultaneously viewed as vocal advocates for youth and legitimate partners with police and governmental authorities. They have earned the trust of both constituencies. According to Harvard scholars Jenny Berrien and Christopher Winship, the TenPoint Coalition created an umbrella of legitimacy for police to work under, whereby police were sheltered from public criticism while engaged in activities deemed by the ministers to be in the interest of the community and its youth.[10]

At the same time the TenPoint Coalition was emerging, another major development was taking place. In 1992 the Boston Police Department would launch a unique model of community policing, by combining crime prevention and law enforcement with close daily work by the police and a broad segment of community-based groups and residents. This model included a major retraining of the police force, with a focus on how to work with diverse cultures and groups. In a series of unprecedented problem-solving retreats, police, elected leaders, community groups, church leaders, and gang members came together to develop a new approach to community safety. Working together, they would build a new model that was unique, influential, and compelling.

During the 1990s the number of homicides in Boston dropped dramatically from a high of 152 in 1990 to 31 in 1999. Indeed, between August 1995 and January 1998 Boston had not one teenage homicide victim. To most reasonable observers, two and a half years with no teenage homicides looked very much like a miracle. Homicides during the 1990s declined by 80 percent. Further, complaints against police dropped by over 60 percent during the same period.[11] The dramatic results that followed received national attention, and Rev. Rivers, one of the visible leaders of the TenPoint Coalition, would find himself on the cover of *Newsweek* in June 1998, and the lead story "God vs. Gangs" would chronicle the Boston Miracle.

Since 1992 the faith community has remained a central figure in Boston's ongoing efforts to address crime, gangs, and youth violence. Though homicides have jumped several times over the years since the collaboration started, the overall rates have remained significantly lower. Collaboration between police and clergy has led to a host of joint efforts that are still active at the present time. For example, weekly meetings at the Ella J. Baker House (a social service ministry of Rev. Rivers's Azusa Church) bring together a wide range of community agencies and groups to strategize about what's working and what modifications may be needed to more effectively address current problems. The TenPoint Coalition has also developed a number of ongoing collaborative programs designed to confront the violence, crime, drugs, and other problems that youth face. These include Crisis Intervention Services, which is integrated into all Boston TenPoint Coalition programs; Fly Girls, which provides street-level support specifically for gang-involved or -affiliated girls and seeks to build personal strength, values, and character and thus help young women avoid violence, abuse, drugs, and prostitution; Gang Mediation and Intervention, which negotiates successful truces and ceasefires through a series of summits; and the Re-Entry Initiative, which provides mentoring and basic services to ex-offenders as they prepare to return to the local community.[12]

Those skeptical of the Boston Miracle have correctly noted there was also a noticeable drop in youth violence in a number of other American cities (e.g., Detroit, Dallas, Houston, Los Angeles, New York, San

Antonio, and San Diego) during the early 1990s. On the other hand, during the same time period, there was little change in the rates of violence in other cities (e.g., Baltimore, Chicago, Las Vegas, Phoenix, San Jose, and Washington, DC). Since some cities saw a drop and others did not, one can argue that the drop in violence in Boston was simply due to chance or some other possible explanation. The best available evidence, however, suggests that the drop in violence and homicides was due to the Boston strategy and not chance. Results of a rigorous and systematic evaluation of the Boston experience by Anthony Braga and other researchers from Harvard's Kennedy School of Government focused on Operation Ceasefire (also known as the Boston Gun Project), a youth gun violence strategy, first implemented in Boston in 1996.[13]

Operation Ceasefire was an interagency intervention that focused attention on a small number of chronically offending gang-involved youth. These high-risk youth were believed to be responsible for a significant portion of the city's youth violence problem. A central component of Operation Ceasefire was regularly scheduled forums involving police, ministers, individuals from social service agencies, and criminal justice personnel. The clergy and congregations associated with the Ten-Point Coalition were a vital component of Operation Ceasefire. Most observers, including the Boston police commissioner, Paul Evans, and other local leaders of city government, have been quick to credit the drop in violence to the pivotal work of a group of ministers and the ongoing influence of the TenPoint Coalition, and the congregations they represent. This is not meant to imply that policing strategies associated with Operation Ceasefire were otherwise ineffective. Quite the opposite: leaders of the TenPoint Coalition were known to publicly praise the outstanding work of the police and regularly honored "good cops."[14] In sum, the Boston Miracle was a team effort, and the success was something all the partners could share equally.

In the spring of 1997 President Bill Clinton traveled to Boston to announce a national community safety and anticrime initiative based on Boston's successful model. President Clinton was keenly aware that the key to the Boston Miracle was a partnership between city government, the Boston Police Department, the district attorney, and a host of highly committed community-based groups, especially the leadership and commitment of the TenPoint Coalition.

Successful violence reduction efforts like Operation Ceasefire in Boston involved the TenPoint Coalition as primary partners from the outset.[15] Because of its documented success in Boston, Operation Ceasefire has been successfully implemented in Los Angeles; Chicago; Washington, DC; Fayetteville, North Carolina; and a number of cities in New Jersey.[16] Early returns generally look very positive for Operation Ceasefire in these other jurisdictions. For example, an evaluation of Operation Ceasefire in Chicago found the program significantly reduced shootings and killings. The Chicago study, funded by the National Institute of Justice, confirms Operation Ceasefire to be an evidence-based intervention, with a moderate to large impact, and with effects that are immediate.[17]

Due to the successful collaboration between the TenPoint Coalition and other agencies and groups, the faith community has become an important ally to city leaders when planning to enact new programs designed to reduce crime and violence in Boston. Leaders within local government and especially law enforcement have continued to intentionally seek out the counsel and contribution of clergy and the faith community.

The Boston Miracle is appropriately named. Though there are thousands of congregations in Boston, just a handful of congregations and clergy working together with police, probation, and other community groups dramatically reduced youth violence. Imagine the possibilities had a significant portion of congregations come alongside the TenPoint Coalition. What if suburban churches had decided to partner with inner-city congregations in Boston, and were fully committed to realizing the TenPoint Coalition's motto: *Reshape Lives—Rebuild Communities*?

The work of the TenPoint Coalition continues, and today the faith-based nonprofit is as vibrant as ever. According to the Reverend Jeffrey Brown, one of the founding pastors and currently the executive director of the TenPoint Coalition, the Coalition continues to work in a coordinated matter with police, probation, the courts, community-based groups, and congregations in order to improve the life prospects of Boston's at-risk youth. Rev. Brown says he can tell stories about young people who have made it as a result of the TenPoint Coalition's intervention, but he thought it was perhaps even more important to tell a story of one who did not make it:

His name was Selvin Brown, and he was the first drug dealer I encountered in Boston in 1992. He was the mentee of Rev. Eugene Rivers and Mark Scott (a minister in Rev. Rivers's church). "Sal," as we liked to call him, also became our mentor of the streets. In his mid-twenties, he ran a crew in Dorchester called the HQ Boyz, and he was our guide, taking us to every crackhouse, whorehouse, and street corner in the community he ruled. Sal felt very strongly that, if we were going to "take his place" in the streets, that we had to understand the street culture. He was extremely bright, and ran his operation like a business (all computerized). He disliked the organized church, but was very open (as we found is often the case) to having extensive discussions about spirituality. We in turn would challenge Sal to change his ways—and he did.

He gave up his leadership position in the gang. We in turn tried to find him a decent job. But that proved to be very difficult. Sal had an extensive criminal past, and many employers were reluctant to take a chance with him. We arranged to get him into a Christian college in the South, but he came back weeks later, unable to stay away from Boston for long. Sal started to feel pressure to "get back into the drug game" because, we found out later, he was supporting his family as a dealer. One weekend, he bought some drugs from his old colleagues to sell and make some quick money. While preparing them that evening, he and his girlfriend decided to use some, and they both overdosed. She eventually woke up, he didn't. What added to the tragedy was that on the following Monday, an internship Gene Rivers fought for came through for Sal. Perhaps the internship would have been a key turning point that finally helped make the difference for Sal to stay the course. Maybe we were that close.

I wanted to tell his story because Sal is typical of the living stories we encounter every day on the streets. We don't tend to encounter situations like this within the four walls of our churches. That is why I hope and pray that others will respond to the same calling—to meet and engage these kids in the streets, neighborhoods, and communities we can no longer afford to ignore.

CONGRESS WANTS TO KNOW WHAT WORKS

In 1996 Congress commissioned a report to determine the effectiveness of Department of Justice (DOJ) funding and the most appropriate way to use funding in the future. Congress essentially wanted to determine which of the approaches to preventing crime worked, which did not, and which were promising. The report would provide an in-depth evaluation of crime prevention programs funded by the Department of Justice.[18] Led by Lawrence Sherman and a team of respected scholars, the results from this exhaustive review were mixed; some prevention programs work, some do not, some are promising, and some have not been tested adequately. The report concludes that the effectiveness of DOJ funding depends heavily on whether it is directed to the urban neighborhoods where youth violence is highly concentrated. Additionally, it concludes that significant reductions in rates of serious crime can only be achieved by prevention efforts in areas of concentrated poverty, where the major-ity of all homicides in the nation occur, and where homicide rates are twenty times the national average.[19]

The report suggests that crime prevention efforts directed to these high-risk areas are not well understood and that there is a need to pro-vide better guidance about what works, especially in these high-crime areas. Consequently, the report recommends significant crime preven-tion funds be dedicated to rigorous scientific testing. The results of such research would make it possible to isolate the factors behind programs' effectiveness and provide a road map for replicating these exemplary practices across the nation.

The report investigated six key institutional settings believed to be important: community, family, school, labor markets, places, and the criminal justice system. I was not surprised to see that religion was missing from this list of important institutions that the research team would be investigating. I found it troubling, however, to learn that the report contains virtually no references to the work of religious institu-tions, faith-based organizations, and religious or spiritual programs that have long been engaged in efforts to reduce crime and delinquency. This balance is especially noteworthy since faith-based institutions and so many of the programs they offer to combat crime and delinquency tend to occur in exactly the high-risk areas the report reminds us are not well understood and acknowledges should be the primary focus of programs and research addressing crime reduction and prevention.

In fairness to the report, it is largely based on scientific evaluations of programs and interventions that the DOJ previously funded. While a substantial and growing body of empirical research links increasing religiosity to crime reduction (as is documented in chapter 7), government-funded evaluations of faith-based organizations and initiatives attempting to reduce or prevent crime have been rare. Without federal funding, not surprisingly, social scientists have rarely conducted rigorous evaluations of faith-based efforts. Consequently, Sherman and colleagues did not have DOJ-funded evaluation research on faith-based organization to include in the report.

If faith-based approaches to social problems are not new and are prevalent, the obvious question is, why has the government, at a minimum, not asked for evaluations of faith-based initiatives purporting to reduce crime, treat drug addicts, and rehabilitate prisoners? I contend that the failure of the federal government to call for the study and evaluation of the role of religion in crime reduction is yet another example of the last acceptable prejudice outlined in chapter 1. Like the academy, the federal government has exhibited a long-standing antireligious sentiment.

Vincent Phillip Munoz, a political scientist, maintains that governmental hostility toward religion is not new and can be found in the rulings of the Supreme Court. Munoz writes, "The Supreme Court of the United States remains primarily responsible for the continued legal hostility towards religious expression in the public square." Munoz also argues that the Supreme Court has interpreted the Establishment Clause in a manner that encourages and sometimes demands hostility toward religion.[20]

This governmental bias against religion and faith-based organizations was documented in a report published by the White House itself, not long after the Office on Faith-Based and Community Initiatives was established in January 2001. The report, *Unlevel Playing Field*, documents the paltry funding of faith-based organizations (FBOs). The scarcity of funding to FBOs is glaring when one considers the overrepresentation

of FBOs in the provision of many social services and crime reduction efforts in poverty-stricken communities—the same at-risk places
the report to Congress suggested should be the focus of intervention.[21]
Simply put, FBOs have not been treated fairly by the government, and
Unlevel Playing Field was an admission of this fact as well as a wakeup
call that the bias had to end. This indictment of the government's hostility toward religion is summed up best in the conclusion of *Unlevel
Playing Field*:

> The Federal Grants process, despite a few exceptions and a
> growing sensitivity to and openness toward both faith-based
> and community groups, does more to discourage than to wel-
> come the participation of faith-based and community groups.
> That is the overwhelming message trumpeted in the reports of
> the Centers for Faith-Based & Community Initiatives at HUD,
> HHS, Justice, Education, and Labor. Too much is done that
> discourages or actually excludes good organizations that sim-
> ply appear "too religious"; too little is done to include groups
> that meet local needs with vigor and creativity but are not as
> large, established, or bureaucratic as the traditional partners of
> the Federal government. This is not the best way for govern-
> ment to fulfill its responsibilities to come to the aid of needy
> families, individuals, and communities. Government must do
> a far better job at equipping and empowering America's social
> entrepreneurs—the quiet heroes, from North Central Phila-
> delphia to South Central Los Angeles, that are conquering
> social ills in every corner of America.[22]

Perhaps the idea of studying faith-based approaches never entered
the minds of those working within federal agencies, or worse, it did, but
was assumed to be irrelevant. Either explanation reflects a strong bias
against religion. The same could be said for criminologists and social
scientists who have designed major longitudinal studies of crime and
delinquency over the last three or four decades and have all but excluded
religion and religious variables. It's hard to study religion when religion
variables are missing from so many of our main data sets. Since 2001
this unfortunate oversight has been slowly changing as federally funded

evaluations of faith-based efforts are no longer an oddity. Though progress has been made, much more systematic evaluation is needed on the
role of religious and faith-based organizations in confronting crime and
delinquency.

Because of the willingness to consider a sacred-secular partnership
that was coordinated and comprehensive, something special happened
that captured the hearts and minds of people not only in Boston but
elsewhere around the country. We do not know how many youth turned
from crime, violence, and drug abuse to pursuing a crime-free life, but
the number is not small. Rev. Jeffrey Brown sums things up this way:

> Looking back on these experiences over the last several
> decades, I have learned that faith calls us to action, and that
> also means faith calls us to take risks. After all these years, I
> can see Peter's paradox: Being on the rough water with Jesus
> is safer than riding in the boat with the other eleven. I went
> from being one of the eleven disciples remaining in the boat—
> afraid to move—to being more like Peter, and willing to get
> out of the boat to walk on the rough water. All these years later,
> it's still about having the faith to take risks. I think respond-
> ing to God's calling really boils down to being willing to take
> risks. That's why after twenty-two years of being a full-time
> pastor, I resigned from my church to be the executive direc-
> tor of the TenPoint Coalition. The important collaboration we
> have enjoyed with so many groups is not something I was even
> thinking about twenty-two years ago. Back then, it was all
> about how the church itself could matter. I've come to realize
> that we're called to be there, in the community itself. Though
> I don't shepherd a congregation at this time, I'm still minister-
> ing and being a pastor, just on a completely different path than
> the one I was originally trained to follow.

## CHAPTER 3

Children of Prisoners: People of Faith Mentoring Children of Promise

Amachi—who knows but what God has brought us through this child.

IMAGINE FOR A MOMENT that you are a young child and that your mother was in and out of prison your whole life, and at the same time your father was largely absent. Imagine you were raised in a housing project or some other impoverished neighborhood and that your grandmother was left with the task of raising you. Imagine that as a child you were raised in an environment where you were regularly exposed to crime, drugs, violence, and abuse. Imagine being raised in a community where many youth do not complete school and the expectation is that young girls have children very early in life and young boys assume they may well end up in prison or be dead before they reach the age of twenty-five. This scenario is not far-fetched for many kids and adolescents today. This chapter discusses a program designed to counter these tragic realities and concludes with a true story that could have had a similarly tragic ending if not for the program highlighted in this chapter. Let me explain.

In 2007 an estimated 744,200 state and federal prisoners in the United States were fathers to 1,599,200 children under the age of 18.[1] Factor in female prisoners who have children, and some researchers have suggested that as many as 2 million children in the United States currently have an incarcerated parent. When one thinks of crime victims, however, children of prisoners do not typically come to mind. Neglect, abuse, poverty, and others challenges confronted by children of prisoners make them one of the most disadvantaged groups in our society. As might be expected, children of prisoners go on to be overrepresented in the criminal justice system.[2]

What is worse, the estimate of 2 million children of prisoners only represents the tip of the iceberg. Consider that approximately 700,000 prisoners—a little less than half the total U.S. prison population—are released from America's prisons each year.[3] In addition to the current 2 million children of prisoners, add another roughly 1 million children of prisoners who may have a parent leaving prison each year. Over just the last five years, some 7 million children have likely either had a parent in prison or released from prison. Further, these estimates do not consider the large number of children who have or have recently had a parent incarcerated in jail.[4] By any measure, children of prisoners represent a very large group. In order to break the cycle of incarceration, children of prisoners cannot be overlooked any longer.

The cycle of imprisonment among large numbers of individuals, mostly minority men, is increasingly concentrated in poor, urban communities that already have enormous social and economic disadvantages.[5] Most prisoners are confronted with numerous difficulties when leaving prison. Housing, transportation, employment, and trying to reconnect with families are just some of the factors most ex-prisoners are ill-prepared to navigate. To put it bluntly, most ex-prisoners are returning to negative and unwelcoming environments.[6]

So challenging for ex-prisoners is this reentry process that many fall prey to substance abuse and other major health risks.[7] In fact, a recent study of all inmates released from prison in Washington state from July 1999 through December 2003 shows that the risk of death among former inmates was 3.5 times higher than comparable residents during a 1.9-year follow-up period. Even more striking, during the first two weeks after release from prison, the risk of death among former inmates was 12.7 times that among other state residents. The leading causes of death among former inmates were drug overdose, cardiovascular disease, homicide, and suicide.[8] These data provide a gloomy but realistic picture of what many children of prisoners face when an incarcerated parent comes home.

The Plight of Children of Prisoners

When parents are incarcerated, the lives of their children can be disrupted in many tragic ways. A change in the child's caregivers or the addition of a new member to the household can be quite traumatic.[9] For children who reside with a parent who becomes incarcerated, this may result in foster care placement and the introduction of new family members as well as reliance on nonparent adults for care.[10] Repeated changes in family relationships are a common source of disruption in children's lives.[11] The potential instability and insecurities surrounding caregivers can be deeply distressing for children and youth.[12] Consider that children of prisoners are more likely to observe parental substance abuse, perform poorly in school, and experience extreme poverty and disadvantage.[13] Knowing these formidable challenges, it's not surprising that children of prisoners are more likely to experience aggression, anxiety, and depression.[14]

It gets worse. Children of prisoners are at risk for alcohol and drug abuse, delinquency and crime, gang involvement, and subsequent incarceration.[15] Parental criminality is a correlated risk factor for juvenile delinquency, and the relationship between the incarceration of a parent and a variety of antisocial behaviors among their children is common.[16] Further, research shows that issues of social stigma and isolation are prominent, and that families often deceive children about the whereabouts of incarcerated parents.[17] Taken together, these toxic factors often lead children of prisoners into early and frequent contact with the criminal justice system. For many children of prisoners there is likely little hope for living a full life, and an expectation of following a similar path as their incarcerated parent.[18] Unfortunately, research confirms that such expectations are warranted. Children of prisoners experience much higher rates of criminal behavior and subsequent incarceration.[19] These disturbing statistics are a reminder of the urgent need for intervention strategies to prevent these adverse outcomes for children of prisoners. Finally, we need systematic research to help us determine the effectiveness of these interventions.[20]

The Need for Mentors and Purpose in
the Lives of Children

Research has shown that the personal effects of purposelessness can result in a sense of drift that may lead to problem behaviors, including depression and addictions. Stated simply, the absence of purpose may result in deviant or destructive behavior. In contrast, we know that mentors and the development of purpose in the lives of youth can prevent problem behaviors. Having purpose during adolescence is a predictor of positive behavior, moral commitment, achievement, and high self-esteem.[21]

Children find purpose through role models and participation in mentoring groups, which provide the means to discover and commit to purpose. Mentors, parents, and other positive role models are potential sources of purpose for children and youth. Access to these positive role models is essential to motivating youth to develop plans for their life. Like role models, positive environments allow youth to develop purpose. Religious congregations, for example, have the potential to help youth develop purpose as well as a way to feel connected to their community.[22] Members of houses of worship can help youth develop purpose, character, and moral values. Youth impacted by incarceration may find inspiration for developing purpose through relationships with mentors who model prosocial behavior.[23]

We know mentoring matters in the lives of at-risk youth.[24] Mentoring may also help youth to develop life plans with a sense of purpose and meaning.[25] There is additional evidence that children who have longer-lasting relationships with mentors (i.e., relationships lasting at least a year) have higher levels of self-competence and school engagement, have more positive relationships with their parents, and are less likely to use drugs and alcohol.[26] In general, youth mentoring programs are effective at increasing children's well-being, improving academic competence and achievement, and reducing problem behaviors.[27] In a systematic review of fifty-five studies of mentoring programs, it was concluded that nearly 90 percent of the analyses resulted in positive effects for youth.[28] We know that resilient youth—those who successfully transition out of disadvantaged backgrounds to the world of work and good citizenship—tend to be set apart by the presence of a caring adult in their lives.[29] In sum, the best research supports the notion that strong mentoring relationships encourage positive youth development and deter risky youth behavior.[30]

This knowledge begs the more important question, is it possible to create a partnership that intentionally engages very large numbers of children of prisoners and then matches them with caring adult volunteers in one-on-one mentoring relationships? If so, is it possible that interventions reaching so many children of prisoners could also provide the screening, training, and management necessary to sustain these mentoring relationships? No precedent exists for such a massive infusion of mentors, especially considering that the target—children of prisoners—is one of the most at-risk and difficult populations to locate and match with mentors.

MENTORING CHILDREN OF PRISONERS: A PHILADELPHIA EXPERIMENT

During the fall of 1999 John DiIulio Jr. recruited me to join him in launching the Center for Research on Religion and Urban Civil Society (CRRUCS) at the University of Pennsylvania (Penn). A prominent political scientist and public policy expert, DiIulio had just returned to Penn (his alma mater) after thirteen years in the Department of Politics at Princeton University. DiIulio and I had become good friends as a result of our shared interests in the role of religion in combating crime and delinquency.

DiIulio had a number of ambitious plans surrounding the launch of CRRUCS at Penn, but one of them was particularly striking—a comprehensive strategy to provide one-on-one mentoring to children of incarcerated and formerly incarcerated parents in Philadelphia. DiIulio envisioned a plan that would bring together churches, a top mentoring organization, a faith-based prison ministry, an organization for creating programs that improve the lives of low-income communities, a major university research center, and last, a foundation that might consider backing this collaborative effort with substantial funding.[31]

The ambitious plan would seek to attract a number of unlikely partners:

(1) inner-city congregations (mainly African American churches); (2) Public/Private Ventures (P/PV), a well-known and respected research and evaluation firm; (3) Prison Fellowship, a national prison ministry founded by Chuck Colson; (4) Big Brothers/Big Sisters—a national leader in the mentoring of children; (5) CRRUCS, the new Penn center dedicated to producing research on religion and urban society; and (6) the Pew Charitable Trusts, a Philadelphia-based foundation.

Pulling this unlikely group of sacred and secular organizations together would not be easy. Being privy to these initial deliberations, I remember how excited and uneasy people felt about such a partnership. For example, Big Brothers/Big Sisters (BBBS) was more than a little reluctant to partner so intentionally with churches. Prison Fellowship, an overtly Christian prison ministry, had obvious reservations about such a unique collaboration that would be led by a secular organization (P/PV). Finally, there was concern it might not be possible to gain the trusts of key African American clergy and churches in the city of Philadelphia.

In the end, most of the reservations people had about the project gave way to the enormous good most believed was possible to achieve through this partnership. BBBS got over its fear of partnering with churches shortly after DiIulio suggested (tongue-in-cheek) if a deal couldn't be reached with BBBS, it may be necessary to start a separate organization—Big Brother/Big Sisters in Christ—to provide the mentoring component. After months of meetings, the Pew Charitable Trusts would agree to provide significant funding to Public/Private Ventures to oversee this unprecedented collaboration. The project would be called Evergreen Youth Ministries, and would be launched at a special event on September 15, 2000, at Greater Exodus Baptist Church.[32] However, only days after the launch, there was a setback, and Prison Fellowship ceased to be a partner in the project. P/PV made the necessary adjustments and quickly scramble for a new name for the collaboration. The new name would be Amachi, a Nigerian Ibo word that reportedly means "who knows but what God has brought us through this child." By November 2000, Amachi was officially ready to move forward. Drawing on the central role of faith-motivated volunteers for mentors to bring hope to children of prisoners, Amachi's motto would become, "People of faith mentoring children of promise."

The Amachi Team and Plan of Action

The plan was that Public/Private Ventures would implement and oversee the Amachi project, provide administrative oversight and financial management, and take the lead in recruiting congregations as well as children of prisoners.[33] P/PV would also collect the data used to monitor the mentoring relationships, gauge the overall progress of Amachi, and troubleshoot problems as they developed.

Perhaps the most important task confronting P/PV was to find the right person to lead Amachi. It was essential to attract someone who was comfortable with the partnership between BBBS and Philadelphia's African American congregations, a person with credibility in both the secular and faith-based communities. Dr. W. Wilson Goode Sr., formerly the mayor of Philadelphia (1984–1992) but now a reverend, would be the perfect pick. Rev. Goode had worked with black churches and inner-city congregations for years, and already had established relationships with many pastors and churches. Rev. Goode brought immediate credibility to Amachi and was able to bring together secular and faith-based partners in a respectful way. He also played a vital role in getting Amachi off the ground quickly. His leadership would be pivotal in not only recruiting churches and mentors, but in working with local correctional facilities in identifying children of prisoners in Philadelphia. As P/PV understood all too well, effective mentoring does not just happen, and solid partnerships between secular and sacred groups can be difficult to navigate. Rev. Goode's leadership was critical in making both of these things happen in tandem.[34]

Beyond being the source for volunteers, congregations became critical partners in Amachi. When a church decided to participate in Amachi, this decision sent a very clear message that there was buy-in from the pastor as well as the congregation. Each participating church committed to recruiting ten volunteers from its congregation who would be willing to meet at least one hour a week for a year and mentor a child of a current or former prisoner. Each church was also responsible for collecting and submitting monthly data on how often those matches were meeting. By signing on, congregations were committing to nurture and support the volunteer mentors, and to step in if they were not meeting their commitment. Each participating church received a small stipend

for a Church Volunteer Coordinator, who was responsible for oversee-
ing the Amachi effort within the congregation.[35]

We know that inner-city congregations are involved in many outreach
efforts covering a host of social service areas (housing, job training, day
care, after-school programs, etc.). In a census of Philadelphia congregations (n=1376) focusing on the provision of social services, it was discovered that 88 percent of congregations (n=1211) provide at least one
social program. On average, each congregation provides 2.41 programs
and serves 102 people per month. This study concluded that the financial
replacement value of all congregational social services in Philadelphia
was $246,901,440 annually.[36] Amachi was viewed as another program
whereby urban churches would be in the front lines in breaking the cycle
of imprisonment.

Research on mentoring children documents that positive outcomes
are achievable when mentors and mentees meet regularly for a sufficient time period (e.g., at least a year) and there is the necessary program infrastructure to support the mentoring relationship.[37] What's
more, programs that carefully screen, train, monitor, and support mentors have positive effects.[38] This is exactly why Big Brothers/Big Sisters,
the nation's oldest and most experienced mentoring organization, was
intentionally recruited to participate in Amachi.

BBBS case managers were responsible for screening the volunteers
and providing supervision and support for the matches by staying in
touch with mentors, children, and caregivers. Interestingly, Amachi was
viewed as another program for BBBS, but it was seen as a ministry for
the churches. However, when it came to self-identification, mentors
might use the term "Amachi" or "BBBS" interchangeably—a positive
indication of the integration achieved through this unusual partnership.

It was decided that Amachi would focus attention on four disadvantaged communities within Philadelphia: Southwest Philadelphia, West
Kensington, North Philadelphia, and South Philadelphia. An effort
was made to recruit ten churches in each of the four areas, and each of
the churches was asked to provide ten volunteers who would become
mentors for children in the community immediately surrounding the
church. Community Impact Directors (CIDs) were hired in each of
these communities to provide oversight.

One of the key challenges was actually locating children of prisoners in Philadelphia. As Rev. Goode would later state, "There's no record of these children anywhere." A breakthrough occurred when Goode was allowed to go directly into the Philadelphia prisons and speak to the parents in person. He recalls, "I went to a prison and saw a grandfather, a father, and a grandson, all in prison at the same time, and they told me they met for the first time in prison." During a period of four months, incarcerated prisoners completed enrollment forms for almost two thousand children who would become potential candidates for Amachi and a faith-based mentor. After the necessary contact information and permission to move forward were received, an attempt would be made to contact the caregiver for children of prisoners. Contacting caregivers was done with great sensitivity since some caregivers had a strained relationship with the incarcerated parent. In general, however, most of the caregivers welcomed the opportunity for the child to have a mentor from a local congregation.

CONNECTING WITH CONGREGATIONS

Churches were targeted based on a number of factors, but particularly important was identifying churches that had a significant percentage of members who lived in the community and did not commute from the suburbs. Half the congregations that participated were Baptist, and the other half included Pentecostal, United Methodist, A.M.E., Lutheran, Seventh-Day Adventists, and other nondenominational churches. The forty-two original churches participating in Amachi were Protestant congregations ranging in size from less than one hundred to more than one thousand.[39]

Pastors are busy people, and making contact with them was not easily accomplished. After contact was finally made, Rev. Goode would meet individually with the pastor at each church to talk about Amachi and learn whether the pastor was interested. Rev. Goode not only discussed the great need for mentoring the estimated twenty thousand children of prisoners in Philadelphia, but gave a strong theological foundation for taking on this ministry. In the end, many pastors accepted the invitation to be part of Amachi.

The Amachi message hit close to home for the pastors of Philadelphia's inner-city congregations. They knew their churches were located in neighborhoods impacted by incarceration. Many clergy admitted that they had failed to consider the plight of children of prisoners, and Goode's message represented a profound wake-up call. They knew Goode was correct when he stated, "We have to break the cycle." In addition to the compelling message, Amachi was bringing a structure for local churches to work within as well as resources to support the effort. Amachi had clearly defined roles and responsibilities, and churches would simply be asked to provide ten mentors who would each commit to meeting with a child for at least one hour a week for one year. Rev. Goode made an offer difficult to turn down.

BBBS would handle recruiting children, screening or training mentors, making the matches, or providing the forms of support and supervision. Amachi would provide funding for the coordinator's position in the church as well as cover expenses. Taken together, the Amachi message resonated with most congregations, plus Amachi would bring the necessary resources to help oversee it. The buy-in from the pastors was the first step in the process. Next, the pastors had to convey the message to their congregations and inspire members to reach out as mentors. Some spoke individually to members of the congregation whom they believed would make good mentors. Other pastors invited Rev. Goode to come to the church and speak about Amachi.

Though the Pew Charitable Trusts generously funded the initial demonstration of Amachi in Philadelphia, they did not fund a major impact study. This is unfortunate, because among other things, a rigorous study would have made it possible to conduct ongoing interviews to determine (1) the influence of faith-based mentors over time on children of prisoners, (2) how parents and caregivers felt about the impact of the Amachi program on them and their children, and (3) how mentors were impacted by participating in Amachi. Like so many other new interventions, we are left with largely anecdotal insights to these three important areas. My own interviews with Amachi mentors, mentees, and program managers from around the country confirm what I have heard from Dr. Goode as well as others who have been central to the implementation of Amachi over the last ten years: (1) the influence of faith-based mentors on children of prisoners tends to be remarkably positive if the relationship can be sustained for at least a year, (2) parents (and caregivers) of children of prisoners tend to be incredibly appreciative of the involvement of faith-based mentors, and (3) most mentors believe they benefit more from the relationship than do the children they mentor. To follow I highlight the story of one Amachi match that took place in Philadelphia shortly after the program's launch. I do not argue it is representative of all Amachi matches, but it is a story that accurately highlights the complexity and the amazing possibilities that no doubt have been realized for thousands of others who have participated and continue to participate in this program.

MARIE AND ERICKA: A PHILADELPHIA MATCH

Ericka Dill, a twenty-eight-year-old college student living and working in Philadelphia, recounted to me how she was stirred by an appeal she heard one Sunday at New Hope Temple Baptist Church. Pastor John Coger asked members of the congregation if they would prayerfully consider being a mentor to a young boy or girl who had a parent incarcerated. Pastor Coger asked members of the congregation to consider investing in a child whom society had largely neglected. Rev. Coger shared how everyone needs a role model in life, but he went on to point out that many children are raised without that kind of influence. Coger stated, "Our church is going to participate in a new program called Amachi, because we believe a caring adult can make a big difference in the life of a child. The old adage is true—there but by the grace of God go I. Some of you need to consider becoming a big brother or big sister and help mentoring a child in this community who has a parent in prison." The pitch was simple and straightforward and immediately touched the heart of Ericka Dill.

Ericka had been raised by a hard-working single mom and knew that Pastor Coger was right: young people do need to have resources of caring adults in their life, someone willing to invest in them. According to Ericka, "I listened that Sunday, and knew I wanted to give someone what I wish I had as a child. I knew immediately I was supposed to do it." Ericka signed up that Sunday and went through all the steps necessary to qualify to be a mentor through Big Brothers and Big Sisters.

While Ericka was going through the process to become a mentor, Marie Gilliam, an eighth-grade student, was told by her grandmother who was raising her that Marie's mother, currently in prison, had signed her up to participate in a mentoring program called Amachi. Marie didn't think this was a good idea, but her grandmother did. End of discussion. Marie and Ericka met soon thereafter in May 2001, and both have similar recollections of that initial meeting. Ericka recalls that Marie didn't really want to be there—a fact Marie readily admits was accurate. As Marie stated to me, "I had put all these walls up and wouldn't let anyone get close to me." In addition to her mom being in prison, she stated her father was MIA (missing in action). Marie would occasionally see her father on the streets of their Philadelphia neighborhood, but there really wasn't any relationship between them.

To say that Marie and Ericka's match got off to a slow start would be an understatement. By both of their own admissions, their backgrounds were very different, and the match, on the surface, did not seem to be the perfect fit. Knowing that Marie was less than thrilled about the match, however, did not deter Ericka, because she knew God had called her to be a big sister. Ericka would plan activities she knew Marie would enjoy. "We would go shopping, do hair and makeup stuff, you know girly things." There would be many ups and downs in our relationship, Marie would concede, "but Ericka would never give up on me." Although the Amachi guidelines required mentors to spend at least one hour a week with their mentee, Marie and Ericka far exceeded that basic threshold as it was not uncommon for them to spend well over three or four hours together in just one week. As months turned into years the relationship ever so slowly grew. Ericka gives much of the credit not to herself, but Marie's grandmother, whom she called "Grammy," because she was fully supportive of the relationship. "Without Grammy's support, Marie and I may not have learned the lessons of cherishing our relationship during the hard times. She truly influenced us to maintain our sisterhood."

A turning point came approximately two years after they were matched; Grammy agreed to let Marie go to church with Ericka. It would not be long before Marie became a Christian, and she eventually went forward in front of the church to be baptized. "That was one of the most important days of my life," Marie stated. This step marked one of several key turning points in Marie's life. For the first time, she began to pull down the walls that had prevented her from letting anyone get too close. Marie's faith, coupled with the support she received through

Pastor Coger and the congregation, became very important in her journey. Indeed, church members provided a valuable network of support and a second family of sorts for Marie. People like Yvonne Addison, the Amachi coordinator for New Hope Temple Baptist Church, were an endless source of encouragement not only to Marie but Ericka. Indeed, Ericka argued that she herself was the beneficiary in this relationship, that God was changing them both through this experience.

After two to three years, Ericka began to feel she really was part of Marie's family. It was about this time that Ericka told Marie, "I will always be there for you, period." Today, almost a decade later, Marie chokes up when she recalls the day she heard those words spoken for the first time from Ericka. It was a promise Ericka would keep—even beyond the contractual opportunity to end her Amachi obligations past the mentee's age of eighteen years old.

Over the ten years of this match, Marie has experienced a number of tragedies. In addition to her mother being in and out of prison, sadly, she has suffered the losses of her aunt, uncle, and father—all suicide victims. While Marie attests to having a loving family, she is greatly appreciative to the Amachi program for providing her a vital source of social and emotional support. As Marie recalls, "When I felt that no one else was there, Ericka was. Whether a family reunion, a funeral, it didn't matter, she was there for me—always. When people in my family passed away, she was there. When I turned sixteen, she got balloons for me and we celebrated, and no one, outside of my family, had ever taken time for me like that. It's made me a better person to have her by my side." Marie agrees that without Ericka, the Amachi program, and a determined grandmother, she could have been among the ranks of those girls who drop out of high school and get pregnant, but she is glad that she's had the opportunity to bypass that dreadful prospect. The best available data would suggest Marie's prediction to be quite realistic.

But Marie didn't drop out. She graduated from high school in 2006 and is currently a fashion design and marketing major in college. Marie now lives on her own in Virginia and is building her portfolio through the retail industry. Ericka is a recruitment coordinator working for Comcast in Philadelphia. Both Marie and Ericka readily acknowledge that their story is one showing that God knew they needed each other. From bringing them together in the spring of 2001 God has helped to sustain them and their match since then. They still maintain a sister-hood today.

I also interviewed Elizabeth Gilliam, Marie's mother, so she could offer her recollections of the Amachi program. She indicated she heard Wilson Goode promoting Amachi and how excited he was about the program when he visited the facility where Elizabeth was incarcerated. "Perfect!" That was Elizabeth's first response to the advertisement of the Amachi program. According to Elizabeth, "I saw how emotionally dis-traught Marie was, and I was worried about her and I knew she was wor-ried about me. I wanted her to have comfort and support. When I heard Wilson Goode say it was a Christian-based program, I thought, *I'm all for it*. I was brought up in the church, and I knew Marie would benefit from contact with people in the church."

When asked what would have happened if there had been no Amachi program, Elizabeth responded, "We wouldn't have grown to be close like we are today. Ericka was the key. Without Ericka, we would not have the relationship we do now." Elizabeth also added that connecting Marie to the church and the people who constitute the church community was especially important for Marie's development. Finally, Elizabeth indi-cated that simply knowing Marie had a big sister in her life gave her an enormous peace of mind while in prison. "When I heard all the things they were doing together, I would draw comfort from that knowledge." Indeed, Elizabeth went on to tell me that Ericka is a member of their family, and she was definitely Marie's sister. "She has helped our entire family. In fact, I still call her for advice today." Elizabeth concluded her comments by stating, "I would recommend the Amachi program to any-one in prison who happens to have a child."

These accounts represent my own observations and interviews with individuals since the founding of the Amachi initiative. Systematic research on Amachi is much needed to determine if my observations will be supported or possibly refuted. Until such research is completed and published, we are left with this remarkable fact: Amachi's spectacu-lar growth over the last decade provides overwhelming evidence that faith-based individuals and communities are able to respond by bring-ing unprecedented numbers of volunteers to bear on a key and previ-ously unaddressed social problem.

CONCLUSION

Amachi is a unique partnership involving secular and faith-based organizations working together to provide mentoring to children of incarcerated parents. Amachi began recruiting urban churches in Philadelphia in November 2000; by April 2001 the first mentors were meeting with their mentees.[40] By the end of January 2002 Amachi was operating through forty-two churches and had made almost 400 matches. During the initial two years of operations, 517 children were paired with mentors. The spectacular growth of Amachi in Philadelphia in such a short period of time represents an unprecedented development in the field of mentoring.

P/PV concluded from tracking data that Amachi was able to recruit volunteers who could be effective mentors and that its highly structured partnership was successful in supporting the relationships, enabling them to develop and endure. Importantly, P/PV's data also suggested the children involved in Amachi benefited in ways comparable to the children whose outcomes were measured in previous BBBS evaluations.[41]

Amachi has spread rapidly across the country, and there are now some 350 Amachi-modeled programs in more than one hundred U.S. cities, partnering with some six thousand congregations.[42] To date, these programs have served more than one hundred thousand children of prisoners. P/PV continues to work to see that new mentoring-children-of-prisoners programs benefit from the lessons learned in the Amachi initiative. Sixty-seven sessions of the Amachi Training Institute have been held, and Amachi staff regularly visit programs to provide on-site technical assistance.[43]

In September 2009, in partnership with Dare Mighty Things, P/PV launched the Amachi Mentoring Coalition Project, which was awarded $17.8 million in Office of Juvenile Justice and Delinquency Prevention funding to provide financial resources, training, and technical assistance to mentoring organizations in thirty-eight states. The project will assist these agencies with creating jobs (i.e., positions to staff their mentoring effort), improving program capacity, generating new mentoring matches, forming statewide coalitions, and developing strategic partnerships for sustainability. The three-year grant is expected to create some twenty thousand new mentoring matches for children impacted by incarceration.

The Amachi story is a remarkable one, providing proof that churches and faith-motivated volunteers can effectively partner with secular organizations like BBBS and P/PV to achieve scale in addressing one of the most pressing problems of our time. Launched in 2000, and in less than a decade, Amachi has been the driving force behind a national movement to mentor more than one hundred thousand children of prisoners.

The Amachi experiment would not have succeeded without each of the partners. This fact is a critical reminder that faith-motivated volunteers can play a central role in confronting some of society's most pressing social problems, and that volunteers should not be overlooked when experts and decision makers seek to devise future programs and interventions. Amachi should also be a wake-up call to people of faith that these "armies of compassion" need training, support, monitoring, and management. In other words, faith-based efforts need proper oversight and evaluation if they are to be viewed as key partners in the future.

## CHAPTER 4

The Center for Neighborhood Enterprise and the Violence-Free Zone

The successful programs and interventions that I've discovered over the years were not from people within civil rights groups, government bureaucracies, or higher education institutions, but were people that are working quietly within these communities. Some of these people were in poverty but not of it, meaning they were former criminals and/or drug addicts, but their lives were transformed and now serve as role models for others in the community.

ROBERT WOODSON

T HE MISSION OF the Center for Neighborhood Enterprise (CNE) is to transform lives, schools, and troubled neighborhoods from the inside out. CNE is a nonprofit organization, and most of its work assists churches and local neighborhood ministries to grow and expand. Because CNE operates within public structures, such as public school systems, the focus is not on the Christian content of what it does, but the secular outcome that is produced because of its faith in Christ. CNE believes it is more important to be "explicitly Christian" as witnessed by its deeds than it is to express it in its name. Since Robert Woodson believes labels can be an obstacle for reaching people, he goes the extra mile in making sure CNE does not get labeled as a faith-based organization.

Robert Woodson, a tall and slender man, looks far too young to have been an activist in the civil rights movement. A lifelong community organizer, Woodson seeks to help the residents of low-income neighborhoods by identifying capable community and faith-based organizations and then providing the training, technical assistance, and support necessary to become more effective in confronting the social problems in their communities. Societal problems addressed by CNE's grassroots network include youth violence, substance abuse, teen pregnancy, homelessness, joblessness, family dissolution, poor education, and deteriorating neighborhoods. Woodson has led projects that improved poor neighborhoods by tapping the talents of entrepreneurial individuals within them. He is the author of *The Triumphs of Joseph: How Community Healers Are Reviving Our Streets and Neighborhoods.*

When asked if this approach is important because of the bias against faith-based organizations, Woodson responded, "It's not just bigotry against faith-based approaches. Oftentimes it has been churches that have screwed up and unfortunately given religion a bad name. Some of the resentment toward the efforts of faith-motivated individuals is a result of self-inflicted wounds by people in churches and faith-based organizations. As a result, we can't just simply blame secular folks for all the hostility toward faith-based efforts."

CNE's message resonates well within the religious community, as the majority of the community leaders and organizations CNE assists have expressed some type of religious base and belief in God. Since its founding in 1981 CNE has provided training and technical assistance to leaders of more than twenty-six hundred community-based groups in thirty-nine states. The overwhelming majority of these organizations are faith-based. The Center also has been a strong advocate for religious freedom and the rights of faith-based groups in the public policy arena.

Having worked for the left-of-center National Urban League as well as the right-of-center American Enterprise Institute, Woodson believes traditional approaches to addressing social problems are all too often wrongheaded. According to Woodson, "If I am the administrator of a social welfare agency and I have two hundred kids to serve and my budget is $2 million, I can come back to the Congress and argue I'm now serving four hundred kids and request my budget be doubled." Woodson suggests these are simply perverse incentives. Woodson's experiences led him to conclude that 80 percent of all dollars spent on poor people go to those who serve poor people. Instead of asking which problems are solvable, groups supposedly helping the poor would rather ask which problems are fundable.

Another problem Woodson sees with contemporary approaches to social problems is a bias against utilizing social entrepreneurs. "In our social economy, Person A can raise five children successfully and send them all to college, but she could not get certified to operate a daycare center. Person B never had children, can hate kids, can get a master's in early childhood development, and be certified to run a daycare center. I am not against standards, but there should be some correlation between certification and qualification. For heart surgery I want to see board certification. If I want to be delivered from demons, the evils of drug addiction, or prostitution, I need spiritual renewal." As Woodson articulates in his book *The Triumphs of Joseph*, "Grassroots Josephs may not have degrees and certifications on their walls, but they do have this— the powerful, uncontestable testimonies of people whose lives have been salvaged through their work. The undeniable fact that lives have been transformed through the work of modern-day Josephs must be appreciated even by observers who may be skeptical about their approach."[1]

Woodson, therefore, believes it is transformation that we must strive to achieve as an outcome. "If I'm killing myself, I do not need to be rehabilitated. I need to be transformed. I need to become a new person. Therapy does not make you another person. Rehabilitation rarely removes bad stuff. Transformation, on the other hand, replaces the bad stuff with good stuff. That is the difference."

As a result of this commitment, Woodson and CNE have brought national attention to the effectiveness of faith-based programs and identified barriers that they face, saving some important faith-based programs from unfair regulatory actions. In 1996 the state of Texas threatened to close down Teen Challenge and Victory Temple because they did not have licensed professionally trained counselors. As one headline famously quoted one of those trying to close the faith-based program, "We don't care the program is effective—they are not licensed." CNE led a demonstration at the Alamo involving three hundred born-again drug addicts. After receiving major coverage in the media, the state relented. Following a meeting CNE had with then-governor George W. Bush, he signed into law a bill that exempted faith-based drug treatment programs from state regulations.

From years of experience working in largely disadvantaged communities, Robert Woodson learned that solutions to difficult social problems could be found in local residents and local community and faith-based groups. Woodson may or may not agree that all politics is local,[2] but his approach to social problems might best be summed up this way: all solutions are local. The Center for Neighborhood Enterprise is focused on finding these organic leaders and groups—what some have called "social entrepreneurs"—and helping them grow their work. This is why the word "enterprise" is in its name: because Woodson believes strongly that the principles that operate in a market economy ought to operate in our social economy. Indeed, this perspective remains prominent in the three founding principles established to govern and direct Woodson's organization for the last thirty years:

1. Those suffering from the problem must be involved in the creation and implementation of the solution.
2. The principles of the market economy should be applied to the solution of societal problems.
3. Value-generating and faith-based programs and groups are uniquely qualified to address the problems of poverty.

CNE's philosophy and approach are based on the recognition that effective, community-based programs originate in those same communities, not from ivory towers or subject matter experts who often have very little practical or firsthand knowledge of these communities.

In recent years CNE has developed a major focus on youth violence intervention and prevention called the Violence-Free Zone. According to Woodson, "Unless there is civil order there can be no activity in the city, so we have been concentrating on reducing youth violence." Working closely with school safety officers and local police, the Violence-Free Zone (VFZ) now has active sites in Milwaukee, Dallas, Richmond, Atlanta, and Baltimore.

THE VIOLENCE-FREE ZONE INITIATIVE—
ITS ORIGINS

The VFZ initiative is a youth violence prevention and reduction program located within middle or high schools. It was developed and formulated outside of the public school environment. Woodson already had a great deal of knowledge about gang behavior and youth violence from his days studying and working with faith-based and community organizations in a number of different cities. Woodson was able to apply his knowledge on addressing youth violence and gang-related issues in January 1997 at Benning Terrace, a public housing development in Washington, DC, where youth violence had led to more than fifty youth deaths in a several-year period, culminating with the shooting death of a twelve-year-old boy.

Woodson and CNE helped to craft a peace agreement between the warring youth factions and helped bring life skills, job training, and job placement services for youth seeking an alternative to their drug- and crime-filled lifestyle. This peace accord was possible as a result of CNE's openness to learn from and collaborate with local community organizations and leaders in addressing particular community problems and issues. One of the key things that emerged from these efforts was the knowledge of how much influence these violent youth leaders had on young people in their neighborhoods. Unfortunately, in Benning Terrace, they used it in a negative way to control and harm the community. Following CNE's intervention, a remarkable development took place in which these same youth leaders underwent a transformation that would enable them to use their power to help turn the community in a positive direction. Former gang leaders became positive role models and motivated younger kids to pursue normative behavior and academic achievement. Woodson and CNE saw how youth leaders could become highly influential role models, affecting their younger peers in prosocial rather than antisocial ways.

A key contributor to the development of the VFZ initiative was Omar Jahwar, who worked with the youth population as a prison gang specialist in a Dallas prison. In 1996 Jahwar invited Woodson to speak to the youth he was working with at the prison. Woodson was so impressed with Jahwar's approach and connection to these youth that he encouraged and supported him in starting a community-based organization, named Vision Regeneration Inc., to serve as a partner with CNE on violence prevention activities within the community.

The general premise for Woodson was to convince Jahwar they should work "upstream" with youth not yet imprisoned but at risk of becoming so. Jahwar began by working in the neighborhood surrounding Madison

High School in Dallas, Texas. In the spring of 1999 the school's principal, Robert Ward, had expelled fifty youths from the school for disruptive behavior. Jahwar, with private funding obtained through CNE, provided summer jobs for these youths, both in an effort to make connections with these youth and also as a way to get rival gang members to begin talking to one another.

Before the beginning of school that next fall, Jahwar met with Ward, both to discuss the future of the expelled youths and to offer a proposal to help the principal deal with the overall issue of violence in the high school. As Jahwar described the meeting, "During the summer, we had built some momentum in terms of building relationships with the kids and getting them to at least talk to one another. We asked the principal to accept these kids back, and we would assume the responsibility for their behavior and bring it under control."

The principal took Jahwar up on his offer, providing Vision Regeneration with space within the school and one hundred thousand dollars for one semester to hire six youth advisors, whose job was to establish and grow their relationship with a select number of the youth who previously were the cause of much of the school violence. However, they were sure to also add youth to their caseload who demonstrated more exemplary behavior and academic performance, so as not to brand their effort as only being about working with delinquents.

By the fall of 2000 the principal saw dramatic improvements to the school in its safety and overall atmosphere, and offered a strong recommendation to the Dallas superintendent of schools, who made Vision Regeneration a listed vendor. The program, subsequently called the Violence-Free Zone (VFZ), received five hundred thousand dollars annually for its work in fourteen Dallas middle and high schools.

THE 10 PERCENT RULE

One of the central challenges to public schools is the disruption of the educational environment and educational process resulting from instability within the school, often a product of neighborhood rivalries or gang-related conflicts occurring during school time. What Jahwar and Woodson had both learned from their previous experiences working with gangs and violent youth was the importance of identifying and reaching out to the leaders. Kwame Johnson, national coordinator of the VFZ programs, described it this way:

> If you have a high school of one thousand or more kids, there are usually about 10 percent of those kids responsible for most of the incidents and disruptions occurring within the school. About 10 percent of these kids, in turn, are the leaders that orchestrate much of the disruptions, usually in the form of one gang acting out on another gang. Much of the VFZ strategy boils down to first identifying, and second, trying to develop relationships with these ten or so leaders. So, the 10 percent rule is really about the 10 percent of kids causing the disruption at school, and then drilling down to the 10 percent of those that are really the driving force behind those con-flicts. By engaging and redirecting these leaders, we have seen significant reductions in incidents, particularly gang-related incidents, in the schools where the VFZ initiative is operating.

The VFZ model entails recruiting and training Youth Advisors, who are generally mature young adults from the same neighborhoods as the students in the schools they serve. VFZ sites in Baltimore, Chicago, Dallas, Milwaukee, and Richmond, Virginia, are led by ordained pastors. These Youth Advisors command trust and respect because they have faced and overcome the same challenges these youth are facing. They serve several roles, including as hall monitors, mentors, counselors, role models, and peacemakers when conflicts flare up in the school.

Woodson describes the type of people sought out to serve this Youth Advisor role as "community healers" or "grassroots Josephs," the latter in reference to the biblical character and the trials he endured, as well as his subsequent transformation as a leader in the service of Pharaoh and helping Egypt during a time of famine.

In order to gain a more complete understanding of the effectiveness of the VFZ, it was necessary to conduct preliminary field research in two different locations, Milwaukee and Richmond.[3] In both cities, in-depth interviews were completed with

- Staff from the VFZ
- Members of community-based organizations partnering with VFZ

- ▶ Leaders from the faith-based organizations teaming with VFZ
- ▶ Select officials from the Milwaukee and Richmond public schools
- ▶ Representatives of the foundations funding the VFZ initiative
- ▶ Others with knowledge of the VFZ initiative in Milwaukee and Richmond (these face-to-face interviews were transcribed and excerpts appear throughout this chapter)
- ▶ Data provided by the Milwaukee Public Schools (on total suspensions, suspension rates, and the number of violent and nonviolent incidents)[4]
- ▶ Data from the Richmond Public Schools as well as the Richmond Police Department were also analyzed.[5]

FINDINGS FROM MILWAUKEE

The VFZ initiative in Milwaukee has its roots in a 1993 request to CNE from the Milwaukee-based Lynde and Harry Bradley Foundation. The Bradley Foundation asked CNE to help it identify faith-based and community organizations (FBCOs) as a part of a civic-focused initiative the foundation was launching. Over the years, CNE provided training and technical assistance to many faith-based and community groups in Milwaukee's central city. One group that CNE met in 2003 was the Latino Community Center (LCC), located on the south side of Milwaukee, which was already doing work with the local high school to help it with gang-related incidents within the school. As Woodson explained,

> The Latino Community Center had already negotiated an agreement with the South Division High School to have some of their youth staff in the building when we discovered them. That helped us to know that we were already on the same page with the Center and so, with the initial support of the Bradley and other local foundations, we decided to launch the VFZ program in Milwaukee.

Beginning in September 2005 CNE and LCC formed a partnership to implement the VFZ initiative in South Division High School, which had been plagued with escalating youth violence and gang-related conflicts in recent years. The first year of VFZ was funded entirely with private foundation dollars, through a consortium of local foundations coordinated through the Bradley Foundation. CNE deliberately follows this approach of using initial private funding when beginning the VFZ initiative, so it can demonstrate actual results before approaching public agencies for funding. This approach hearkens back to one of CNE's founding principles—*The principles of the market economy should be applied to the solution of societal problems*—with the program outcomes representing the "goods" provided through the VFZ initiative. Woodson described their reasoning:

> We don't even approach the school or other public agency for funding until we can show the impact and cost savings associated with reducing suspensions and gang-related incidents within the schools. We feel this is central to the integrity of our organization and the community partners to sell our program on results.

Community Partnering

CNE is very particular when selecting a local faith-based/community organization to entrust the operational responsibilities for the VFZ initiative. Another of CNE's founding principles—*Those suffering from the problem must be involved in the creation and implementation of the solution*—is also represented in the process by which CNE identifies, or sometime creates, the local community partners that assume the responsibility for implementing the VFZ initiative. Woodson stated,

> When we come into a city looking for the right community partner, I generally start networking through any contacts—family, friends, and colleagues—about community-serving organizations already working with youth. We will also walk into barber shops and local restaurants to find out where people go to get help in times of trouble. This searching mostly takes place through informal community networks, among people who "know each other," and generally not through public social service agencies or local elected officials.

Sometimes the search process yields organizations such as the LCC in Milwaukee with whom CNE partners to implement the VFZ initiative. At other times, CNE's search efforts produces individuals, such as Omar Jahwar in Dallas, with whom CNE literally helps to build (or "create") the partner organization to implement the program. In either instance, CNE provides technical assistance (i.e., capacity-building organizational and financial management, resource development, and staff training) to assure that the organization is able to implement and sustain the VFZ initiative in that city.

CNE's high standards for its local partners are not indicative of a typical corporate franchise mentality, where one size fits all. On the contrary, the Center's approach to partnering with, or helping to create, its community VFZ partners also reflects a degree of humility within the CNE organizational culture by providing guidance, but delegating practically all of the operational decision making for a local VFZ site to these partners. Furthermore, these local partners are the ones knowledgeable on how to adapt the principles for the VFZ to work within their particular context, with CNE serving as enablers and facilitators of these organizations' implementation of the CNE vision and model.

Typically CNE identifies only one community partner per VFZ site, through which all Youth Advisors are recruited, trained, and monitored. However, given the scope of VFZ Milwaukee, which is currently in eight high schools and growing to as many as twenty in the coming years, and the distinct demographics between the primarily Latino south side and the primarily African American north side of the city, CNE chose two community partners: the Latino Community Center (LCC) on the southern side and Running Rebels Community Organization (RRCO) on the northern side.

Latino Community Center

The Latino Community Center is only an eight-year-old organization, but it has made rapid strides over the past five years to establish itself as a key resource for its community, particularly the youth. What Woodson found particularly noteworthy of the LCC, aside from its initial outreach to the local South Division High School prior to VFZ, was its direct effort to expand outreach into the community by having its staff walk the streets two days out of each week. LCC staff members simply walk up to youth and adults, introduce themselves, and listen to them about the challenges and issues they see their community facing. They have also developed strong relationships with the pastors of local churches, who often join them on these community walks.

LCC's success, both through this outreach as well as from its programming in response to those needs, bore strong resemblance to CNE's early violence intervention work at Benning Terrace in Washington, DC, whereby faction leaders were identified, engaged, and redirected from criminal activities toward more positively focused career development and community services. In fact, LCC's success in addressing youth violence and gang-related incidents in the community naturally led them to seek out a relationship with the local high school, where gang-related incidents were on the rise. Jorge Perez, interim director for the LCC, reported,

> As we were succeeding in addressing gang-related conflicts in the community, we noticed that these problems were continuing and growing in the local high school. That was a little frustrating for us, because we weren't in the schools and didn't have any continuity with the kids during that time. This is a real problem at South Division, where there are eight gangs represented in the student body, all in close contact with one another. By getting into the schools, we were able to maintain our connection, relationship, and most importantly the accountability with the kids, because now they see us and have to deal with us all day.

Initially, the principal at South Division would have only brought LCC into the schools in response to gang-related incidents, such as fights and other disruptions. However, after a student was stabbed to death during school in September 2005, the principal agreed to give LCC an ongoing presence in the school, laying the groundwork for the VFZ program, which officially began in September 2005. After one year of the VFZ initiative the safety at the high school improved significantly and the school received an award as one of the safest schools among the twenty Milwaukee public high schools.[6] VFZ then took these and other positive outcomes to a meeting brokered by the Bradley Foundation with William Andrekopoulos, the superintendent of the Milwaukee Public School System. Andrekopoulos was so impressed that within three months of that first meeting he provided funding through the school system to expand VFZ to five additional high schools, beginning in September 2007. Andrekopoulos stated,

> We are expanding the Violence-Free Zone Initiative because it works. This pilot program, using community engagement and the support of key community organizations, has proven to be a proactive way to support the needs of young people in lieu of having them get trapped in the criminal justice system.

LCC managed the Violence-Free Zone in two of the first six schools, which included South Division, while CNE's other community partner, the Running Rebels, assumed management of the other four.[7]

Running Rebels Community Organization

Running Rebels Community Organization (RRCO), originally named for its athletic programs in track and field, was founded in 1980 with the mission of providing high-risk youth on the north side of Milwaukee with athletic, academic, life skills, and career training services. One of the strengths of the RRCO was its strong working relationship with the courts for youth in the community. As with LCC, RRCO was always looking for opportunities to collaborate with government agencies. As Dawn Barnett, executive director for RRCO, explained,

> We are always working hard to develop good working relationships with the courts, the police, and other public agencies that deal with our kids. We felt the lack of continuity and connection we had with the schools, so we welcomed the opportunity to work with the schools, and place staff within the schools, which is what VFZ allows us to do. Being a partner with CNE on the Violence-Free Zone initiative also helps to legitimize the role of our organization with these youth and in the community.

RRCO has also seen improvements in working relationships with the police and district attorney's office in terms of a greater openness to community input provided through their organization. However, similar to LCC, RRCO was frustrated by the lack of continuity and connection with the local high schools. Even though the local high school, Marshall, had implemented a school safety improvement program in 2005, there was no community participation, oversight, or liaison associated with the program.

The Foundation Community

The other distinctive feature of VFZ Milwaukee as a public-nonprofit-private collaboration is the active support it received from the foundation community, led by the Lynde and Harry Bradley Foundation. The Bradley Foundation coordinated with other foundations in Milwaukee to support the VFZ entirely during its pilot implementation in South Division High School. Dan Schmidt, vice president for programs at the Bradley Foundation, described the role Woodson played in getting the Milwaukee Public School System to buy into the program:

> Woodson played an essential role in bringing VFZ about. Although their partner organizations were already skilled and knowledgeable to do the work, it was Woodson and CNE's credentials, particularly their experience in engaging school systems. What made these negotiations particularly successful, however, was that they not only gained access to the schools for the VFZ staff, but also got them to invest financially in the operations of the program.

THE MILWAUKEE PUBLIC SCHOOLS AND VIOLENCE-FREE ZONE INITIATIVE

In the years preceding the arrival of the VFZ initiative, many Milwaukee observers believed the Milwaukee Public School System (MPS) represented one of the most troubled school districts in the state, with the dubious distinction of having the highest school suspension rate in the nation. In 2008 MPS received grant funding from the Safe Schools/

Healthy Students grant program from the U.S. Department of Justice, which it used to cover some of its investment in the VFZ program.

Principals and other school officials have observed positive changes in the school environment with the presence of the VFZ Youth Advisors in the schools. As Mark Kuxhause, principal for the South Division High School, explained, "The climate of the school has definitely changed over the past two years. The VFZ complements the efforts of the school faculty and is an instrumental component to the other services offered at South Division."

The Youth Advisors represent a vital support system for teachers, in that they are able to spend less time trying to maintain order and more time providing educational instruction. Gregory Y. Ogunbouwale, principal of the High School of Expeditionary Learning, reported that

> Having the extra bodies in school has been very helpful in providing support to safety assistants, administration, and general school staff in the school. The ability of the Violence-Free Zone team to build relationships with our youth has allowed them to obtain information and to notify staff of altercations before they happen, conduct effective mediations, and assist in crisis prevention. It is very helpful to use the Violence-Free Zone staff to get to the bottom of situations before they escalate to violent incidents.

Finally, the Youth Advisors bring with them a sense of cultural competency, insofar as they live in the community and lived through many of the challenges the youth face, which impact how school staff interacts with students during school.

Youth Advisors

The Youth Advisors are the cornerstone of the VFZ model. Most VFZ staff members are between the ages of nineteen and thirty, come from as well as continue to live in the same neighborhoods as the students, and have struggled with the same issues (e.g., gang-related crime and substance abuse). They are employed by CNE's community partner organization(s) within the city where VFZ is operating. Table 1 shows some of the contrasts in the work and mind-set of youth advisors, as compared with school social workers or counselors.

TABLE 1. Youth Advisors and Social Workers/Counselors

	Youth Advisors	Social Workers/Counselors
They generally relate to students as . . .	Friends	Clients
Make themselves available to students . . .	24/7	9 to 5
The daily work activities are . . .	Driven by student needs	Generally predetermined through position descriptions
Skills and knowledge primarily based on . . .	Similar background and experiences/ struggles as faced by students	Professional licensure/ certification

The VFZ model is simple, but the work is not easy. Youth Advisors provide the following duties in a typical day:

- ▶ Walking the streets. The Youth Advisors walk around within about one thousand feet outside the school before the day begins. The advisors encourage students toward school and pick up information on any brewing gang conflicts, touching base with any police officers in the immediate vicinity.
- ▶ Greeting the students as they come in to school. The advisors offer any support they can to school security personnel, making themselves visible and available to any students who may have issues from home or for other reasons.
- ▶ Participating in tardy hall. For students arriving late to school, Youth Advisors meet with chronically late youth to find out why the student is continually tardy. Sometimes, advisors also make calls to home for late or absent students to identify issues affecting their attendance.
- ▶ Walking the halls. Between classes, Youth Advisors walk around the halls, redirecting students; maintaining a presence/keeping

radar up for any possible individual beefs, neighborhood rivalries, or gang-related conflicts; and touching base with teachers on any behavior issues in the classroom.

▶ Spending lunchtime with students. A critical relationship-building opportunity for the youth advisors with the students, building trust and maintaining visibility.

▶ Actively particpating in mediation meetings. As scheduled throughout the day, Youth Advisors participate in teacher-student, parent-student, and student-student mediation to surface and resolve issues causing disruption within the school and classes.

In addition to these services supporting the whole school, each Youth Advisor carries a caseload of anywhere between ten and twenty-five students, many of whom are referrals from the principal, teachers, or counselors. However, the Youth Advisors also seek out other students who may not have behavioral issues, but instead are clearly academic or social leaders in the school. This type of diversification of caseload also counteracts any stigma for a youth assigned to a Youth Advisor as solely because of delinquency and issues associated with high-risk youth.

DATA FROM THE MILWAUKEE PUBLIC SCHOOLS

The impact the VFZ initiative has had within and around the schools is not only descriptive, but is captured through changes in data and outcomes from the Milwaukee Public School System and the Milwaukee Police Department. In the long run, the VFZ initiative in Milwaukee hopes to see improvements in academic performance resulting from a safer, more orderly school environment. In the near term, however, the VFZ is demonstrating its impact in terms of

▶ Reductions in the number of violent and nonviolent incidents reported in high schools with the VFZ program.

▶ Decreases in both suspension rates and the overall number of suspension days reported by high schools with VFZ programs.

▶ An improved climate within the schools, as measured by improvements in student perceptions of the school's safety, order, and overall environment.

The most immediate impact of the VFZ program is measured by the reductions in the number of violent and nonviolent incidents for VFZ high schools, as compared with MPS high schools as a whole. Violent and nonviolent incidents at MPS high schools as a whole increased 15 percent and 19 percent, respectively, between academic years 2006 and 2008.[8] In contrast, among the VFZ schools, the number of violent incidents actually decreased by 11 percent from pre-VFZ levels, while nonviolent incidents decreased by 21 percent.[9] The VFZ also influenced the suspension rate, as there was a decrease in overall number of suspensions between academic years 2007–2008 and 2008–2009. For MPS as a whole (excluding VFZ schools), the number of suspensions decreased by 9 percent (64,393 to 58,572), while VFZ school suspension dropped approximately 30 percent from pre-VFZ levels (23,666 to 16,662).

Increasing emphasis has recently been placed on student responses to school climate surveys as an important indicator of the quality of a school's outcomes. MPS administers an annual survey to high school students between October and December of each year. The following analysis is based on questions that most strongly correlate to the impact that the VFZ program expects to make on the school environment. Students from VFZ schools were much more likely than students from non-VFZ schools to view the school as a welcoming and learning environment, report the school and grounds were safe, and state the school was orderly and that students were more likely to adhere to rules.

FINDINGS FROM RICHMOND

The origins of the VFZ in Richmond date back to 2005, when Rodney Monroe was hired as chief of the Richmond Police Department. Prior to this, Chief Monroe was the Area 6 commander in the Washington, DC, Metropolitan Police Department. While there he worked closely with CNE to better conditions in the Benning Terrace community and facilitated communications and building trust between law enforcement and youth. At the time, Richmond was still recovering from the dubious distinction of having the highest per-capita murder rate in the nation in 1999, and Chief Monroe was determined to transform the image to work more closely with the community. Chief Monroe was particularly concerned with the rising tide of youth violence, mostly gang-related, that was plaguing the city. In 2001 the violent crime rate for youth under eighteen years old in Richmond was almost four times the state average.

One organization that Chief Monroe and the police came across on numerous occasions was an organization known as the Richmond Outreach Center (ROC), which was developing after-school programs and a Saturday program in which they reached out to youth across the city via a bus ministry, engaging youth in social enterprises aimed at redirecting their time and efforts away from gangs and related criminal activity. In 2004 Chief Monroe asked the ROC to provide outreach for a community carnival so the community at large could see the ROC staff, which had already forged strong ties with youth and their families, working alongside the police at this event.

The ROC

The ROC began in April 2001, when Geronimo Aguilar and Ronnie Ortiz, also known as Pastor G and Pastor Rsen, respectively, left Southern California, where they were involved in a variety of outreach ministries, and settled in Richmond. Both Aguilar and Ortiz were raised in the streets as youth, becoming involved in gangs and criminal activity as the only means of survival that they knew, before experiencing their own personal transformations, and with it a passion for reaching out and helping those faced with similar life challenges. The vision for the ROC was to facilitate community-serving programs and ministries among faith-based and community organizations throughout the city.

The ROC began with the acquisition of a warehouse, which they renovated into basketball courts and program space to house a variety of programs, with a primary emphasis on serving youth from five to twelve years in age. However, the 144 ministries currently operated by the ROC also include programs on and for parenting, Hispanics, seniors, substance abuse, marriage, job readiness, and prisoners. Roughly 80 to 85 percent of the ROC's current staff and volunteers come from among those who were originally served through one or more of ROC's ministries.

Although the ROC originated as an outreach center, in 2004 it also became a church, and has since been one of the fastest-growing churches nationally. The mainstay program for the ROC has been what it terms its bus ministry, whereby a fleet of twenty buses pick up between nine hundred and twelve hundred youth (ages five to twelve) for activities every Saturday afternoon. Through this and other after-school programs, the

ROC provides fourteen hundred backpacks filled with school supplies, provides over twenty-four hundred children with Christmas gifts, and involves over one hundred kids per month in one of its youth sports programs.

The ROC is unapologetically evangelical in its various program offerings, but its workers are also skilled in collaborating and coordinating with various public agencies, a skill that Pastors G and Rsen learned from life experiences:

> One of the things we learned personally from living in the streets is the need to be adaptable, which we carry over into our collaboration with public agencies. For example, our prison ministry works closely with the prison chaplain, and also sponsors breakfasts and dinners with the sheriffs and chaplains. Our goals as a ministry is to "be all things to all people," whether ministering to a kid or working with the police in the community.

CNE and Woodson relied on Chief Monroe and his recommendation of the ROC as the VFZ community partner. Based on his relationship with Chief Monroe, as well as the opportunity to meet and visit with the ROC, Woodson agreed to the partnership. As Chief Monroe explained,

> I saw the ROC and CNE as the ideal partnership. The ROC had a well-established reputation of working with the youth in the city, and had staff with experience running various youth programs already. CNE had the experience in working with school superintendents and other staff to ensure that the right conditions were in place for the VFZ to succeed.

Support from the Corporate Foundation Community

Chief Monroe first introduced the VFZ program to the Richmond School Department back in 2005, which began a long courtship process for winning over their support for the program. CNE invited a number of police and school officials to Washington, DC, for a presentation of the work CNE had done in Benning Terrace, and also met with principals in Washington and Baltimore about their experience working with the CNE on youth violence prevention efforts. A couple of years later, one of those school officials, Larry Evert, specialist for truancy for the Richmond School Department, had become the informal designee for evaluating the potential of a VFZ program in Richmond. Evert spoke to students, principals, teachers, and VFZ staff about the VFZ program; he was impressed with the impact that the program was having and made a favorable report back to the school superintendent in Richmond.

The next step for Chief Monroe was to raise the start-up funding through private sources to pilot VFZ at one of the more troubled, violence-plagued high schools. Consistent with one of CNE's founding principles—namely, that *the principles of the market economy should be applied to the solution of societal problems*—CNE did not approach school systems for funding to support VFZ until and unless they demonstrated results, in the form of reduced levels of truancy, nonviolent/violent incidents, and unexcused absences.

Chief Monroe targeted the corporate foundation community, using the Richmond Police Foundation, a dormant 501(c)3 organization, through which he was able to raise $450,000 to fund VFZ at one school for two years. Among those funders was the MeadWestvaco Foundation, associated with an international packaging and office supply company headquartered in Richmond, with annual giving of approximately $4.1 million. The interest in supporting VFZ was the manner in which it tied in two of its funding objectives, as Kathryn Strawn, company vice president and executive director for the foundation, explained:

> We want to help make a real difference in student success for young people attending Richmond Public Schools. Clearly academic achievement requires a safe and secure learning environment. VFZ has an established track record of positive impact. We are pleased to help seed a program we believe can be effective and worthy of sustaining through longer-term funding from the school system.

For Chief Monroe, there was a clear connection between supporting VFZ and public safety:

There is a clear short-term and long-term rationale for funding VFZ's start-up through the police foundation. In the short term, the VFZ program would free up police resources in terms of the frequent service calls we've had to respond to at certain schools from violent incidents, and the associated labor hours for responding officers. In the long term, the VFZ, involving the ROC, is an opportunity to reach and redirect kids away from a lifestyle of crime and violence that we are otherwise going to have to deal with.

VFZ Richmond Implementation

With the funding and community partner (i.e., the ROC) in place, CNE, Chief Monroe, and the school system settled on George Wythe High School, with an enrollment of about eleven hundred students, as the VFZ pilot site. This choice was based, among other things, on the school's 2006–2007 truancy rate (as measured by the percentage of students with six or more unexcused absences) of 66 percent, more than triple the 20 percent average for the other seven high schools. In addition, George Wythe was tied for the most youth ages fourteen to nineteen who were arrested between January and June 2008, comprising 36 percent of all youth arrests among Richmond high schools during that time period.

Another factor for selecting George Wythe as the pilot site was the fact that a new principal, Willie Bell, would be coming into the school for the 2008–2009 academic year. Principal Bell had developed a niche for turning around troubled schools, and this appointment represented the fourth school in his eight-year career as a principal. The unique opportunity for the VFZ program to start fresh with a new principal would allow VFZ to be a part of an overall culture change that was to take place within the school, as opposed to trying to fit in to a preexisting modus operandi from a principal who had already been there.

The Richmond Police Foundation funding for the VFZ supported six Youth Advisors for two years. However, the ROC leadership was so enthused by the opportunity to work within the school that they redirected five of their youth ministry staff to augment the number of youth advisors to eleven. Pastor Rsen said,

We jumped at the opportunity to increase the staffing for the VFZ, because it would give us more time to interact with the kids. Without VFZ, we had to work time in around the school. VFZ helps to blur the distinction between school and the community in a positive way. Our general philosophy is that, given enough time with them, we can effectively counteract the negative influences of peer pressure and impact these kids' lives, and so improve the school environment in the process.

The added staff also allowed VFZ Richmond to have a penetration rate (as measured by the percentage of VFZ caseload students to overall high school enrollment) about twice as high as for a typical VFZ site. With an average caseload of twenty students per Youth Advisor, this came to about an 18 percent caseload to total enrollment, as compared to the typical VFZ penetration rate of about 10 percent.

In actuality, CNE did not get the official green light from the Richmond school system to begin at George Wythe until a week before the start of the 2008–2009 academic year. In fact, the VFZ program had been operating for a month in the school before they were even introduced to teachers and other school staff. However, the Youth Advisors worked diligently to reach out to teachers and let them know they were there to support them.

At the same time, Evert worked internally during the initial months with social workers, teachers, and security staff to hear their concerns and clarify roles and responsibilities as it related to the work of the VFZ program and staff. Evert explained,

It took a bit of massaging with various personnel at Wythe regarding the introduction of the program. Because of the challenges we have had historically at Wythe, there are a lot of people who wanted to provide help, so we just needed to make sure there was coordination and communication of those efforts as it related to the VFZ program. I think the VFZ staff have done a good job of navigating these relationships and, most importantly, did not try to take all the credit for the turnaround in the school when we started to see results.

In 2008 Chief Monroe left the Richmond Police Department (RPD) to assume a similar role for the city of Charlotte, North Carolina. However, the RPD continued to support the VFZ program, which included sending representatives to VFZ sites in other cities, and has publicly credited the VFZ program with reductions in crimes such as motor vehicle thefts in the area around the Wythe High School (described further in the findings below).

Differences You Can Measure

The impact of the VFZ in George Wythe, both qualitatively (from interviews of school staff and students) and quantitatively (through the comparison of a wide range of data) between academic years 2007–2008 and 2008–2009, has been immediate and significant. Many teachers who were initially skeptical and sometimes intimidated by the presence of the Youth Advisors have, over time, come to see their value and have referred disruptive youth to the YAs, or requested their presence in the classroom.

Qualitatively, the principal, teachers, and other school staff observed positive changes in the school culture with the presence of the Youth Advisors in the school. For Principal Bell, VFZ helped him bring about the turnaround faster than he had experienced in his previous placements:

> We've had surprising success in just the first year here at the school, and the VFZ was a big part of that. In particular, the VFZ Youth Advisors have accelerated our efforts to strengthen what I call the school-home connection. Now, when a parent comes in with their child following a suspension, as is required, we have a Youth Advisor there, and an opportunity to give the parent information about the VFZ and possibly "recruit" the student into the program, thus providing them with the additional support and mentoring to prevent future suspensions and get them back on track as a student.

The philosophical/strategic alignment between Principal Bell and the VFZ is further reflected in their shared views on the students' need, and therefore the school's need, for more discipline and organization. As Pastor Rsen described,

> Our experience in working with these kids helped us see that their home and family life is often unsettled and chaotic. Therefore, we understand and supply their need for more structure in their lives through our after-school and Saturday programs, and hope to bring that into the school environment as well through the VFZ.

Assistant Principal Riva Green, who was at George Wythe the prior year, also saw the benefits of VFZ coming aboard at the same time as the new principal:

> I think it was perfect timing to have VFZ starting at the same time we had a new principal, because they were able to work together to reshape the school and make positive changes. I also think that the ROC's high visibility among many of the students, based on the work they do in the community, helped them hit the ground faster and begin to impact the kids' lives and behaviors.

Teachers have also responded positively to the presence of the VFZ. As Ahad Allah, an art teacher at George Wythe, explained,

> You could see kids that were on the verge of being disruptive getting redirected and making better choices. I have seen attendance in the class improve, with fewer kids cutting classes, and becoming more teachable in the classroom. I think that the reward system they use for their caseload kids, where they get an opportunity to go on a field trip for meeting certain academic or behavioral benchmarks, has helped a lot. As a result of all this, I have fewer disruptions, my classes are more productive, and I have more self-directed students to work with.

Youth Advisors

The Youth Advisors are the cornerstone of the VFZ program. They generally share similar life experiences as the youth they serve, in terms of having a past history of crime and substance abuse. In contrast with VFZ programs in other cities, the majority of the Youth Advisors in Richmond are white, whereas the majority of the students they serve are African American. However, as explained by Kwame Johnson, this distinction proved to be a nonfactor:

> At first we were challenged with the fact that the VFZ staff shared and understood the life experiences faced by these youth, in terms of some of the things they have gone through, but generally did not share a similar cultural or ethnic background. However, once you see the kids interacting with the VFZ staff, you realize that these kids don't see color; they see people who truly care for them. What the students are really looking for is someone to be real with them. That's all we needed to see to know that this program would succeed.

The VFZ model is simple, but the work is not easy. The day for Youth Advisors for VFZ Richmond begins at 6:30 a.m. when they meet as a team, discuss issues with particular students from the previous day, and get updates on school policies and/or activities. At 7:00 a.m., they go to their morning post to prepare to greet the students into school, and make themselves visible and available to students as the day begins. Kelly Williams, one of the Youth Advisors, explains the important role of morning posts as follows: "Monday mornings are especially important, because that's when we learn about what happened in the neighborhood over the weekend that may spill into the school." During the course of the day, all Youth Advisors assist security with monitoring the halls between periods, and also are present in the cafeteria during lunchtime.

Each Youth Advisor carries what they call a formal and an informal caseload of students. The formal caseload, of about twenty students, has the VFZ program track interventions and outcomes, both in terms of academic performance (i.e., GPA) and behavior-related data (e.g., fights, truancy, etc.). The VFZ caseload students are roughly made up of students specifically targeted by VFZ staff, principal, or teachers; students enrolled during reinstatement after a school suspension; and word-of-mouth referrals. The informal caseload constitutes students reaching out for relationship and connection with one or more Youth Advisors, since the VFZ staff always wants to be available to whomever needs their time and attention. The VFZ Richmond strategy, which also embraces the broader goals of the ROC after-school and Saturday programming, is not to eliminate gangs per se, but to reengineer them. Williams explains,

> With more time together with the kids through the VFZ, we can take what's good about gangs, as a social support network, and make it something positive. For example, through the after-school program at the school, which we just started this year [the 2009–2010 academic school year], we can remix the kids, so we have kids from different neighborhoods sitting together and doing activities together and re-form their groups to reduce the conflicts that might otherwise occur between different kids.

When conflicts do occur, the VFZ employs a formal mediation process, whereby the Youth Advisor brings the two students together; lays out the ground rules for communicating with one another; gives both students a chance to speak their piece, including an apology; and has them sign a mediation contract, where they pledge to not fight with one another in the future. During the 2008–2009 academic year, VFZ Richmond enacted 133 mediation contracts.

Impact on Students

The impact of the VFZ program on the students, as described by students, echoes the comments made by the ROC on how the program offers them additional time with, and exposure to, the students, as the key difference. As one student said,

> My youth advisor has helped me to stop being a follower, and to take responsibility for my actions, instead of just going with

the crowd. I've been involved with the ROC since I was in elementary school, but having them here in the school really makes a big difference, and helps to remind me of what I need to be doing to stay out of trouble and focus more on my schoolwork.

Another student talked about how the VFZ program gave him a reason to show up at school, and to focus more on learning: "Once I got involved with the VFZ, I stopped skipping school and changed my attitude about school and got my grades up."

Looking Forward

Plans are currently under way to expand the VFZ to another high school, which has also struggled with disruptive behavior and violence. The VFZ program is also expected to be operated by ROC as the community partner. For year two at George Wythe, the VFZ is looking forward to another year of successes and positive changes. As Williams reported,

There were a lot of adjustments we had to make the first year, but now we have a clearer understanding of our scope of work, and can build on the relationships we've developed with both staff and students. We believe there is room for more improvements and positive changes at George Wythe this coming year.

Assessing Data from the Richmond Public Schools and the Richmond Police Department

The impact the VFZ initiative has had within George Wythe High School is not only descriptive, but is captured through changes in data and outcomes tracked through the Richmond Public Schools. In particular, the Richmond VFZ demonstrated an impact after just one year of operation in the three following areas:

1. *Improved safety within the schools*, as measured both by changes in the number of incidents and the number of students involved in those incidents.

2. *Increased presence of students in school*, as measured by the number of unexcused absences, total absences, suspensions, suspension days, and truancy rates.

3. *Reduced need for police intervention*, as measured by changes in the number of calls for service, arrests, and motor vehicle thefts within one thousand feet of the George Wythe High School.

The long-term outcomes that VFZ hopes to achieve, whose impact is not shown after one year, are improvements in the school's overall GPA, as compared to the other Richmond high schools that do not have a VFZ program. Keep in mind, however, that VFZ staff is not directly involved in the education of youth, although the expectation is that a safer school environment will lead to improvements in academic performance.

When researchers evaluate programs, simply comparing outcomes before and after an intervention is not enough. Stated differently, it is necessary to ask if the pre- and post-outcome results are significantly different from a comparable group not receiving the intervention under study. Therefore, several comparisons were made between George Wythe High School and a comparable high school without the VFZ program. The Armstrong High School is similar to George Wythe in terms of the income and demographics from which it draws its students.

The number of school incidents and the number of students involved in those incidents at Armstrong both increased from academic year 2008 to 2009. For George Wythe, both decreased during the same time period (13 percent and 12 percent, respectively). Though we do not have a research design in place that would allow us to address cause and effect relationships, it is compelling nonetheless to observe the impressive differences presented between the two comparable Richmond schools.

Increased Presence in the School

Making the school safer is clearly a precursor for increasing student attendance. Table 2 shows the changes in trends in unexcused absences, total absences, suspensions, suspension days, and truancy rates for the two schools between AY 2008 and AY 2009.

Most notable in these comparative trends is in total absences, which increased by 68 percent at Armstrong from AY 2008 to AY 2009, while decreasing by 9 percent at George Wythe. Truancy rates increased 37

TABLE 2. Comparative Trends on Student Absence
from School (AY 2008 to AY 2009)

School	AY 2008	AY 2009	% Increase (Decrease)
Unexcused Absences			
Armstrong	13,428	15,916	19%
George Wythe	14,177	9,161	(35%)
Total Absences (days)			
Armstrong	22,641	37,988	68%
George Wythe	22,972	20,949	(9%)
Suspensions			
Armstrong	1,430	1,375	(4%)
George Wythe	1,001	994	(1%)
Total Suspension Days			
Armstrong	5,209	5,456	5%
George Wythe	4,438	3,978	(10%)
*Truancy Rate**			
Armstrong	29.84	40.91	37%
George Wythe	33.87	19.85	(41%)

*Truancy rates are calculated as the percentage of students absent from school for more than ten days in a given school year.

percent at Armstrong, while decreasing by 41 percent at George Wythe. These findings are consistent with comments by VFZ staff and students at George Wythe, in which the close relationships forged between students and staff make attending school more desirable. A striking benefit to reducing student absences is the dramatic change in the number of teaching days for both schools.[10] For example, total student absences at Armstrong reflect a total loss of 14,887 teaching days, while George

Wythe experienced a net gain of 1,776 teaching days between AY 2008 and 2009.

CONCLUSION

Our public schools are facing enormous challenges, especially in our urban centers where poverty is concentrated. Robert Woodson argues that a number of key foundations presently working with our inner-city schools are missing the boat when trying to address the problems that failing inner-city schools face. For instance, instead of devising strategies where people are intentionally involved with students firsthand as mentors, he believes these foundations are misguided when they come into a community and decide that reform means taking large schools and breaking them down into smaller schools. "They came into one Baltimore inner-city school and broke it into three multiplexes. The kids on the top floor have computers and uniforms. The first month, those kids get beaten up by the kids on the other two floors because they never took into consideration the civil environment. The result? "The worst schools become multiplexes where chaos prevails," states Woodson.

Alternatively, Woodson believes money should be invested in vouchers and that competition should be sought: "Take a lot of these disaffected schoolteachers and let them work with some of these faith-based groups that are already located in these communities and know how to be engaged in a positive way with our youth. We must operate in the social economy the way we operate in our regular economy, where competence is actually rewarded. In our market economy, it is not one's credentials that determines who leads, it is all about outcomes. In our social economy, this ought to apply also."

Woodson has put his time and talent where his mouth is. Drawing upon local faith-based leaders and groups, the Violence-Free Zone has become a force for youth violence prevention within middle and high schools across the United States. Believing that all solutions are local, the VFZ model has recruited and trained Youth Advisors from the same neighborhoods as the students in the schools they serve. These faith-motivated Youth Advisors have actively engaged public school students in these communities—24/7—and have become a stabilizing influence in the lives of these youth.

## CHAPTER 5

A Systematic Review of the Literature:
1944 to 2010

PLENTY OF GOOD research exists on delinquency, gang activity, drug use, domestic violence, and a host of other crime-related topics. Not surprisingly, crime remains a topic of concern for politicians, scholars, decision makers, and the general public. There is also growing interest in research on religion, spirituality, religious practices, and belief. In recent years there has been a great deal of interest in the role of religious institutions and faith-based organizations in confronting social problems and in the provision of social services to those most in need in our society.

Though crime and religion are hot topics, one might be surprised to learn an extensive research literature addressing the relationship of religion to crime does not exist. This is unfortunate, since properly understanding the nature of the relationship between religion and crime holds considerable implications for operating a more effective criminal justice system. Further, a more developed literature would provide valuable feedback and ongoing assistance to faith-motivated individuals, houses of worship, parachurch organizations, and faith-based groups in implementing programs and providing networks of support in order to more effectively reduce crime and delinquency. Understanding how religion might prevent crime, or help youth from bad neighborhoods to be resilient in spite of their surroundings, is profoundly important. Because faith-based programs focusing on mentoring, drug treatment, restorative justice, cognitive restructuring, or spiritual transformation already exist in most communities, rigorous evaluation and ongoing research will make it possible to not only understand how faith might matter but how these faith-informed approaches can be modified and improved. In order for this to happen, there must be sufficient interest in independent research from officials within the criminal justice system. Additionally, faith-motivated volunteers and organizations must also be open to the notion that objective research is something they should consider if for no other reason than it is an act of stewardship. Research like this will make it possible to improve programs in order to achieve better and more effective outcomes. Additionally, this kind of research will help us determine how and why faith might matter for some, but not for others.

A Systematic Review of the Literature

An idle mind is the devil's workshop. This widely recognized adage is not found in scripture, as some might assume. Rather it is an English proverb.[1] There are a number of variations of this proverb, but they tend to follow the same basic theme: people who don't have something particular to keep them occupied will likely be tempted to commit some kind of inappropriate behavior. Translating this old English proverb into a research proposition to test might read something like this: *The more one is involved in religious activities, the less likely one will be involved in criminal acts.* Propositions or hypotheses like this have been the subject of many studies, and this chapter turns a spotlight directly on these studies. Taking an objective look at all the published studies in a particular area is an arduous and time-consuming task, but it adds particular weight if one is able to assess an entire research literature. In fact, an exhaustive and objective review will make it possible to determine whether or not there is support for the notion that various measures of religiosity provide an effective antidote to crime and delinquency. In this chapter I review the existing literature in a systematic fashion and thus make it possible to assess and summarize the current state of our knowledge regarding the relationship between religion and crime.

Contemporary research on the relationship between religion and crime is generally traced to Travis Hirschi and Rodney Stark's important study titled "Hellfire and Delinquency," published in 1969.[2] Unexpectedly, the study became the subject of considerable debate and speculation. Hirschi and Stark's primary finding was that religious commitment among youth was not related to measures of delinquency. The study generated a great deal of interest among academics and beyond. Empirical evidence documenting that religion held little or no influence over the behavior of youth was greeted with positive and negative reactions.

Controversial publications are typically replicated to determine if the findings hold, and the "Hellfire and Delinquency" study would be no exception. A number of scholars replicated the study, and the replications both supported[3] and refuted[4] Hirschi and Stark's original finding. Rather than clarifying the situation, these initial replications seemed to muddy the waters. After a series of studies over a decade or so, we were still not able to answer the question of whether religion helped reduce delinquency. Stark and colleagues would later return to the issue and suggested that these contradictory findings were likely the result of the moral makeup of the community being studied. That is, areas with high church membership and attendance rates represented "moral communities," while areas with low church membership were more "secularized communities."[5] Stark predicted religion would deter delinquency in moral communities, but there would be little or no effect of religiosity on individuals residing in secularized communities.

The moral-communities hypothesis provided an important theoretical framework for understanding why religion reduced delinquency in some studies, while other studies found religion had no significant impact on delinquency.[6] Over the last twenty years, scholars have approached the religion-crime relationship from a number of different perspectives and have helped us understand the nature of the relationship between religion and crime.

One of the first studies to shed new light on the religion-crime relationship was conducted not by a criminologist, but by an economist, Richard Freeman, at Harvard University. Freeman was writing a book on the employment crisis among young black males raised in poverty in urban America.[7] Since delinquency and crime tend to be most heavily concentrated in poverty-stricken areas or what social scientists like to call socially disorganized communities, Freeman focused on poverty-stricken communities.[8] Decaying urban communities provide many hardships for residents, and consequently, many living in housing projects and similar poor areas become involved in illegal activities.

What is less well known, however, is the fact that the majority of urban black youth do not turn to crime and deviance, even though they live in communities where crime occurs all around them. Freeman's study is particularly helpful in turning our attention to one of the factors helping at-risk youth become resilient youth—kids who stay out of trouble in spite of the bad neighborhoods in which they reside.

Analyzing data collected by the National Bureau of Economic Research (NBER) on black male youth living in poverty tracts in Philadelphia, Boston, and Chicago, Freeman found that church-attending youth were significantly less likely to engage in a series of illegal behaviors than youth who did not attend church. Additionally, Freeman found that frequent church attendance was also associated with improved academic performance as well as positive employment indicators.

More than a decade later, several colleagues and I would replicate Freeman's 1986 study and find strong empirical support for his conclusions.[9] Results indicated that the frequency of attending religious services significantly lowered the likelihood that young black males living in poverty would commit illegal activities, use drugs, or be involved in drug selling.[10] Specifically, we found that the probability of committing a nondrug crime was reduced by 39 percent for youth who attended church more than a once a week when compared to youth who did not attend church. Similarly, when comparing at-risk youth who frequently attended church to comparable youth who did not attend church, the probability of drug use decreased by 46 percent. Finally, the probability of youth selling drugs was reduced by 57 percent when comparing regular church attendees to nonattendees.[11]

But can we draw the conclusion that church attendance is responsible for keeping these youth residing in housing projects in Boston, Chicago, and Philadelphia out of trouble? For example, could it be that those youth who attended church regularly actually came from stronger families or two-parent households where they were monitored and supported more closely? It is not possible to completely answer this question, but we do know that many of these youth came from households headed by only one parent—a factor that otherwise increases the likelihood of criminal activity. I found, however, that youth from single-parent households were similarly protected by frequent church attendance. Consequently, active participation in a church appears to play a critical protective role in fostering social control as well as making youth resilient to the negative influences of living in disadvantaged environments.[12]

There is also mounting evidence that religious involvement may lower the risks of a broad range of delinquent behaviors, including both minor and serious forms of criminal behavior.[13] Aided by a number of important delinquency studies and several systematic reviews of this literature, it has become increasingly clear that the research literature is not as inconclusive as some scholars have asserted.[14] In a systematic review of forty studies focusing on the relationship between religion and delinquency, my colleagues and I found that most of these studies reported an inverse relationship between measures of religiosity and delinquency (i.e., increasing religiosity is related to decreasing delinquency).[15] Several studies found no relationship or reported mixed findings, and only one found a positive link between greater religiosity and increasing delinquency (i.e., increasing religiosity is associated with increasing delinquency). Systematic reviews often examine the methodology and research design of the studies reviewed, essentially making it possible to compare one study to the next in terms of research quality. We found that among those studies with the most sophisticated research designs, there was an increased likelihood that higher levels of religiosity were linked to decreases in delinquency. On the other hand, those studies reporting inconclusive results tended to employ less sophisticated research designs.

In another systematic review, Baier and Wright review sixty studies within the religiosity-delinquency literature and reach much the same conclusion as our previous study.[16] Baier and Wright find that studies using larger and more representative data sets are more likely to find significant inverse effects (i.e., increasing religiosity and decreasing delinquency) than studies that utilize smaller, regional, or convenient samples. In a third systematic review, we reviewed studies examining religion and multiple outcome areas, including several that are relevant for our current discussion (i.e., alcohol abuse, drug use/abuse, and crime/delinquency). Among the ninety-seven alcohol studies reviewed, only two studies found religiosity to be associated with deleterious outcomes. Another ten studies reported inconclusive findings, while eighty-five studies found an inverse relationship, indicating increasing religiosity was associated with a lowered likelihood of alcohol abuse. We also found a similar pattern among the fifty-four studies reviewed examining drug use or abuse. Fifty of the fifty-four studies found increasing religiousness linked to decreasing drug use or abuse, while only one study found a positive relationship. Finally, we reviewed another forty-six studies within the crime and delinquency literature that examine the influence of religion, and the same trend is obvious—increasing religiosity is associated with lowered likelihood of criminal or delinquent behavior (thirty-seven studies), while religiosity is positively related to delinquency in only one study.[17]

In sum, these reviews confirm consistent and mounting evidence suggesting increasing religious commitment or involvement helps individuals avoid crime and delinquency. But are these research findings consistent with the more recent research literature on religion and crime? In order to answer this question, I report findings from the most thorough systematic review conducted to date of the relevant research literature on religion and crime. This comprehensive review utilizes multiple research strategies to locate studies from diverse disciplines and varied methodological perspectives. All totaled, this review located 272 studies on religion and crime that were published between 1944 and 2010, making the current systematic review the most extensive to be undertaken on this topic. In this systematic review I examine the type of study (e.g., cross-sectional, prospective cohort, retrospective, experimental, case control, or descriptive); the sampling method (e.g., random, probability, systematic sampling, convenience/purposive sample); the number of subjects in the sample; population (e.g., children, adolescents, high school students, college students, or adults); location; religious variables included in the analysis (e.g., religious attendance, scripture study, subjective religiosity, religious commitment, intrinsic religiosity, extrinsic religiosity, etc.); controls; and findings (e.g., no association, mixed evidence, beneficial association with outcome, or harmful association with outcome).[18]

The results of this current review are presented at the end of this chapter in Table 3. Consistent with previous systematic reviews, the vast majority of these studies find religion and religious involvement to be associated with decreases in various measures of crime and delinquency. Specifically, I found that 90 percent of the studies (247 of 272) report an inverse or beneficial relationship between religion and some measure of crime or delinquency. Only 9 percent of the studies (24 of 272) found no association or reported mixed findings, whereas only 2 out of 272 studies report that religion was associated with a harmful outcome.[19]

Until recently there has been a lack of consensus about the nature of this relationship between religion and crime. Based on our exhaustive review of studies utilizing vastly different methods, samples, and research designs, increasing religiosity is consistently linked with decreases in various measures of crime or delinquency. As expected, these findings are particularly pronounced among the more methodologically and statistically sophisticated studies, especially those relying upon nationally representative samples. Put simply, we find increasing religiousness to be associated with decreases in crime or delinquency. The weight of this evidence is especially intriguing in light of the fact that so many researchers continue to overlook religion.

For many, I suspect this review will prove very little. Some might argue, for example, that the majority of studies reviewed do not utilize longitudinal or experimental designs and rely upon mainly cross-sectional samples. The problem with criticisms like this is that they ignore the fact that social scientists have had a very bad habit of leaving religion variables out of research plans when longitudinal studies were designed and implemented. The fact that religion variables are either missing from so many important data sets, or contain only minimal religion measures when included, obviously limits the possibilities for researchers interested in conducting studies on the role of religion. This is why my mentor and landmark religion researcher David B. Larson often argued that religion was the "forgotten factor." I think Larson was being polite. The only real reason that religion is the forgotten factor is the bias against religion held by so many within the academic community.

The fact that 90 percent of these methodologically and theoretically diverse studies found beneficial associations between religion and crime reduction will not be enough to convince some people of the linkage. Until we are able to complete a more rigorous meta-analysis of this same literature, we will not be able to document effect sizes across studies.[20] Meta-analyses allow a more meaningful interpretation of the weight of the evidence presented in the systematic review. Since meta-analysis allows for a more standardized and valid assessment of the research literature, it is important to consider conducting meta-analyses. As a result of the value attributed to this methodological innovation, colleagues and I are now completing a detailed meta-analysis of this same literature to be published in 2012. Because of the obvious trends we see in the current as well as previous systematic reviews, we will be surprised if the meta-analysis we are currently conducting does not generally support the conclusions drawn for the systematic reviews reported here.

Assume for a moment the present systematic review found just the opposite—that 247 of the 272 studies (or 90 percent) found increasing religiosity to be associated with increasing crime or delinquency, and only 9 percent of the studies found religion to be associated with decreasing crime. Findings like this would likely be the lead story on the nightly news and appear on page one of most major newspapers. No doubt commissions would be put in place and Congress would be asked to investigate why religion was linked to increasing crime and delinquency, and what might be done to combat the deleterious impact of religion. But documenting an empirical link between religiosity on the one hand and harmful outcomes on the other has befuddled social scientists for decades. And systematic reviews of the research literature, like the one found in this chapter, provide ample evidence of that fact.

As evidence of this observation, consider the attention given to a questionable 1995 publication which concluded that the most religious societies in the world were more likely to suffer from higher rates of crime, homicide, sexually transmitted diseases, teenage pregnancies, and other social ills.[21] Further, the article drew the conclusion that more secular societies and jurisdictions were significantly less likely to experience these same social problems. The paper's author is an obscure writer without a college degree or any apparent training as a social scientist. However, media accounts of the study mistakenly refer to the author as a social scientist and even an expert. As was quickly discovered as soon as the article was released, it is by no means an example of serious scholarship, and it is inconceivable that it could have been published in a top or reputable social science journal that is peer-reviewed. However, the "study" was covered in newspapers around the world. It was featured prominently on radio and television, and was lauded by many observers and journalists as evidence that the influence of religion may well be harmful.

In sum, based on an exhaustive and objective review of 272 studies comprising the religion-crime literature published between 1944 and 2010, there is overwhelming empirical evidence of an inverse relationship between religion and crime. Simply stated, there is clear support for the central thesis of this book: more God equals less crime. In fact, I find that regardless of the methodology employed, the sample selected, or the measures utilized, the faith factor matters in important ways for crime reduction and prevention.

But how do we reconcile the fact that we have such consistent empirical evidence linking religion to crime reduction and yet there remains little acknowledgment of this fact? Two possibilities seem to emerge as reasonable explanations. First, scholars have not done a very good job of communicating these realities to the public at large. Second, persistent stereotypes, anecdotes, and sweeping generalizations of religion as bad seem to be much more newsworthy than do empirical studies that are not readily accessible to the public. Both of these explanations would suggest *More God, Less Crime* may be a much needed corrective to these two shortcomings.

TABLE 3. A Systematic Review of the Religion and Crime Literature

No.	Investigators	Type	Method	N	Population	Location	Religious Variable	Control	Findings
1	Adamcyzk (2008)	PC	R	1,449	Ad	National US	SR, ORA, RE	MC	B
2	Adelekan (1993)	CS	S/R	636	CS	Nigeria	SR, D	N	B
3	Adlaf (1985)	CS	R	2,066	Ad	Ontario	D, ORA, SR	N	B
4	Albrecht (1977)	CS	C	244	Mormon teens	UT, ID, LA	SR, ORA	MC	B
5	Albrecht (1996)	PC	R	12,168	HS	National US	ORA	MC	B
6	Alford (1991)	PC	C	157	Ad, PP	NE	Misc.	N	B
7	Allen (1967)	CS	S	179	HS (16–18)	Youth fac.	D, ORA, SR	MC	B
8	Amey (1996)	CS	R	11,728	HS	National US	OR, SR, D	MC	B
9	Amoateng (1986)	CS	R	17,000	HS	National US	SR, ORA	MC	B
10	Bahr (1993)	CR	C/P	322	Ad	3 west counties US	SR	MC	M
11	Bahr (1998)	CS	R	13,250	HS	UT	ORA, SR	MC	B
12	Bahr (2008)	PC	R	18,517	Ad	National US	A, SR	MC	B
13	Barnes (1994)	PC	R	658	Ad	Buffalo, NY	ORA	MC	B

14	Barrett (1988)	CT	S	326	Ad	TX	ORA	MC	B
15	Bell (1997)	CS	R	17,952	CS	National US	SR	MC	B
16	Benda (1994)	CS	R	1,093	HS	OK, MD, AR	ORA, SR	MC	B
17	Benda (1995)	CS	S	1,093	HS	AR, MD	ORA, SR	MC	B
18	Benda (1997a)	CS	S	724	HS	AR, OK	ORA, SR	MC	B
19	Benda (1997b)	CS	R	1,093	HS	5 US cities	ORA, SR	MC	B
20	Benda (1999)	CS	R	1,093	Ad	OK, MD, AR	Misc.	MC	B
21	Benda (2000a)	CS	R	1,057	HS	OK, MD, AR	Misc.	MC	B
22	Benda (2000b)	CC	C	600	Prisoners	AR	ORA, SR	MC	B
23	Benda (2001)	CS	R	837	HS	Southeast	Misc.	MC	M
24	Benda (2002)	CS	C	326	M (15–24)	AR	SR	SC	B
25	Benda (2006)	CS	R	3,551	Ad	Southern state	SR	MC	B

Type: CC case control; CR case report; CS cross-sectional; CT clinical trial; D descriptive; Exp experimental; PC prospective cohort; RS retrospective. **Method** (sampling): CP convenience/purposive sample; P probability, or population-based sample; R random; S systematic sampling.

N: number of subjects in sample; Cs controls. **Population:** Ad adolescents; C children; CDA community dwelling adults; CS college students; HS high school students. **Location:** city, state, region, or country. **Religious Variables:** CM church membership; D denomination; ER extrinsic religiosity; I intervention; IR intrinsic religiosity; M mysticism; NORA (scripture study); O orthodoxy; ORA organizational religious activities (religious attendance and related activities); Q quest; R religious coping; RB religious belief; RC religious commitment; RE religious experience; SR subjective religiosity; SWB spiritual well-being.

Controls: MC multiple controls; N no controls; NS no statistical analysis; SC some controls. **Findings:** B beneficial association with outcome; H harmful association with outcome; M mixed evidence; NA no association.

No.	Investigators	Type	Method	N	Population	Location	Religious Variable	Control	Findings
26	Benson (1989)	CS	R	>12,000	HS	National US	SR	MC	B
27	Bjarnason (2005)	CS	R	3,524	HS	Iceland	SR	MC	B
28	Bliss (1994)	CS	C	143	CS	OH	ORA, SR	N	M
29	Bowker (1974)	CS	R	948	CS	College	ORA, D	N	B
30	Brizer (1993)	CC	C	65	PP	N	ORA, NORA	N	B
31	Brook (1984)	CS	C/P	403	CS	College in NJ	ORA	MC	B
32	Brown T L (2001)	CS	R	899	Ad	OH, KY	ORA, IR, Misc.	N	B
33	Brown T N (2001)	CS	R	188,000	HS	National US	RCM	MC	B
34	Brownfield (1991)	CS	C/P	800+	HS	Seattle	SR, ORA, D	MC	B
35	Burkett (1974)	CS	C	855	HS	Pacific NW	ORA	SC	B
36	Burkett (1977)	CS	S	837	HS	Pacific NW	ORA, RB	SC	B
37	Burkett (1980)	CS	S	323	HS	Pacific NE	ORA, SR, RB	N	B
38	Burkett (1987)	PC	C	240	HS	Pacific NW	ORA, SR, RB	MC	B
39	Burkett (1993)	PC	R	612 and 428	HS	Pacific NW	RB, SR, ORA	MC	B
40	Cancellaro (1982)	CC	C	74	Drug addicts	KY	NORA, RE	N	B

41	Caputo (2004)	PC	R	1,911	Ad	National US	Misc.	MC	B
42	Caputo (2005)	PC	R	1,911	Ad	National US	Misc.	MC	B
43	Carlucci (1993)	CS	R	331	CS	Eastern US	D	N	B
44	Carr-Saunders (1944)	CC	C	276–551	Delinquents	London, UK	ORA	N	B
45	Cecero (2005)	CS	C/P	237	CS	NE University	Misc.	MC	B
46	Chadwick (1993)	CS	R	2,143	Ad (Mormons)	Eastern US	ORA, RB	MC	B
47	Chandy (1996)	PC	R	1,959	Ad	National US	SR	MC	B
48	Chawla (2007)	CS	R	1,442	CS	West Coast	SR	MC	B
49	Chen (2004)	CS	R	12,797	HS	Panama & DR	D, ORA	MC	B
50	Christo (1995)	PC	C	101	Poly-drug abuse	London	RB	N	B
51	Chu (2007)	PC	R	1,725	Ad	National US	ORA, SR	MC	B
52	Cisin (1968)	CS	R	2,746	CDA	National US	ORA, RC, RB	MC	B
53	Clark (1992)	CS	R	2,036	Medical students	Great Britain	D	N	B
54	Clear (2002)	PC	S	769	Prisoners	DE, TX, IN, MS	SR, D	MC	B
55	Cochran (1989)	CS	R	3,065	Ad	Midwest US	ORA, SR, D	MC	B
56	Cochran (1991)	CS	R	3,065	Ad	Midwest US	ORA, SR, D	MC	B
57	Cochran (1993)	CS	R	3,065	Ad	Midwest	Misc.	MC	B
58	Cochran (1994)	CS	C	1,600	HS	OK	ORA, SR	MC	B
59	Cohen (1987)	PC	S	976	Mother/caretaker	NY	ORA	MC	B

No.	Investigators	Type	Method	N	Population	Location	Religious Variable	Control	Findings
60	Coleman (1986)	CC	S	50	Opiate addicts	Philadelphia	ORA, SR	MC	M
61	Cook (1997)	CS	R	7,666	Youth (12–30)	United Kingdom	RCM	N	B
62	Coombs (1985)	PC	C	197	Ad	Los Angeles	RB, ORA	N	B
63	Crano (2008)	PC	R	2,111	Ad, HS	National US	RA	MC	B
64	Cretacci (2003)	CS	R	6,500	Ad, youth	National US	SR, ORA, RCM, D	MC	B
65	Cronin (1995)	CS	C	216	CS	ND	D, SR	N	B
66	Dennis (2005)	Q	D	1,725	15–21	National US	SR	SC	B
67	Desmond (1981)	PC	C	248	PP addicts	San Antonio	Misc.	N	B
68	Desmond (2009)	PC	R	1,725	Ad	National US	ORA, SR	MC	B
69	Dudley (1987)	CS	R	801	SDA Youth	National US	ORA, NORA, CM	SC	B
70	Dunn (2005)	CS	R	6,029	HS	National US	SR	MC	B
71	Ellifson (1983)	CS	R	600	Ad, HS	Atlanta, GA	RB, SR, NORA	SC	NA
72	Ellis (1989)	CS	C	354	CS	ND	RB, Misc.	SC	B
73	Ellis (2002)	P	C	11,000	CS, R	US & Canada	D	SC	B
74	Ellison (1999)	CS	R	13,017	CDA	National US	ORA, D, Misc.	MC	B
75	Ellison (2001)	CS	R	13,017	CDA	National US	ORA	MC	B
76	Ellison (2007)	CS	P	3,666	CDA	National US	ORA	MC	B
77	Engs (1980)	CS	S	1,691	CS	Australia	D, SR	N	B
78	Engs (1996)	CS	C	12,081	CS	National	SR, D	N	B

#	Study								
79	Engs (1999)	CS	C	4,150	CS	Scotland	D, SR	N	B
80	Evans (1995)	CS	S	477	CDA	Midwest US	OR, SR, RB, D	MC	B
81	Evans (1996)	CS	R	263	HS	Midwest City	ORA, SR, RC	MC	B
82	Fernquist (1995)	CS	—	180	CS	—	ORA, NORA	N	B
83	Forliti (1986)	CS	C	10,467	Ad/parents	United States	RB, ORA, SR	NS	B
84	Forthun (1999)	CS	R	526	CS	Southwestern	ORA	N	B
85	Foshee (1996)	PC	R	1,553	Ad	Southeast US	ORA, RB, SR, D	MC	B
86	Francis (1993)	CS	S	4,753	HS	England	ORA, RB	N	B
87	Francis (1994)	CS	S	16,734	Ad	England & Wales	A, D	N	B
88	Fraser (1967)	CS	R	282	Ad	New Zealand	Misc.	MC	B
89	Free (1992)	CS	C/P	916	CS	SW & Midwest	ORA, SR	N	B
90	Free (1993)	CS	C/P	916	CS	SW & Midwest	ORA, SR	N	B
91	Free (1994)	CS	C/P	916	CS	SW & Midwest	ORA, SR	N	B
92	Freeman (1986)	CS	R/R	4,961	Ad	Boston, Chicago, Philadelphia	ORA	MC	B
93	Galen (2004)	CS	C/P	265	CS	—	D, MD	MC	B
94	Gannon (1967)	CS	C/P	150	Ad	Chicago, IL	Misc.	N	M
95	Gardner (2007)	CC	C/P	202	Ad	Jamaica	Misc.	MC	B
96	Garis (1998)	PC	R	25,000	Ad	National US	ORA	MC	B
97	Grasmick (1991a)	CS	R	304	CDA	Oklahoma City	D, ORA, SR	SC	M

No.	Investigators	Type	Method	N	Population	Location	Religious Variable	Control	Findings
98	Grasmick (1991b)	CS	R	285	Adults	Oklahoma City	D, SR	MC	B
99	Grunbaum (2000)	CS	R	441	HS	TX	ORA	MC	B
100	Guinn (1975)	CS	S/R	1,789	HS	TX	ORA	N	B
101	Hadaway (1984)	CS	R	600	Ad, HS	Atlanta, GA	ORA, SR, NORA	SC	B
102	Hamil-Lucker (2004)	CS	PC	2,509	14–22	–	Misc.	N	B
103	Hammermeister (2001)	CS	C/P	462	CS	Pacific Northwest		N	B
104	Hansell (1990)	PC	R	908	Ad	NJ	ORA	MC	B
105	Hanson (1987)	PC	R	6,115	CS	US	D	N	B
106	Hardert (1994)	CS	C	1,234	HS, CS	AZ	ORA, SR	MC	NA
107	Hardesty (1995)	CS	C	475	HS, CS (16–19)	Midwest US	Family religiosity	SC	B
108	Harris (2003)	CS	R	1,393	Ad, LDS	7 US states	ORA, SWB, RE	MC	B
109	Hater (1984)	CS	S	1,174	PP	National	ORA, SR	MC	NA
110	Hawks (1994)	CS	R	293	Ad and parents	3 Utah counties	D	MC	NA
111	Hays (1986)	CS	R	1,121	Ad (13–18)	National	Religiosity scale	MC	B
112	Hays (1990)	CS	–	415	HS	–	D	MC	B
113	Heath (1999)	PC	R	1,687	Twins only	MO	Misc.	MC	B
114	Hercik (2004)	PC	C	413	Prisoners	FL	Religious program	MC	B

							Misc.		
115	Herronkohl (2005)	CS	R	680	HS	Pacific NW		MC	B
116	Higgins (1977)	CS	R	1,410	HS (10th)	Atlanta, GA	ORA	SC	B
117	Hill (1999)	PC	R	808	HS (1985–1993)	Seattle	ORA	N	M
118	Hillman (2000)	CS	C/P	292	HS	Midwest	D, SR	N	B
119	Hirschi (1969)	CS	R	4,077	HS	Northern CA	ORA	N	NA
120	Hodge (2001)	CS	R	414	HS	NM	ORA, RB	MC	B
121	Humphrey (1989)	CS	R	1,097	CS	Southeastern US	ORA	MC	B
122	Hundleby (1982)	CS	C	231	HS	Ontario	ORA, NORA	N	NA
123	Hundleby (1987)	CS	C	2,048	HS	Ontario	ORA	MC	B
124	Isralowitz (1990)	CS	R	7,671	CS	Singapore	RB	N	NA
125	Jang (2001)	PC	R	1,087	Youth (13–22)	National US	ORA, SR	MC	B
126	Jang (2003)	CS	R	2,107	CDA	National US	ORA, NORA, SR	MC	B
127	Jang (2004)	CS	R	659	CDA	National US	ORA, NORA, SR	MC	B
128	Jang (2005)	CS	R	659	CDA	National US	ORA, NORA, SR	MC	B
129	Jang (2007)	PC	R	1,250	CDA	National US	ORA, NORA, SR	MC	B
130	Jang (2008)	PC	R	1,044	Ad	National US	D, ORA, SR	MC	B
131	Jang (2010)	PC	R	1,033	Ad	National US	ORA, SR, D	MC	B

No.	Investigators	Type	Method	N	Population	Location	Religious Variable	Control	Findings
132	Jessor (1973)	PC	R	605–248	HS, CS	CO	ORA	N	B
133	Jessor (1977)	PC	R	432–205	HS, CS	CO	ORA, NORA, SR	N	B
134	Jessor (1980)	CS	R	13,122	Ad	National US	ORA, SR	MC	B
135	Jeynes (2006)	PC	R	18,726	Ad, HS	US	R	MC	B
136	Johnson (1987)	RS	S	782	Former prisoners	FL	ORA, SR	MC	NA
137	Johnson (1997)	CC	S	201–201	Former prisoners	NY	ORA, NORA	MC	B
138	Johnson (2000a)	CS	R/R	2,358	Youth	Boston, Chicago, Philadelphia	ORA	MC	B
139	Johnson (2000b)	PC	R	207	Ad	National US	ORA	MC	B
140	Johnson (2001a)	PC	R	1,087	Ad	National US	SR	MC	B
141	Johnson (2001b)	PC	R	1,305	Youth	National US	ORA, SR	MC	B
142	Johnson (2002)	CC	S	148–247	Former prisoners	Brazil	Religious program	SC	B
143	Johnson (2003)	PC	C	177–177	Former prisoners	TX	Religious program	MC	B
144	Johnson (2004)	CC	S	201–201	Former prisoners	NY	ORA, NORA	MC	B
145	Jones (2004)	CS	R	3,395	HS	Midwestern state	Misc.	MC	B

	Study								
146	Junger (1993)	CS	R	788	Ad	Netherlands	ORA	MC	B
147	Kandel (1976)	PC	R	1,112	Ad	NY	ORA	MC	B
148	Kandel (1982)	CS	R	1,947	Ad	NY	D	MC	B
149	Kandel (1986)	PC	R	1,004	Ad/Young adults	NY	ORA	MC	NA
150	Kerley (2005)	RS	R	386	Prisoners	MS	ORA, SR, RB	MC	B
151	Kerley (2005b)	RS	R	386	Prisoners	MS	ORA	MC	B
152	Kerley (2006)	RS	R	386	Prisoners	MS	ORA	MC	B
153	Kerley (2009)	RS	C/P	63	Prisoners	MS	ORA, SR, RB	MC	B
154	Kvaraceus (1944)	CS	S	700+	Ad	NJ	ORA, D	N	NA
155	Lee J (1997)	CS	R	7,658	Ad/Parents	US & Canada	ORA, Misc.	MC	B
156	Lee M (2004)	CC	R	1,889	Homicide	National	D	MC	B
157	Leigh (2005)	CS	R	196	CS	Intro Psych Class	Misc.	MC	B
158	Linville (2005)	CS	R	235	Teens	VA	ORA	MC	B
159	Litchfield (1997)	PC	R	>1,500	Ad	—	ORA, RB, RCM	MC	B
160	Lo (1993)	CS	R	160	CS	Deep South	D	MC	B
161	Long (1993)	PC	R	625	HS	MT	CM, ORA, SR	MC	B
162	Longest (2008)	PC	R	1,680	Ad	National US	ORA, SR, NORA	MC	B
163	Longshore (2004)	PC	R	1,036	Drug offenders	5 US cities	RB, SR, D	MC	B

No.	Investigators	Type	Method	N	Population	Location	Religious Variable	Control	Findings
164	Lorch (1985)	CS	S/R	13,878	HS	Colorado Springs	CM, ORA, SR	MC	NA
165	MacDonald (2005)	CS	R	5,414	HS	SC	ORA	MC	M
166	Mainous (2001)	–	P/C	191	Ad, HS	KY	A,R	MC	B
167	Marcos (1986)	CS	R	2,626	HS	Southwest US	ORA, RCM	MC	B
168	Mason (2001)	PC	R	840	Ad	NY	S, A, D	MC	B
169	Mason (2002)	PC	L	6,504	Ad	National US	Misc.	MC	B
170	Mauss (1959)	CS	S	459	HS	CA	D	N	B
171	McIntosh (1981)	CS	R	1,358	HS	TX	D, ORA, SR	MC	B
172	McLuckie (1975)	CS	R	27,175	HS	PA	D, RA	MC	B
173	Merrill (2001)	CS	R	1,036	CS	US	RCM	MC	B
174	Merrill (2005)	CS	C	1,333	CS	Utah	D, A, R	MC	B
175	Middleton (1962)	CS	–	554	CS	CA, FL	RB, ORA, SR	N	B
176	Miller (2000)	CS	R	676	Ad	National US	ORA, NORA, RE	MC	B
177	Miller (2001)	CS	C	279	C	NY	ORA, RCM, D	MC	B
178	Mitchell (1990)	CS	R	694	CS	2 universities	ORA	MC	B
179	Montgomery (1996)	CS	–	392	HS	Great Britain	NORA	SC	B
180	Moon (2000)	PC	R	788	Mother/child	National US	ORA	MC	M
181	Moore (1995)	CS	C	2,366	Ad	Israel	D, SR	N	B

182	Morris (1981)	CS	C	134	CS	TN	IR, ER	N	B
183	Mullen (2001)	CS	R	1,534	HS	Netherlands	D, ORA, RB	N	B
184	Muller (2001)	PC	P	—	HS	US	ORA	MC	B
185	Nelsen (1982)	CS	R	4,531	HS	NE US	ORA, D	N	B
186	Newcomb (1986)	PC	R	994	Ad	Los Angeles	SR	N	B
187	Newman (2006)	CC	C/P	827	HS	Thailand	D	N	B
188	Nonnemaker (2003)	PC	R	16,306	Ad	National US	IR, ER	MC	B
189	O'Connor (2002)	CS	C/P	1,597	Prisoners	SC	ORA, NORA	SC	B
190	Oetting (1987)	CS	S	415	HS	Western US	SR, ORA	MC	B
190	Oetting (1987)	CS	S	415	HS	Western US	SR, ORA	MC	B
191	Oleckno (1991)	CS	C	1,077	CS	Northern IL	ORA, SR	N	B
192	Onofrio (1999)	CS	C	1,127	C, Ad, HS	US-Mid Atlantic	D, R	MC	B
193	Parfrey (1976)	CS	R	444	CS	Ireland	ORA, RB	N	B
194	Park (1998)	CS	R	1,081	HS	National US	RB	MC	B
195	Park H (1999)	PC	R	7,692	HS	National US	D	MC	B
196	Parsai (2008)	CS	C/P	1,087	Ad	Southwest	ORA, D	MC	B
197	Patock-Peck-ham (1998)	CS	C/P	364	CS	AZ	D, IR, ER	MC	M
198	Pearce M (2003)	PC	R	10,444	Ad & mothers	US	SR, D	MC	B

No.	Investigators	Type	Method	N	Population	Location	Religious Variable	Control	Findings
199	Pearce L. (2004)	PC	R	1,703	6th & 8th grade	Northeastern US	ORA, NORA, SR	MC	B
200	Peck (1985)	PC	R	817	HS	National US	RCM	MC	M
201	Perkins (1985)	CS	S	1,514	CS 17-23	New York	D, S	MC	B
202	Perkins (1987)	CS	S	860	CS	New York	SR, D, Misc.	MC	B
203	Pettersson (1991)	CS	R	118	Police districts	Sweden	ORA	SC	B
204	Petts (2007)	PC	R	1,259	National survey	US	Misc.	MC	B
205	Petts (2009)	PC	R	2,472	National survey	US	SR, Misc.	MC	B
206	Piko (2004)	CS	R	1,240	PV	Szeged, Hungary	ORA, prayer	MC	B
207	Piquero (2000)	CC	C/P	150	PV	Detention facility	Misc.	MC	B
208	Pirtle (2006)	PC	R	929	PV	National US	SR	MC	B
209	Powell (1997)	CS	S	521	HS high risk	Birmingham, AL	ORA, SR	MC	B
210	Preston (2005)	CS	R	516	HS	Southern US state	ORA, RCM, RB	MC	B
211	Pullen (1999)	CS	R	217	PV	Southeast US	ORA	MC	R
212	Regnerus (2003a)	PC	R	9,667	HS	National US	ORA, SR	MC	B
213	Regnerus (2003b)	PC	R	9,234	HS	National US	ORA, IR	MC	B

214	Regnerus (2003c)	PC	R	9,200	HS	National US	ORA, IR	MC	B
215	Regnerus (2003d)	PC	R	11,890	Ad, Parents	National US	ORA, RC, D	MC	B
216	Resnick (1997)	CS	R	12,118	Ad	National US	SR	MC	NA
217	Ritt-Olson (2004)	CC	C/P	382	HS	CA	ORA, RB, SR	MC	B
218	Rhodes (1970)	CS	R	21,720	HS	TN	ORA, D, Misc.	MC	B
219	Rohrbaugh (1975)	CS	C	475–221	HS/CS	CO	ORA, RB, RE	N	B
220	Ross (1994)	CS	R	271	CS	Seton Hall	Misc.	MC	M
221	Schiff (2006)	CS	R	600	HS	Jerusalem	ORA	MC	B
222	Schlegel (1979)	CS	R	842	HS	Ontario, Canada	ORA, D	N	B
223	Scholl (1964)	CC	C/P	52–28	Ad delinquents	IL	RB, RE	N	B
224	Schulenberg (1994)	PC	R	3,399	HS	National US	ORA, RC	MC	H
225	Simmons (2004)	CS	R	451–867	Families/ children	IA	Misc.	MC	B
226	Singh (1979)	CS	C	54/59	CA/HS	Ottawa, Canada	SR	N	B
227	Sinha (2007)	CS	R	2,004	Ad	National US	ORA, SR	MC	B
228	Sloane (1986)	CS	R	1,121	HS	National US	ORA, SR	MC	B
229	Sorenson (1995)	CS	R	1,118	HS	Seattle	ORA, D	MC	B

No.	Investigators	Type	Method	N	Population	Location	Religious Variable	Control	Findings
230	Stark (1982)	CS	R	1,799	Ad M	National US	RB, SR, ORA	N	B
231	Stark (1996)	CS	R	11,955	Ad	National US	D, ORA	SC	B
232	Steinman (2004)	CS	C	705	HS	Midwest City	ORA	N	B
233	Steinman (2008)	CS	R	33,007	Ad	Columbus, OH	ORA	MC	B
234	Stewart (2001)	—	C/P	337	CS	Southern US	SR, RB	N	B
235	Stewart (2002)	CS	R	2,317	Ad	National	ORA, SR, NORA	N	B
236	Stylianou (2004)	CS	R	275	CS	Pacific NW	RCM	MC	B
237	Sussman (2005)	CS	R	501	Ad	Southern CA	Misc.	MC	M
238	Sussman (2006)	CS	R	501	Ad	Southern CA	Misc.	MC	B
239	Taub (1990)	CS	R	3,500	HS	National US	ORA, SR	MC	B
240	Tenent-Clark (1989)	CC	C	25–25	Ad	CO	SR	N	B
241	Templin (1999)	CS	C/P	277	CS	Catholic college	RC	MC	B
242	Tibbetts (2002)	CS	C/P	598	CS	Into courses	SR	MC	B
243	Tittle (1983)	CS	R	1,993	15 and older	IA, NJ, OR	ORA, SR	MC	B
244	Travers (1961)	—	C/P	223	10–17	NE urban area	RCM	MC	B
245	Trawick (2006)	—	R	120	Counties	KY	Misc.	N	B
246	Turner C (1979)	CS	R	379	CS	Private school, NJ	Misc.	N	B
247	Turner N (1994)	CS	R	247	HS	Austin, TX	D, ORA	MC	B

248	Vakalahi (2002)	CS	R	4,983	Ad	UT	D	MC	B
249	Valliant (1982)	PC	R	456	Ad	Boston	ORA	N	B
250	Van den Bree (2004)	CS	PC	14,133	Ad, CS	National US	ORA, SR, Misc	MC	B
251	Veach (1992)	CS	C	148	CS	NV	RE, Misc.	N	H
252	Vener (2003)	CS	C	4,220	Ad, CS	3 Midwest cities	RB	N	B
253	Walker (2007)	CS	R	1,273–812	Ad, HS	New York City	ORA, SR	MC	B
254	Wallace (1991)	CS	R	—	Ad	National US	ORA, SR	N	B
255	Wallace (1998)	CS	R	5,000	HS	National US	D, ORA, SR	MC	B
256	Wallace (2003)	CS	R	47,738	HS	UW	SR, ORA, D	MC	B
257	Wallace (2007)	CS	R	16,595	HS	National US	ORA, SR, Misc.	MC	B
258	Walsh (1995)	CS	R	480	CS	Boise State	ORA, SR	MC	B
259	Wattenburg (1950)	CS	S	2,137	Ad	Detroit, MI	ORA	N	B
260	Welch (2006)	CS	R	350	CDA	Midwest	ORA, SR	MC	B
261	Wechsler (1979)	CS	R	7,170	CS	New England	D, ORA	N	B
262	Wechsler (1995)	CS	R	17,592	CS	National	SR	MC	B
263	Weill (1994)	PC	R	437	HS	France	ORA	N	B
264	White (2008)	PC	R	825	CS/Ad	Washington	ORA	MC	B
265	Wickerstrom (1983)	CS	C/P	130	CS	4 states	IR, ER	MC	B
266	Wills (2003)	PC	R	1,182	Ad	NY	RB, SR, Misc.	MC	B

No.	Investigators	Type	Method	N	Population	Location	Religious Variable	Control	Findings
267	Windle (2005)	PC	R	760	Ad	NY	ORA, SR	MC	B
268	Wright (1971)	CS	C	3,850/ 1,574	CS	England	RB, ORA, Misc.	N	B
269	Yarnold (1995)	CS	R	1,694	Ad	Dade County, FL	SR	MC	B
270	Youniss (1997)	CS	R	3,119	HS	National US	ORA, SR	MC	B
271	Zhang (1994)	CS	C	1,026	CS	China, Taiwan, US	SR, NORA, ORA	MC	B
272	Zimmerman (1992)	—	C/P	218	Ad	Inner-city Baltimore	Misc.	MC	B

## CHAPTER 6

Can a Faith-Based Prison Reduce Recidivism?

IT IS NOT a new idea that the life of even the worst prisoner can be transformed. Clergy and religious practitioners have proclaimed this message as long as prisons have existed. In recent years, however, there has been considerable interest in going beyond traditional prison ministry, to establishing faith-based prison programs, dorms, or even entire faith-based prisons. One of the rationales for the emphasis on faith-based prison interventions is the common criticism that traditional prison programs are simply not effective in rehabilitating inmates or helping former prisoners become law-abiding citizens once they are released back into society. Many prison wardens and correctional administrators would wholeheartedly agree with this assessment and quickly add that the purpose of correctional institutions is not rehabilitation, but custody and public safety. This observation is not meant to suggest prison officials are opposed to the idea of rehabilitation. Rather, it is more a recognition of the elusive nature of authentic rehabilitation, especially considering the finite resources available to prisons. What do the data tell us about the effectiveness of prisoner treatment programs?

PRISONER REHABILITATION: WHAT WORKS?

Robert Martinson's widely cited study, "What Works? Questions and Answers about Prison Reform," addressed the question of whether secular treatment programs are effective. This study, or at least many of the subsequent interpretations of it, seemed to answer this question emphatically in the negative: nothing works.[1] However, subsequent research has more accurately answered the question this way: some programs do reduce recidivism for some offenders, in some settings.[2] Over the last two decades a number of studies have systematically evaluated the effectiveness of various correctional treatment programs to reduce recidivism. These research reviews draw very similar conclusions about what is effective in reducing recidivism following release from prison.[3] The rehabilitation programs that were most effective included at least one of the following components: academic skills training (e.g., adult basic education), vocational skills training (e.g., acquiring and maintaining employment), cognitive skills programs (e.g., goal setting, problem solving, and self-control), and drug abuse treatment.

It should be noted, however, that the amount of recidivism (reincarceration) reduction for those in secular programs when compared to prisoners not receiving the program tends to be rather small (e.g., 5 to 10 percent).[4] Unfortunately, most evaluations of these programs are underfunded, which makes interpretation of the results less definitive. For example, some research only reports on program completers without consideration of matched or comparison groups. Such research presents insurmountable challenges to both validity and reliability. In sum, there is research evidence that some secular programs can reduce recidivism, but these reductions tend to be quite modest. This observation begs the question: can faith-based prison programs aid in reducing recidivism?

FAITH-BASED PRISON PROGRAMS AND RECIDIVISM

Prison Fellowship (PF) has the most pervasive outreach of existing prison ministries.[5] At the core of PF's mission is the premise that crime is fundamentally a moral and spiritual problem requiring a moral and spiritual solution.[6] Some of the earliest prisons in America were also based on the belief that crime was a moral and spiritual problem, and that prisoners needed religion to reform. Consequently, intensive religious instruction and training were integral in some of America's earliest prisons. It should not come as a surprise, then, that a significant percentage of today's prison vernacular as well as philosophy draw from religious concepts or perspectives (e.g., corrections, penitentiary, solitary confinement, reform, and restorative justice).[7]

Prison Fellowship and many other prison ministries still believe religion is the critical ingredient in offender rehabilitation and helping former prisoners to lead a crime-free life. PF offers prisoners a variety of in-prison programs. Through one- to three-day seminars and weekly Bible studies, inmates are taught to set goals that prepare them for release. These programs teach concepts such as "surviving the prison environment, beginning a relationship with God in prison, overcoming obstacles, building better families, sharing the Gospel behind bars, and preparing for life on the outside." Weekly Bible studies usually last an hour, and one- to three-day seminars might be offered several times a year at a particular prison. The level of prisoner exposure to such religious programs would probably be a maximum of fifty hours of Bible study and several days of intensive seminars annually—a relatively modest correctional intervention.

There is, however, preliminary empirical evidence that regular participation in volunteer-led Bible studies is associated with reductions in recidivism.[8] For example, during a one-year post-release follow-up study I found that prisoners from four different New York prisons who attended ten or more Bible studies during a one-year period prior to release were significantly less likely to be arrested. In a more recent study tracking these same prisoners for an additional seven years, I found that regular participation in volunteer-led Bible studies remains significantly linked to lower rates of recidivism for two years and even three years postrelease.[9] Even for a substantial intervention it is noteworthy to observe an effect two or three years after release, but for a minor intervention like volunteer-led Bible studies, it is unheard of.

If participation in relatively small doses of religious programs can have a measurable and beneficial effect on inmates, imagine the effect an extended faith-based prison program might have. Believing that a much more intensive intervention could lead to even better outcomes, PF began to strategize how it might be possible to create an unapologetically faith-based community within prisons in the early 1990s.

THE TEXAS IFI PROGRAM

In the mid-1990s Prison Fellowship decided to pursue an unusual correctional experiment. PF's plan was to locate a willing prison partner that would allow PF to launch a program replacing occasional volunteer efforts with a completely faith-based approach to prison programs. The ultimate goal would be to reform prisoners as well the prison culture. Charles Colson, founder of PF, unsuccessfully pitched this idea to a number of governors, before finding an enthusiastic partner in then–Texas governor George W. Bush. PF moved quickly and introduced the concept of a faith-based program to the Texas Department of Criminal Justice (TDCJ) in January 1996. The concept described a program with a distinctly Christian orientation, "emphasizing restorative justice, in which the offender works through several phases of treatment to reshape his value system."[10] Shortly thereafter, the seventy-fifth Texas Legislature directed TDCJ to develop a rehabilitation tier of programs that would be evaluated on its success in reducing recidivism."[11] The InnerChange Pre-Release Program, as it was originally named, was officially launched in April 1997.

The collaboration between TDCJ and PF represented a first for Texas, if not the country.[12] According to Prison Fellowship, the InnerChange Freedom Initiative (as it was later called) is different than other prison ministries in that it represents the first full-scale attempt to offer religious programs in a prison environment virtually "around-the-clock." The InnerChange Freedom Initiative (IFI) promotes adult basic education, vocational training, life skills, mentoring, and aftercare, while linking each of these components in a setting permeated by faith.

IFI is a "faith-saturated" prison program whose mission is to "create and maintain a prison environment that fosters respect for God's law and rights of others, and to encourage the spiritual and moral regeneration of prisoners."[13] According to the IFI promotional material, the program is a "revolutionary, Christ-centered, Bible-based prison program supporting prison inmates through their spiritual and moral transformation beginning while incarcerated and continuing after release."[14]

IFI was officially launched in April 1997, at the Carol Vance Unit, a 378-bed prison in Richmond, Texas.[15] The Vance Unit, one of over one hundred prisons located throughout Texas, was selected because of its custody level as a prerelease facility and its proximity to the Houston area—the focus of aftercare resources and volunteer recruitment. Only offenders from Houston or surrounding counties were considered for participation in the program.[16] Two hundred beds in the Vance Unit, or essentially half the facility, were reserved for participants in the IFI program.[17]

Simply stated, IFI is responsible for inmate programs, and TDCJ is responsible for security and custody. Prison Fellowship was so optimistic that IFI would be successful in reducing recidivism, it agreed to fund the entire program with private dollars—an offer Texas was quick to accept.[18] The Texas Department of Criminal Justice covers the security and operating costs of the Vance Unit. Together, Prison Fellowship and the Texas Department of Criminal Justice formed a unique private-public partnership—one designed to test the proposition that this sacred-secular collaboration could achieve the civic purpose of reducing recidivism and thereby increase public safety.

Anchored in biblical teaching, life skills education, and group accountability, IFI established a three-phase program involving prisoners in sixteen to twenty-four months of in-prison biblical programs and six to twelve months of aftercare while on parole. Phase I provides a spiritual and moral foundation from which the rest of the program is based. Phase II tests the inmate's value system in real-life settings in hopes of preparing him for life after prison. Commonly referred to as aftercare, Phase III is the reentry component of IFI and is designed to help assimilate the inmate back into the community through productive and supportive relationships with family, local churches, and the workplace.

Phase I of IFI lasts approximately twelve months and focuses on rebuilding the inmate's spiritual and moral foundation as well as providing educational and survival skills. A heavy emphasis is placed on

▼ Biblical education, GED, tutoring, substance abuse prevention, and life skills

▼ Work (jobs are similar to those of other prisoners in the general population)

▼ Support groups designed to increase one's personal faith (Survival Kit, Heart of the Problem, Experiencing God, and Masterlife)[19]

▼ Support groups for enriching relations with family members and crime victims

▼ Mentoring

▼ Peer groups (Community Bible Study)

Phase I is designed to transform the criminal thinking process and establish a new foundation for growth. Six months into Phase I, IFI participants are supposed to be matched with a mentor. Mentors are

Christian men from the Houston community who meet with IFI prisoners one-on-one for a minimum of two hours per week.

Phase II of the IFI program lasts six to twelve months and seeks to continue the educational, work, and support-group aspect of the program. The main difference in Phase II is that IFI participants are allowed to perform community service work during the day at off-site locations, such as Habitat for Humanity. IFI members in Phase II continue with Christian-based education, Bible study courses, mentoring, and support groups, but with a special emphasis on leadership issues. Since IFI operates under the assumption that the program encourages spiritual growth, it is expected that in Phase II participants will begin to take on leadership roles within the program.

Evening programs are also offered to IFI participants throughout the week with support groups focusing on a different topic each night: Personal Faith, Mentoring, Substance Abuse, Family/Crime Victims, Community Bible Study. Additionally, intensive spiritual weekend retreats are offered periodically through Kairos, a nationally recognized prison ministry.

Phase III of IFI is the aftercare component of the faith-based program and lasts for an additional six to twelve months. The mission of the aftercare program is to assist participants in their reentry into society by helping with housing and employment referrals, facilitating the mentoring relationship, and making connections between the offender and local church communities that will provide a nurturing environment to continue the former prisoner's spiritual growth. Aftercare workers recruit new churches and volunteers to assist in the mentoring of IFI participants, and to help with other critical reentry needs such as housing, transportation, and employment.

IFI made the decision early on that the target of aftercare services would be directed toward those offenders completing at least sixteen months of the IFI prison program at the Carol Vance Unit. Therefore, those offenders who did not complete the program because of an opportunity for early parole, or who are asked to leave the program early (typically for disciplinary reasons), for example, were not guaranteed reentry assistance from IFI's aftercare workers. The justification for this controversial decision was that PF wanted to encourage and reward successful behavior (completing the program) with additional assistance beyond the prison walls. Arguably, those offenders most in need of aftercare may well be those who did not receive aftercare since they did not complete the program. IFI leadership ultimately decided it was more prudent to "invest" already limited aftercare resources in only those program participants who had exhibited the most progress by completing the program, rather than investing in individuals who had not shown progress in the program.[20]

Evaluating the Texas InnerChange Freedom Initiative

The seventy-fifth Texas Legislature directed the Texas Department of Criminal Justice to develop a rehabilitation tier of programs, and required these programs to be monitored and evaluated by the Criminal Justice Policy Council (CJPC).[21] However, in addition to documenting outcomes like recidivism, PF felt it vital to commission an independent evaluation that would focus more on the IFI participants and the program itself.[22] The findings of the evaluation reported here relied on the recidivism and outcome data generated by the CJPC, as well as data I collected on the IFI program, participants, staff, volunteers, and correctional staff.[23]

The evaluation approach combined both a quantitative study and a qualitative study (see chapter 7). Like the CJPC evaluation, the quantitative aspect of the independent evaluation essentially focused on recidivism outcomes, namely arrest and incarceration of former IFI participants. The qualitative component, however, relied largely upon observational work and field interviews. This approach helped to document the workings of the faith-based prison program, the spiritual changes in the participants as well as the prison environment, and the experiences of IFI participants following release from prison. Appendix B provides a detailed and systematic discussion of the research methodology including selection criteria for admission to IFI, a thorough explanation of the match design utilized, discussion of IFI participants—the study group, selection bias, graduating from the IFI program, measuring recidivism, and monitoring the role of mentoring. The following are the results from the quantitative study.

Findings presented in Table 4 compare the measures of recidivism between the total sample of IFI participants and each of the three comparison groups. As can be seen, 36.2 percent of IFI participants were arrested during the two-year period following release. Similarly, 35 percent of the matched group, 34.9 percent of the screened group, and 29.3 percent of the volunteered group were arrested during the two-year follow-up period. Likewise, there is little difference between IFI members (24.3 percent) and the matched group (20.3 percent), the screened group (22.3 percent), and the volunteered group (19.1 percent) in terms of the percentage of former prisoners who were once again incarcerated in the two-year postrelease period.

TABLE 4. Recidivism Data among IFI Participants and the Match Group

RECIDIVISM	COMPARISON GROUPS			
	IFI Participants	Match Group	Screened but Did Not Enter	Volunteered but Did Not Enter
Percent Arrested within Two Years of Release	36.2% (n=64)	35.0% (n=614)	34.9% (n=378)	29.3% (n=164)
Percent Incarcerated within Two Years of Release	24.3% (n=43)	20.3% (n=356)	22.3% (n=242)	19.1% (n=107)
Sample Size	177	1,754	1,083	560

Since IFI was launched in early 1997, representatives of both IFI and PF have maintained that in order for the program to be effective in reducing recidivism, participants would have to complete all three phases of the program. This rationale is based on the premise that each phase of the program builds upon the previous phase. Stated differently, IFI participants will find it difficult to live a crime-free life and survive parole if they do not complete all three phases and graduate from the program. Table 5 documents that 75 of the 177 IFI participants (42 percent) completed all program phases and graduated from the program, while 102 members (58 percent) did not complete all three phases of the program. Hispanics are most likely to graduate from the program (61 percent), and African Americans are least likely to complete all the components of IFI (37 percent). Prisoners over the age of thirty-five are

TABLE 5. Demographic Characteristics of IFI Noncompleters and Completers

CHARACTERISTICS OF OFFENDERS	IFI GROUPS	IFI Participants	Percent Completing Program ("Graduate")	Percent Not Completing Program
		42%	58%
Race/Ethnicity				
African American		67%	37%	63%
Hispanic		16%	61%	39%
Anglo		18%	45%	55%
Age Group				
≤35		48%	35%	65%
>35		52%	52%	48%
Offense Type				
Violent		12%	46%	54%
Property		36%	41%	59%
Drug		50%	42%	58%
Risk Score				
High Risk		31%	42%	58%
Medium Risk		54%	47%	53%
Low Risk		15%	57%	43%
Sample Size		177	75	102

more likely than those under thirty-five to have graduated or completed all three phases of the IFI program (52 percent vs. 35 percent, respectively). Inmates with low salient factor risk scores were more likely than those with high salient factor scores to graduate from the program (57 percent vs. 42 percent).

Among the 102 who did not graduate from the IFI program, 51 (50 percent) were released via parole or mandatory release before they could finish all phases of IFI. Early release on parole was a significant problem for several of the first few cohorts or groups entering IFI, as the Texas Parole Board came under pressure in 1998 and 1999 to stabilize the size of the prison population. Not surprisingly, among the first to be paroled early were minimum-custody prisoners, including those from IFI. The problem of early release on parole was subsequently minimized after the first several cohorts were removed before they could complete the IFI program for the following reasons: 19 for disciplinary reasons, 4 at the request of IFI staff, 1 for medical problems, and 24 at the voluntary request of the applicant.

DOES PARTICIPATION IN IFI REDUCE RECIDIVISM?

Table 6 presents the recidivism findings comparing IFI participants to various comparison groups. As mentioned earlier, there is no difference between the total IFI sample and the matched group on either measure of recidivism. Simply stated, participation in the IFI program is not related to recidivism reduction. Many of the IFI participants were paroled early by TDCJ and did not have the benefit of staying in the program. As one might expect, program graduates are much less likely than IFI participants who did not complete the program to be arrested within the two-year tracking period (17.3 percent vs. 50 percent). In a similar pattern, IFI graduates are significantly less likely to be incarcerated within two years of release than those IFI members not completing the program (8 percent vs. 36.3 percent).

IFI program graduates have significantly lower rates of arrest than the matched group (17.3 percent vs. 35 percent), or either of the two comparison groups—the screened group (34.9 percent) and the volunteered group (29.3 percent). Similarly, those completing the IFI program have

TABLE 6. Results of IFI Texas Two-Year Recidivism Analysis

	Full Sample (n=1931)		IFI Sample (n=177)		IFI Graduates (n=75)		IFI Noncompleters (n=102)	
RECIDIVISM TYPE	(1a) IFI vs.		(1b) IFI Graduates vs.		(1c) < 16 months vs.		(1d) < 16 months vs.	
	(2a) Match Group		(3b) Noncompleters		(3c) > 16 months		(3d) > 16 months	
	(1a)	(2a)	(1b)	(3b)	(1c)	(3c)	(1c)	(3c)
Arrest								
% Arrested	36.2%	35.0%	17.3%	50.0%	15.0%	20.0%	46.5%	68.8%
# Arrested	64	614	13	51	6	7	40	11
Sample Size	177	1,754	75	102	40	35	86	16
Chi-Square	0.09, p = .76		19.98, p < .0001		0.33, p < .5652		2.67, p < .1023	
Incarceration								
% Incarcerated	24.3%	20.3%	8.0%	36.3%	5.0%	11.4%	34.9%	43.8%
# Incarcerated	43	356	6	37	2	4	30	7
Sample Size	177	1,754	75	102	40	35	86	16
Chi-Square	1.57, p = .21		18.79, p < .0001		1.05, p < .3059		0.46, p < .4982	

Note: All tests used the Pearson X2 statistic with one degree of freedom for a 2 X 2 table.

significantly lower rates of incarceration than the matched group (8 percent vs. 20.3 percent), as well as the screened group (22.3 percent) and the volunteered group (19.1 percent).

The fact that IFI graduates are significantly less likely to be either arrested or incarcerated during the two-year period following release from prison represents initial evidence that program completion of this faith-based initiative is associated with lower rates of recidivism of former prisoners. As noted earlier, it is not unusual to observe 5 to 10 percent reductions in recidivism for inmates who complete various in-prison treatment programs. The recidivism reductions found in the current two-year postrelease study of IFI are over 17 percent for arrest and 12 percent for incarceration. Though the number of offenders in the current study group is quite small (n=177), the results are nonetheless promising and considerably higher than most reported within the correctional literature.

That program completion is significantly linked to reductions in recidivism is an important observation. This finding, however, does not by itself reveal if it is program completion or merely the length of time in the program that is most related to recidivism reduction. In order to examine this issue more completely, we specifically focused on length of time in the IFI program for program completers. The findings presented in Table 6 indicate that those participants graduating from IFI with less than sixteen months in the program had lower rates of arrest (15 percent vs. 20 percent) and incarceration (5 percent vs. 11.4 percent) than those graduates who remain in the program for sixteen months or more. Similarly, noncompleters with less than sixteen months in the IFI program had lower rates of arrest (46.5 percent vs. 68 percent) and incarceration (34.9 percent vs. 43.8 percent), than those noncompleters with sixteen or more months in IFI. Though IFI participants (both completers and noncompleters) with less than sixteen months in the program have lower recidivism rates, the difference is not statistically significant. More research is needed to examine the intriguing question of optimum program length. Is it possible that after a certain time period in such an intensive program there is a point of diminishing or even negative returns? As more program participants go through the program, a larger sample will make it possible to answer this question.

As mentioned earlier, we also decided to examine a fourth comparison group—those IFI participants who were paroled early before they could complete the IFI program. This comparison group comprises former prisoners who were not removed from the program for disciplinary reasons and may represent a more suitable comparison group than any of the three listed above. The only possible criticism of this comparison group is that by virtue of the parole board's decision to release them early, this group could be viewed as prisoners posing less of a recidivism risk than other IFI nongraduates. As can be seen in Table 7, IFI graduates are significantly less likely than the comparison group of IFI nongraduates paroled early to be either arrested (17.3 percent vs. 62.7 percent) or incarcerated (8 percent vs. 47.1 percent). Interestingly, the differences in recidivism between IFI graduates and IFI nongraduates leaving the prison early via parole are more dramatic than those found with the other comparison groups.

Remember, however, that program graduates were defined as those who successfully complete the in-prison portion of the program as well as maintaining employment and regular church attendance for three months prior to graduation. For obvious reasons the comparison groups cannot be subjected to the same criteria, and this distinction clearly favors the IFI graduates in the recidivism analysis. In other words, the difference in reported rates of recidivism would almost certainly be smaller if the definition of an IFI graduate did not include maintaining employment or regular church attendance for three months prior to graduation. To address this concern we conducted several additional sets of analyses. Since graduates are typically the recipients of resources that nongraduates may not receive during the first six months following release from prison, we reanalyzed the recidivism rates for IFI graduates and nongraduates from month seven through month twenty-four, providing for an eighteen-month tracking period. Stated differently, if the operationalization of graduates is indeed problematic, one would expect this new analysis to somewhat level the field and to reduce substantially the difference in recidivism between IFI graduates and nongraduates. As can be seen in Table 7, however, rates of arrest for graduates and nongraduates during the eighteen-month tracking period (16 percent vs. 42.4 percent) closely resemble those reported for the entire two-year tracking period (17.3 percent vs. 50 percent). Likewise, the rates of incarceration for graduates and nongraduates during the eighteen-month follow-up period (8 percent vs. 34.3 percent) is almost identical to those found in the two-year tracking period (8 percent vs. 36.3 percent). Though the evaluation team still believes that IFI's definition of what it takes to be a program graduate is too restrictive, these additional analyses reduce the concern that the IFI graduate classification skews the findings in favor of those IFI participants who complete the entire program.[24]

TABLE 7. Additional Results of IFI Texas Recidivism Analysis

RECIDIVISM TYPE	18 Month Recidivism Rates for IFI Participants (Excluding first 6 months following release)		24 Month Recidivism Rates for IFI Program Graduates and Non-Completers Paroled Early	
	(1a) IFI Graduates vs. (2a) IFI Noncompleters		(1b) IFI Graduates vs. (2b) IFI Noncompleters—Paroled Early	
	(1a)	(2a)	(1b)	(2b)
Arrest				
% Arrested	16.0%	42.2%	17.3%	62.7%
# Arrested	12	43	13	32
Sample Size	75	102	75	51
Chi-Square	13.81, p < .0002		27.27, p < .0001	
Incarceration				
% Incarcerated	8.0%	34.3%	8.0%	47.1%
# Incarcerated	6	35	6	25
Sample Size	75	102	75	51
Chi-Square	16.81, p < .0001		27.54, p < .0001	

Note: All tests used the Pearson X2 statistic with one degree of freedom for a 2 X 2 table.

MENTORING AND AFTERCARE

After release from prison, IFI participants continue on parole in Phase III of the program for another six to twelve months. During this aftercare phase of the program, IFI participants, like any other offender released from prison, are expected to meet regularly with their parole officer. What is different, however, is that IFI mentors were also encouraged to attend these meetings, especially during the critical weeks and months following release from prison. As can be seen in Table 8, when comparing those cases where the mentor was known to the parole officer versus those cases where the mentor was not known to the parole officer, the IFI participant was less likely to be arrested (20 percent vs. 30 percent, respectively) or incarcerated (8 percent vs. 17 percent, respectively). Further, if the parole officer had documented regular contact versus little or no contact between the mentor and the IFI participant, then the IFI member was also less likely to be arrested (17 percent vs. 28 percent, respectively) or incarcerated (9 percent vs. 15 percent, respectively).

To summarize, the quantitative analysis yields the following recidivism findings:

▼ There is no statistical difference between the total sample of IFI prisoners and the matched group on either measure of recidivism during the two-year tracking period.

▼ A high percentage of IFI participants (58 percent) were not able to complete the program (half were paroled early, and another 25 percent voluntarily withdrew), and these noncompleters were much more likely than the comparison group to be arrested or incarcerated.

▼ IFI program graduates were significantly less likely than the matched group to be arrested (17.3 percent vs. 35 percent) during the two-year postrelease period.

▼ IFI program graduates were significantly less likely than the matched group to be incarcerated (8 percent vs. 20.3 percent) during the two-year follow-up period.

▼ Mentor contact is associated with lower rates of recidivism.

TABLE 8. The Role of Mentors in the IFI Texas Recidivism Analysis

Mentor Contact (IFI Sample) n=177					
RECIDIVISM TYPE	Mentor Known to Parole Officer vs. Unknown		Regular vs. Little or No Contact		
	Known	Unknown	Regular	Little	
Arrest					
% Arrested	19.8%	29.5%	16.7%	28.5%	
# Arrested	18	26	9	35	
Sample Size	91	88	54	123	
Chi-Square	2.30, p = .13		2.79, p = .09		
Incarceration					
% Incarcerated	7.7%	17.0%	9.3%	14.6%	
# Incarcerated	7	15	5	18	
Sample Size	91	88	54	123	
Chi-Square	3.63, p < .06		0.96, p = .33		

Note: All tests used the Pearson X2 statistic with one degree of freedom for a 2 X 2 table.

DISCUSSION OF THE FINDINGS

Corrections expert Joan Petersilia has identified several major prisoner reintegration practices in need of correctional reform.[25] First, Petersilia argues that it is necessary to alter the in-prison experience and essentially change the prison environment from one fostering antisocial behavior to one promoting prosocial behavior. This shift in philosophy would call for fundamentally changing the prison culture to teach skills and values that more closely resemble those found in society at large. Second, it is critical that relevant criminal justice authorities revise postrelease services and supervision while targeting those with high-need and high-risk profiles. In other words, provide closer supervision and assistance to those most likely to recidivate. Third, there is a need to seek out and foster collaborations with community organizations and thereby enhance mechanisms of informal social control. Stated differently, there is a need to establish partnerships that provide a network of critically needed social support to newly released offenders facing a series of reintegration obstacles.

Interestingly, IFI incorporates all three of these correctional reforms. This unique faith-based program not only attempts to transform prisoners, but as Petersilia suggests, also attempts to change the prison culture from one that tends to promote antisocial behavior to one that is both conducive to and promotes prosocial behavior. Additionally, IFI provides critically needed aftercare services to prisoners following release from prison. Employment and housing are two of the main areas where IFI aftercare workers provide invaluable assistance. Petersilia has also noted the importance of prioritizing risk and providing extra-close supervision and assistance to those most likely to get in trouble. IFI aftercare workers assumed this exact role was the most prudent one for them to play. Indeed, IFI aftercare staff place a great deal of their energies on parolees on their "critical care" list. Central to this process of aftercare is the role of IFI mentors—an asset missing from the vast majority of prisoner reentry initiatives.

Finally, IFI has made a concerted effort to partner with parole officials and congregations throughout the Houston area. Collaborating with parole officials has been important because it has allowed parole officers and IFI aftercare workers to pool their resources in supervising parolees. Partnerships with churches have made it possible to recruit scores of volunteers who teach a wide variety of classes in the IFI program. Similarly, these congregations have been the places IFI has targeted for recruiting mentors and indeed entire congregations to agree to work with prisoners and former prisoners. Without the partnership with these faith-based organizations, IFI would not exist.

Petersilia claims there exists promising in-prison and post-prison programs that help ex-convicts lead law-abiding lives. She argues that community-based organizations, local businesses, and faith-based organizations are showing themselves to be critical partners in assisting offenders with the transition back into society. The key word in this observation, however, is the reference to "promising" rather than "proven" programs. The current study contributes preliminary but important evidence that a faith-based program combining education, work, life skills training, mentoring, and aftercare has the potential to influence in a paradigm-shifting way the prisoner reentry process.

John Braithwaite argues that Americans are quick to apply degradation ceremonies to offenders (e.g., stripping prisoners of many rights), but are often reluctant to embrace programs whose goal is to rehabilitate offenders.[26] The controversial decision in the state of Texas to embrace a faith-based program that claimed it could rehabilitate without degrading prisoners is supported by preliminary research findings linking a faith-based program to subsequent reductions in recidivism in a two-year postrelease study.

## CHAPTER 7

Can a Faith-Based Prison Rehabilitate Inmates?

As demonstrated in chapter 6, we know that completing the IFI program is significantly linked to lower rates of arrest and incarceration during the two-year study period following release from prison. Knowing that recidivism rates are lower is obviously important, but it does not provide an answer to the rather obvious question of why recidivism in the IFI study group is significantly lower than the matched group. In this section we rely upon qualitative methods employed throughout the study in order to shed light on this important question. I begin by providing a qualitative description of the IFI program in hopes that the reader will understand more clearly the workings and nature of the program. The description to follow is based on hundreds of hours of observational work as well as interviews with relevant prisoners, correctional staff, IFI staff, volunteers, mentors, and others. The qualitative description of IFI is followed by a presentation of interview data broken down into observations of five major themes of spiritual transformation. The qualitative findings not only reveal important insights into the spiritual transformation and growth of IFI members but they also provide narratives that help to show how spiritual development both parallels and enhances the process of rehabilitation.

Over the course of the six years spent observing and evaluating the IFI program, I came to the conclusion that this faith-based program was consistently open, positive, supportive, and nurturing. Days begin early and end late. In addition to daily work details typically associated with most prisons, inmates in IFI are expected to participate in classes (offered throughout the day and evening), worship, and devotional times. IFI participants are given homework and are expected to do a considerable amount of reading outside of classes. Many get up as early as 4:30 in the morning to either complete class assignments or to do their own personal Bible study, often referred to as their daily quiet time. Lights are usually out at 10:00 p.m. Unlike the general population inmates, IFI participants do not have televisions in their living areas. This was an area of contention for some within IFI, at least initially, but many have stated that the program was so demanding, there would not be enough time to watch television even if it were allowed.

The research team I led visited the program at all hours of the day and evening and observed traits that many experts in the correctional treatment arena would deem essential for creating an environment that fosters rehabilitation. It is not uncommon to see inmates display affection toward each other, with the staff, and with volunteers that would seem reminiscent of an extended family gathering or reunion. Brotherly hugs are not only common, they are essentially a basic feature of the program. IFI participants were routinely heard greeting volunteers or other first-time visitors to the program with statements like "Hey, man, it's time to hug a thug."

Over the first year or so of its existence, the IFI program began to take on the identity of a church community within the confines of the prison. By design, IFI leadership and staff sought to create an environment that draws upon the best features of a church setting. Some IFI members are selected to assume roles of leadership not unlike those of deacons or elders referred to in scripture. Additionally, special religious meetings with outside speakers are a regular feature of IFI. Often referred to as "revival services" by IFI members and staff alike, feedback from participants who have attended was almost always positive.

> The IFI staff really seem to care about us. I'm Catholic, and they haven't tried to force me to become a Protestant. If people want to get something out of the program, they will.

For at least the first year, there was a concerted effort to largely segregate IFI members from the general prison population. Prison Fellowship believed very strongly that in order to create a healthy spiritual climate in the prison, it was necessary to keep these two prison populations apart. There was concern that if allowed to mingle, the general population inmates would hinder if not contaminate the spiritual progress being made with participants in the IFI program. TDCJ was more than happy to comply with this request, as they too felt this concern was valid.

Before too long, however, IFI and TDCJ had to reconsider the practice of segregating IFI inmates from the general population. IFI members began asking if they could interact with general population inmates. Conversely, many general population inmates, though initially suspicious of the program, began inquiring about potential involvement in the program. Many inmates participating in IFI were eager to share their newfound faith, while general population inmates were more than a little curious about the special programs that regularly took place within IFI. At the request of IFI, TDCJ agreed that the restriction to keep the two populations segregated at all times would be removed. Consequently, where possible, there has been an effort not to deprive general population inmates from some of the spiritual components of the program. This has afforded the opportunity for some IFI inmates to witness (i.e., to share their faith) to general population inmates and to even involve some of them in Bible studies independent of those taking place within IFI.

The ongoing presence of volunteers, facilitators, and mentors bolsters the environment of the IFI program. Prison Fellowship's extensive network and track record made it possible to connect with local congregations and identify volunteers to be trained and to subsequently participate in IFI. Though IFI has full-time staff, it is obvious to any observer that the program could not exist without the participation of a significant number of volunteers. IFI participants repeatedly voiced the critical impact that volunteers made. Indeed, the time commitment of volunteers simply overwhelmed program participants. Some inmates indicated that the presence and dedication of the volunteers had the effect of shattering stereotypes they held of free-world people (i.e., non-prisoners) as harsh, punitive, racist, or self-serving. Many volunteers indicated a similar experience—expressing that mentoring a prisoner actually changed and benefited them more than the benefit the prisoners received. Not surprisingly, the best recruiting tool for volunteers happened to be the volunteers themselves. Churches of all shapes and sizes participated. Contrary to my own initial reservations, the mentoring relationship was not influenced by the racial composition of the mentor-mentee match. The relationship always trumped the issue of race.

Interviews with various members of the custodial staff at the Carol Vance Unit confirmed that IFI participants were not only doing well, but that the IFI program seemed to be influencing the entire prison.

> I have been here since IFI started. Some people have it and some don't. You can see the difference. Some of them just come here to get close to home. Instead they get close to God. . . . I would say that 85 to 90 percent of those who are gone, have left out of here with a completely different perspective. I have noticed that they are even trying to change their families. . . . They learn to take blame for themselves; to face reality. I have heard them say, "I brought myself here and I need to accept responsibility." That's not typical. (Correctional officer, five years with TDCJ)

> Many of the general population inmates envy the IFI inmates because of the special classes, the mentors, the volunteers. The general population inmates can't believe all the free-world people that come in here. All the time and attention they give, and the snacks and refreshments they bring. It's easy to see why general pop inmates would envy IFI inmates. . . . It's interesting, though. I've seen the IFI inmates share the food given to them with the general population inmates. I think that has really won over these other prisoners. (Correctional officer, three years with TDCJ)

> The difference between IFI and, for example, the drug treatment programs I have observed over the years, is the family and community emphasis of IFI. There's a lot of involvement from the outside. And the free-world people are seeing what we're seeing—change. It's intensive. I expect them to do a lot better than general population inmates when they are released. . . . I'd say that 80 percent of correctional officers would say that the IFI program is legitimate. . . . You know prisons often times help create monsters. IFI gives hope. (Major, eighteen years with TDCJ)

Numerous observations and interviews based on visits to the program during day and evening hours as well as aftercare visits confirmed a growing confidence among staff and prisoners alike in the effectiveness of the program. Conversations that have taken place and observations that have been made of IFI employees and volunteers revealed that staff remained very positive about the program, their colleagues, and in general, the progress of the inmates in the program.

SPIRITUAL TRANSFORMATION—
A DEVELOPMENTAL PROCESS

A paramount goal of IFI is to utilize a biblically based program with an overt emphasis on spiritual growth and moral development with the expectation that this approach will substantially enhance achieving the secular and correctional goal of rehabilitation.[1] If the goal of spiritual growth was realized, one would expect to observe changes in attitude and behavior among IFI participants.

A key evaluation goal, then, was attempting to gauge the spiritual development of IFI participants as they proceeded through the program. The evaluation, therefore, focused on observations of program members in various settings such as classes, free time, inmate-mentor sessions, and during individual and group devotionals (e.g., Bible study, prayer, or personal reflection). Direct discussions and interviews with individual IFI members as well as interaction and dialogue in various group settings yielded valuable feedback for the evaluation. Finally, interviews with program staff and volunteers provided additional insights into the spiritual progress of inmates over time.

Augmenting the observational fieldwork, I conducted unstructured interviews with IFI members from different groups and different stages within the program. Rather than having inmates respond to a structured questionnaire with fixed responses, the interviews were intentionally unstructured since the intent was to provide the least threatening environment for the respondent, in hopes they would respond candidly about their experiences. IFI participants were simply asked to share any thoughts they had about the program or their experience in the program. Though responses covered a number of different topics, inmates

overwhelmingly offered remarks that dealt with their spiritual transformation. These interviews were transcribed and the content analyzed.
Five spiritual transformation themes emerged from the narratives of IFI
members and are captured in the following discussion.

Spiritual Transformation Theme 1:
I'm Not Who I Used to Be

IFI participants consistently verbalized themes indicating they are
thankful to have the opportunity to start their life over again. One of the
common statements expressed by IFI participants was that "I'm not who
I used to be" (54 percent of the 125 recorded interviews contained statements reflecting this theme). Their newfound faith or the rediscovery
of a lost faith from their childhood made it possible to begin not just a
new life but a life where they are genuinely loved by God and others and
can view themselves as good people who have been forgiven for their
past mistakes. They have been given another chance or a new lease on
life. Their current positive self-accounts represent a dramatic departure
from their often bleak past. According to research on British offenders, Shadd Maruna states that this process of "willful, cognitive distor-
tion" helps offenders desist from crime and to "make good" with their
lives.[2] For those who have been in prison before, maybe multiple times,
this time they feel like they are on a mission as they prepare to leave
prison. They now have a sense of meaning and purpose they have not
known before. For many, there was a Christian conversion experience
in IFI that marked a turning point in their life—a spiritual awakening or
reawakening that was foundational for them.

> Before IFI, I was kind of at a fork in the road, not knowing
> which way to go. I had a bad attitude and a hard time get-
> ting along with people. I used to get in fights all the time. I
> remember telling myself I didn't want to live like this anymore,
> and I prayed for God to take control and I gave my heart to
> the Lord. I'm beginning to control my thoughts and my anger.
> I'm beginning to find peace for the first time. Something that
> used to get me into a fight, I will now laugh at. I don't curse
> anymore. Instead I try to share God with people. It's nice to

hear positive things being said about me for the first time in my life. When someone tried to help me before, I would deny it. I didn't think anyone cared. I see now they really do. (Len)[3]

The program has awakened me. It has birthed a new me. I'm learning to get along with others and to understand why people do what they do. I am learning more by listening. IFI has made me feel like I am somebody and that I have potential. I have a whole lot more discipline and self-control than before. Being able to be obedient to not just authority, but to everyone. And I'm learning to control my anger. Things out of my control have always bothered me. I struggled with this every day. Change is not overnight and it's not easy to change, but God is changing me. God has shown me what I used to be about and what I'm about now. (Gale)

I have discovered a lot of flaws in myself in the last nine months. I used to always have a lot of anger, but things just don't upset me like they used to, you know. Now I'm trying to turn spiritual knowledge into wisdom. (Stan)

Previous research on active offenders (persisters) as well as inactive offenders (desisters) has found that the differences between the two groups were partly related to the way they defined themselves within their social worlds. Maruna calls this process "rebiographing," and suggests that in order for chronic offenders to refrain from crime, they need to make sense of their past. In rewriting the narratives of their lives, desisting offenders often look to instances in their pasts when their "real" selves showed and when respected members of conventional society recognized their talents and good qualities. Eventually, Maruna argues, these narratives become the building blocks of reform and desistance from crime. Without this rebiographing, or rewriting of one's now reformed identity, the ex-offender will always be an ex-offender.

The experiences of IFI members seem to very much line up with the experiences Maruna describes for crime desisters. In the current study, however, it would seem more accurate to refer to this process as "spiritual rebiographing," since members are taught that spiritually speaking, they are new creations with a new identity. Past behaviors are not something they have to deny or blame on someone or something else; it is simply something tied to the "old" person they used to be. The new person they have become is the focus of the present. The emergence of the new self allows IFI members to make sense of the past, while looking forward.

In order to live crime-free lives they must receive affirmation and validation of the truthfulness of their claim to have changed. Ceremonies and testimonials of respected individuals acknowledging the change in the desister are critical to the strengthening of this new identity and can be a real turning point in societal reintegration. Especially at the early stages, they need outside validation to convince themselves of the authenticity of their conversion. While affirmation from just about anyone helps, those from public officials are the most compelling. Indeed, both Maruna and Wexler[4] believe that graduation ceremonies and other "redemption rituals" should be commonly used in the criminal justice system. These public ceremonies reinforce and contribute to the desister's ability to rebiograph their past. IFI not only encourages regular testimonials, they recognize through various public ceremonies the accomplishments of IFI members.

Spiritual Transformation Theme 2: Spiritual Growth

When IFI participants were asked to share whatever was on their mind, the most common response dealt with their spiritual growth. Indeed, 69 percent of those interviewed indicated that they had grown spiritually as a result of participation in IFI. They spoke of their life in terms of a spiritual journey, a journey that had benefited from important turning points or events that had a profoundly positive impact. For some, the journey was just beginning; for others it was a long journey but with newfound direction. For most, it was a journey that was very much a work in progress. Spiritual growth, then, was something prisoners within IFI very much viewed as a developmental process that was well under way, but was far from where it needed to be. In order to transform their deviant histories into the present good, desisters employ "redemption scripts."[5] This process establishes the goodness of the individual and marks the emergence of the desisting self.

I have learned what life is about since being here. I have learned that life is about helping others to grow like I'm growing. I have found peace for the first time. The change came over me when I saw that other people loved me. Then I wanted to do the same to others. That's when my whole life began turning around. (Lawrence)

I'm becoming stronger in the word of God. You're more into God-type activities here. Instead of a little religion here or there, you're surrounded by it. The program builds your knowledge and hopes. One can never quit growing, and I know I have a long way to go. Church will be a very important part of my life when I get out. My mentor will be a help to me, too. (Dan)

For the first time I have respect for others. I even try to encourage others, and pray for them. The books we use here and the Bible have really helped. Praying has helped. When I stumble, now I repent. When I get out of here, the church is going to be a big part of my life. (Juan)

Spiritual Transformation Theme 3: God Versus the Prison Code

We know from the corrections literature that inmates are profoundly influenced by a unique prison subculture. The existence and adopting of a distinctive prison culture, what has been referred to as "prisonization"—or as some of the IFI members called it, the "penitentiary mentality" or "prison code"—is widely acknowledged by those who live and work in prisons.[6] The existence of gangs, other racially motivated groups, violence, sexual aggression, and other antisocial behavior represent just some of the widely known aspects of the prison culture. There are others. Displays of machismo are often considered acceptable. Showing love, affection, or compassion can be viewed as signs of weakness and are not acceptable. The prison culture provides fertile ground for the breeding of a mentality that supports the notion of rehabilitation or reform as something very much needed by the prison—not the prisoner. The issue of trust, or more precisely the lack of trust, is a central feature of the prison code. For example, a new prisoner learns very quickly that outside of a select group of prisoners, inmates should not trust other people. This is especially true when referring to prison staff or others who work in or represent some aspect of the criminal justice system.

Further, the prospect of opening up or becoming transparent about one's needs or shortcomings—a major feature of the IFI program—can be problematic because it not only shows weakness but it may require one to trust in something or someone else, a prospect that may well run counter to the prison code.

Many correctional experts agree that one of the biggest obstacles to more regularly achieving successful outcomes in various treatment programs is the inability to counteract the deleterious effects of the prison culture. At the core of IFI is the premise that a faith-based program will eventually erode the negative or harmful tendencies of the prison code or penitentiary mentality. In essence, IFI's approach is based on the assumption that the prisoner's spiritual transformation and spiritual growth will help to provide an antidote to the present prison subculture. Thus, a spiritually transformed prisoner will be more likely to choose a prosocial response over an antisocial response when faced with a moral dilemma. The IFI program is based on the belief that spiritually transformed prisoners will, in fact, accept good over evil, or God over the prison code.

How does spirituality counteract the influence of the prison culture? A prime example within IFI is the issue of inmates filing "drop slips" (misconduct reports) on other inmates. The penitentiary mentality says you never snitch on another inmate. Prisoners are supposed to mind their own business. For inmates who have been in prison multiple times (and many in the program had) this is a deeply embedded rule. However, the philosophy of IFI is just the opposite of that promoted via the prison code. Namely, IFI members are taught they have the responsibility to hold each other accountable for various kinds of rule infractions. The issue of trust, therefore, is something that does not come easy for many inmates, since the code teaches otherwise—especially when and where staff is concerned. Particularly among the newest IFI members, there is still the firmly held belief that snitching on another inmate, regardless of the situation, violates the code. However, among members who have been in the program for a longer period of time, they are better able to deal with the tension between these two extremes, often with faith trumping the code. We found that in 34 percent of our interviews, statements were made indicating an offender's decision to respond in a way that prioritized faith or spirituality rather than the prison code. The following are excerpts that capture the struggle in choosing between following one's faith or the prison code.

> I didn't trust anyone before I came here. I thought I knew everything, that I had all the answers. Now I know I don't have anything figured out. And at the same time I'm at peace today with myself. It's changed how I view the world. I'm learning to have more patience. I have found that when I humble myself, I get closer to these guys. (Lowell)

> God is pulling everything back together. I know God's in control. I have to deal with the inmate mentality here, where guys don't want to be confronted about sinful behavior. . . . I now value accountability. I think this is where Christians blow it. They don't want to correct someone else even though they know they're in sin. (Ricky)

> The prison system says that you must play tough. But that's not real. Confession is good for you, according to the Bible. I've come to realize that the inmate code is really nothing but a facade. I can be myself now. (Neal)

Spiritual Transformation Theme 4: Positive Outlook on Life

The longer IFI participants are in the program, the more positive their outlook on life, their current situation, and their future prospects become. Many tend to see the silver lining even when they are the recipients of bad news. They are delighted about their new life, whom they have become, and what the future now holds for them. Because many now believe that they are God's children and that God is in control of everything, they report having developed a new confidence they have not known before. They possess an assurance that they are accepted and loved by God, and they draw peace from the belief that one day they will reside with God in heaven. Interviews revealed that 32 percent of respondents viewed their circumstances positively. Noted criminologists Robert Sampson and John Laub, who work on factors that contribute to the desistance of crime, discuss "transformative action" and "subjective reconstruction of the self"—concepts they found to be quite common among people who develop new commitments, find purpose and meaning in life, and consequently stay out of trouble.[7]

Along the same line, Maruna found that persisters had a much more pessimistic or fatalistic outlook on life and that they tended to attribute this feeling of doom and gloom to a lack of opportunities and hardships stemming from various forms of past social and economic disadvantage. Desisters, on the other hand, like many IFI participants, had a much more positive outlook on life.

> I was just fortunate to get into the program. Before the program I didn't pray, I didn't read the Bible, and I didn't know God. In March of 1997, I prayed in my cell and gave my life to Christ. . . . You know, I just found out that I won't get out in February as planned, but instead November. But that's okay because God wants me to stay in this program longer. (Stuart)

> I'm a stronger believer in God, I have grown in patience, I have a peace of mind that I never had in the world. I have joy. I stopped asking God for parole. Whenever He wants me out is OK, I'm willing to stay in prison another year. My father passed while I was here, but this program has helped me deal with his death. (Phil)

> You know I was so disappointed to get a serve-all [instead of early parole] because it was going to put me back an extra six months, but all in all I really do think it has been worth it. During that time my confidence has really been boosted up and it has forced me to get up in front of people—it's been great. The extra time here has helped me to learn to lean on God, because I know I can't make it by myself. (Gene)

Spiritual Transformation Theme 5:
The Need to Give Back to Society

In order to rationalize their past behavior, inmates commonly state that they are in prison not because they deserve to be, but because the criminal justice system is either unfair or corrupt all together. These techniques of neutralization allow individuals to justify their actions without accepting responsibility for illegal harmful acts.[8] Their incarceration, therefore, can be viewed as an indictment on society rather than on them personally. It is the system, many prisoners have contended, that is in need of reform and rehabilitation.

Conversely, instead of feeling that society owes them, many IFI participants feel an overwhelming need to give back to society and the community when they get out of prison. Many view themselves as people who were down and out until someone cared enough to help them up. Now that they have turned their lives around and have a new and positive identity, they express an unusual sense of gratitude for this new life and they feel compelled to give back to a society that they have never helped before. They feel an overwhelming desire, if not obligation, to make a positive contribution to the community. They believe their experiences of going "to hell and back" especially qualify them to reach out and help others not to make the same mistakes they have made.

> I've always believed in God. But I got away from God as I got into my teens. This program has brought me back to my Christian roots. My feeling and thinking are different from when I got here. I see a big change in myself, I don't see things the way I used to. I used to be a loner, and didn't care about much else. I'm finding myself being more sociable and trying to help others. That wasn't true of me before I got to IFI. Helping others find purpose in their life through God has been a real blessing. (Lou)

> I was a halfway atheist when I came into the program. I came here just to get close to home [Houston]. I didn't come here for spiritual reasons. But about two months ago I gave my heart to Jesus. Everything has changed since then. I know He's real.

I don't want the classes to end now. If this program can help somebody like me, it can help anybody. I'm from the streets. But I know now that God is real. . . . I want to share my testimony with other TDCJ cellmates I have had before I came here, because I wasn't a Christian then. (Harold)

I wish everybody could go through IFI. I came to the program to learn about the Bible. It has taught me that prayer is important. I wish my dad could go through IFI. He's serving twenty-five years in prison. . . . I didn't come up in a spiritual life, but God has done a real work in my life since coming here. Sharing my faith with my family is important to me. Now I have a better relationship with my family, too. (Kerry)

THE ROLE OF SPIRITUAL TRANSFORMATION IN PRISONER REHABILITATION

Several observations from these interviews are worth noting. In general, comments tended to be very positive and supportive of the program. Almost without exception, members indicated they had grown spiritually since coming to IFI. Interestingly, although many indicated they were Christians and had been involved in chaplaincy (i.e., religious programs in prison) prior to IFI, a significant number indicated that they had not experienced a spiritual transformation until entering the IFI program. This is a very important point that may be consistent with Prison Fellowship's belief that the level or intensity of involvement is the critical factor in the spiritual transformation of prisoners. Many of these inmates indicated that they had become believers during their youth, but they quickly followed a different path after leaving church during adolescence. Further, they indicated that the IFI program had brought them back to God and caused them to reevaluate their lives.

Focus groups with prisoners entering IFI seem to support Prison Fellowship's contention that length of time in the program would be associated with spiritual growth. Interviews revealed that the newest members were much more likely to respond negatively to the program. A common set of criticisms consistently emerged from some of the new

IFI participants. For example, some felt the IFI environment was negative, resulting from accountability conflicts, and that favoritism was displayed by staff, especially in the staff selection of IFI leaders. The leaders were referred to by new IFI participants as "show ponies" or "poster boys" who were "faking it." After having been in the program for several months, however, focus groups revealed that most members thought the environment was positive and that there were many opportunities for positive change at IFI. Most realized that positive and negative aspects exist, but the newest program participants seem to be most likely to dwell on the more restrictive aspects of the IFI environment. The newest groups had much more of a negative assessment of IFI staff. New members complained not only about staff favoritism but also what they perceived as the constant changing of rules. On the other hand, members who had been in the program for at least three months generally reported having positive experiences with the staff and claimed IFI staff affirmed and supported them. Finally, IFI members diverged regarding their views on correctional officers. IFI participants new to the program often felt that correctional officers and other TDCJ staff were harsh or tried to provoke them. However, with more time in the program, these same members felt that TDCJ staff tended to treat them in a more positive way than correctional staff in other prisons where they had served time. Clearly, the IFI program, inmates, staff, environment, and correctional officers did not change noticeably from overly negative to positive. The more likely explanation is that new IFI participants actually change themselves, and tend to have more positive feedback all around. These observations are consistent with a point made earlier—namely, that spiritual transformation tends to be a developmental process.

Each of the five spiritual transformation themes discussed above not only corresponds to but also can be seen as providing the impetus for various characteristics and attributes often associated with the process of prisoner rehabilitation. To follow I briefly discuss how these spiritual transformation themes are consistent with elements thought to be essential in order to achieve rehabilitation.

Theme 1—"I'm not who I used to be"—is an important theme because it carries a recognition on the part of the offender that his previous behavior was justifiably unacceptable to society. In fact, the person he has become is now able to condemn his previous behavior because the new person now appreciates and promotes prosocial rather than anti-social behavior. This spiritual theme is powerful because it allows the participant to reconcile his troubled past and move forward.

Theme 2—spiritual growth—is critical because it suggests the person understands he is very much a work in progress. While many report they have made a great deal of progress in putting their life back to-gether, most acknowledge they still have a long way to go. They are quite surprised and encouraged about their own spiritual growth, and this progress is confirmed and validated by staff, volunteers, and mentors— further strengthening their resolve to continue this path of spiritual de-velopment. Particular events like being "born again," or the recognition that God and others actually love and care for them, appear to be criti-cally important turning points in their spiritual development.

Theme 3—God versus the prison code—is particularly significant since many correctional staff already concede that the penitentiary mentality or prison code is so pervasive and strong as to be beyond the possibility of reclaiming. As stated earlier, the prison code runs counter to the various components of offender rehabilitation programs. To be able to successfully oppose or even reverse the influence of the prison code is a remarkable achievement. This evaluation provides a number of observations confirming that the IFI environment successfully opposed if not reversed the prison environment at the Vance Unit.

Theme 4—positive outlook on life—is important because it reflects a paradigm shift for many offenders from a cynical perspective to an out-look on life typified by hope and purpose. Following release from prison many former prisoners relapse or commit new crimes due to minor setbacks with a friend, family member, or employer. Instead of being fatalistic about their circumstances and perhaps making bad decisions, a positive outlook can help them to be resilient in the face of adversity. Believing that their life now has meaning and knowing that they are loved and accepted by God, a mentor, and others, they are much more likely to view their life and circumstances in a positive rather than nega-tive or hopeless way.

Theme 5—the need to give back to society—is something many seemed to feel strongly about. They simply report feeling compelled to give back, to make a contribution to society in a way that improves the situation of others, especially others who come from similar backgrounds and experiences as their own.

In sum, all five spiritual transformation themes reflect behavior and attitudes consistent with those one would hope for in achieving offender rehabilitation.

In general, face-to-face interviews offer subjective evidence that many of the IFI members had made spiritual progress. In free-flowing conversation, inmates responded in ways indicating their lives had changed as a result of their involvement in IFI. The parallels between markers of spiritual development and rehabilitation are intriguing. The relationship between spiritual transformation and rehabilitation is, unfortunately, a grossly understudied topic, but one that may yield important and practical insights for offender treatment inside and outside correctional institutions.

Mentoring Matters

The role of mentors during the vulnerable period following release from prison was predicted to be critical for the success of IFI participants. Focus groups with IFI participants confirmed the many struggles they face following release from prison. In addition, these same focus groups highlighted the centrality of mentors and spiritual growth in succeeding on parole. The men in these focus groups shared how IFI had helped them in a number of ways—from bringing them to salvation, to preparing them for the outside, to resolving their questions about God. The group shared that they had been transformed during their time in the IFI program and that their spiritual growth had been invaluable to them on the outside. Overwhelmingly, the men shared how through IFI they had discovered a new way to live and a new way to look at things. The program has also helped some men realize that people on the outside do care about them, rather than believing that society as a whole has rejected them. Some said that they learned how to be a leader at IFI, how to be held accountable, and even accept responsibility for their words and deeds. These attributes seemed to be helpful during the difficult transition back into society.

Following release from prison, IFI participants did not see much of each other aside from the mandated support group meetings. For most, these meetings were beneficial times of sharing trials and encouraging one another. Without exception the parolees indicated that they missed the fellowship they enjoyed with the other IFI participants while in prison and wished it were possible to get together more often and support each other. This is where the significance of mentors becomes magnified. Without the constant support from others in the program, the mentoring relationship, if it is active and productive, can make the difference toward successful reintegration.

Ex-prisoners indicated that the time immediately following release from prison is a honeymoon of sorts for many of the men. But this honeymoon period dissipates as trials and responsibilities arrive, thus making it more difficult to keep God as a priority in their life. Such trials include temptations from old friends, fatigue, employment difficulties, transportation problems, adjustments to a new environment (e.g., finding their way around again), and "little things" like impatience, relational issues with family members and girlfriends, and financial struggles. Following are excerpts of conversations with IFI mentors that reflect a wide range of perspectives, both positive and negative, on the significance of mentoring in a postrelease environment.

BJ: How's the mentoring going with D?

Tim: D is doing fine. He joined the church the second Sunday of July. I'm the pastor of this church. D's mother, brother, and sister are all members and attend regularly. D has been faithful to the church since his release. I have visited his home on two occasions and have visited his parole officer once or twice as well. And obviously we see each other at church, too. I have always wanted to do prison ministry but never had the opportunity until IFI. Rev. B approached me, and I was very impressed with the prospects of working with the program. The church has been very supportive of D; some know he's been in prison and some don't. On Tuesday nights I also mentor another IFI member at the prison, and have been doing this for the last two months.

~

BJ: Have you been able to meet regularly with S since he's been out?

Gil: I live in Rosenberg, and S lives on the other side of Houston. Therefore, we have not been connecting. I think he is doing fine, but it is just difficult to connect when you are geographically so far apart.

～

BJ: I understand that you and J have not been meeting regularly?

Kim: J and I have not interacted that much, and I cannot say for sure how well he is doing. I contacted J by phone several times, and I have made one home visit. J is attending a different church now, and that has made it certainly less convenient for us to see each other. The real problem is that I was assigned to J after he left prison, and we never had a chance to bond at IFI. He has made several calls to me and clearly has not tried to avoid me. I just think it is more difficult when you don't have that relationship established.

～

BJ: What have you observed since N's release a year ago?

Joe: N has continued to grow spiritually. We have, like a list of scriptures that we keep track of and share. If he has questions, you know, we can have a good exchange and good dialogue as we discuss it, because I don't have all the answers. Even though I'm there to teach him, I have tried to stress to him that he has got to get to know the word of God for himself. What I noticed was that he really took that to heart and started to study. There were times when I would come in, and of course, I would have my notes and I was prepared and I would go on into a discussion and kind of lead our talk and quite often I found he would take the discussion over and then he would really start teaching me the way, you know, just really a blessing. I'd say, after the first ninety days I really started to see that transformation, that change in him. More of a shift toward his really getting into the Word [Bible] and starting to grow.

～

BJ: How often do you see N now?

Sam: We talk anywhere from three to four times a week, and we see each other at least once per week.

BJ: How did you get involved in this whole IFI thing?

Sam: I'm a minister and I got involved in prison ministry in the past when I lived in Dallas, and I really enjoyed it. When I moved to Houston, the church I joined really wasn't involved in prison ministry, but Rev. B came to our church and did a presentation on IFI. He mentioned they were looking for mentors for the program because that's part of what they do—identifying mentors who teach and have a spiritual walk and are interested in being involved in a biblical-based mentoring program with inmates. As it turns out, I knew N because I had gone to school with N's brother. He and I grew up together. I told Rev. B that "I knew this guy," and he said, "Well, great, that's even better because we like to have mentors from the area they are going to go back into." As it turns out, N's church and my church are right around the corner from each other.

Based on interviews held with mentors and IFI participants, the pattern of the mentoring typically follows one of two different paths. First, almost all the mentors said that the two men hit it off during the Tuesday night sessions at the prison. They talked together, prayed with one another, discussed future plans, talked about personal problems, and became friends. However, on the outside of the prison the two divergent paths emerged. For some IFI participants, contact with their mentors continued and even thrived postrelease. These relationships tended to be reciprocal in nature, and a strong bond had been formed. However, for other IFI members the relationship with their mentor was healthy right after release from prison but diminished with time.

Most of the mentors interviewed said they felt comfortable confronting the IFI participant when they were headed down the wrong path. However, one mentor noted that he did not always know when the IFI member was headed in a bad direction. Another mentor told me he showed concern and prayed for the former prisoner when he knew he was making poor decisions, but ultimately believed it was his choice alone to make. Because of lack of contact, some mentors did not always know whether the IFI participant was attending church or Bible study or had little knowledge about other aspects of their spiritual journey. Still, many of the mentors were able to describe struggles the IFI participants faced since they had been released, including professional, financial, relational, and emotional problems.

The mentors offered valuable information concerning IFI expectations of them as mentors, as well as their level of preparedness going into the mentoring relationship. Most of the mentors shared they did not know what was expected of them as mentors. Moreover, several of them did not feel trained or prepared to mentor, especially for the mentoring taking place on the outside. One mentor noted that it was on the outside where the real problems surface. Although they had attended the initial training that IFI offered, they did not feel properly equipped. In sum, mentoring relationships appear to be strong on the inside, but are severely weakened on the outside for many.

As stated earlier, the impact of the volunteers and especially mentors on IFI participants was critical. Following are excerpts of interviews with select IFI participants that capture the significance of these relationships.

BJ: Can you describe some aspect of your relationship with your mentor?

Ron: My mentor is great. We're talking about school and work. I'm getting a lot of encouragement and love. I now find myself talking about my past, which I normally don't like to do because it was just too painful.

∽

BJ: What has been your reaction to the free-world people who come to IFI?

Dan: The volunteers have been extremely helpful to me. The example set by the volunteers has been unbelievable. A lot of volunteers have been victims themselves. They share their own struggles and pains.

The first day I met my mentor [big smile comes to inmate's face], we bonded immediately. I'm planning to go to my mentor's church when I get out.

∽

BJ: Has your mentor been helpful?

Andy: My mentor has really helped and wants to help me when I get out of here. That makes me feel great. I'm only two months from the completion of my GED. And the volunteers have been very important in my spiritual growth.

～

BJ: What do you think about the IFI volunteers?

Wil: The volunteers have really helped. One volunteer had a wife dying in the hospital and he still came to visit me on Tuesday night.

～

BJ: Any thoughts on the volunteers who come in on Tuesday evenings?

Pat: The volunteers stand out. The quality of these people is unbelievable. One of the volunteers that works with me moved from Houston to Austin and still drove back to Houston for the Tuesday night meeting. He has done so much for me. I couldn't let him down for anything.

～

BJ: What do you think about the volunteers and mentors?

Rae: These volunteers mean a whole lot to me and this program. They aren't paid. Bad weather and all they show up, they have a strong commitment. We get so much out of it. I told my mentor I can't believe you'd come into a prison when they have a job, family, and kids. We've become very close and share personal things. We are brothers. We will work together when I'm out, no matter where we have to meet.

～

BJ: What can you tell me about your mentor?

Bob: My mentor stopped by here last night on his way home from Virginia. His wife picked him at the airport and brought him straight here on Tuesday night before going home. Can you believe that? And then his wife waited in the prison parking lot

for two hours while he was in here mentoring me. I can't understand how someone could care that much.

~

The following narratives capture an extended dialogue with IFI participants about their relationship with mentors and general observations
about the program.

BJ: Has your mentor been pretty faithful to this relationship?

Nat: Yeah, yeah. I think he has missed one Tuesday, the week of
        Thanksgiving. Other than that he has been here every single
        Tuesday. He has also brought several mentors in with him on
        extra nights. He has really hung with it. He has volunteered to
        come get me in Huntsville this weekend.[9]

BJ: So, there's no doubt in your mind that the two of you will con-
        nect once you're released.

Nat: Oh, no doubt, no, no! We're already buddies, you know.

BJ: When are you going to meet on the outside. Do you already have
        a regular plan?

Nat: Yes. I got a scheduled date in the parole office for twice a month,
        and my mentor has already indicated he would like to attend
        those meetings and be involved with that. You know, he wants to
        be there with me at the parole office. He's going to buy me a suit
        when I get out. So, we're going to go to the Men's Wearhouse and
        these are the things he wants to do and I'm like, "Sure, okay." He
        wants to do it. And he has said, "Hey, I want you to be like part
        of my family."

BJ: Is this your first time in prison?

Nat: No, it's my third time.

BJ: Have you ever experienced anything like IFI before?

Nat: Oh, no. I have had some supervisors who have given a compli-
        ment as I was leaving that unit, saying something like I was above
        average with some of the guys they had seen come through and
        to take care of myself. It was good encouragement, but no, noth-
        ing like this. I have never set any goals before. Goals are fine,
        but if you don't have an awakening in your soul, in your spirit,
        in your heart, then you're not free from the things that kept you
        there before, and I never was free from my alcohol addiction.

You know, I could never even imagine that I wouldn't, you know, be drinking again. Now I can't even imagine drinking again.

BJ: Did you go through any alcohol treatment programs before IFI?

Nat: Oh, sure.

BJ: Did they have an impact on you?

Nat: Sure they had an impact on me. I stayed sober for a while, you know. I learned a lot about alcoholism. I learned a lot about the AA program, and it was pretty spooky. I learned that I was pretty much helpless and bound to it—a pretty hopeless situation. It always led me back to drinking again or being dry and miserable, I mean I could be sober but not happy. It didn't have anything to it. Until I gave that problem to Jesus Christ, it was still a problem. Now it's something I have to be real careful with; it is something I have to manage. You know I have to stay away from alcohol and the situations that tempt me, but I don't have to worry about drinking again, because that has been relieved— the worry of that and the fear that I might [relapse] is gone. You know, people want to know, "How can you say that?" Personally, the load or the weight has just been lifted off of me so that I don't have to worry about it anymore. People all the time say, "I don't understand how you can tell me, without being out there and you're not facing the temptations, how you can say all this stuff." But I say, "Well, it started by just saying it. You know, just saying it." Once I started saying it, and asking Jesus Christ to help me make it through, and now it feels good to say it. I get more power each time I declare that that is just not me anymore and give the glory to God, I feel charged about it. The times I am tempted, I have the right answer now. And if I should even think about saying anything different, then the conviction would just swoop down on me. You know when you say something to God and you mean it and you make a pact with God and he gives you some peace over it, I don't think you are going to break that pact and be very comfortable.

BJ: Do you feel the same way about your release and your success on release as you do about the whole issue of alcohol and your possible relapse?

Nat: Oh, well, alcoholism has always been my problem. You know, all my employers and everybody have always said that I was a great guy that shouldn't drink. Anything that ever held me back was related to alcohol.

Now, not only do I feel like I don't have to rush out there and warehouse money and things to hedge against. I've got the rest of my life to build something, and I'm not fearful of it disappearing because I'm going to get in trouble again or because I'm going to get drunk. So, now I kind of have a calmness of spirit that says, "Hey, you can go out there and do the little things and by doing them the right way, taking the time and effort to do the things you're supposed to do, the big things will take care of themselves." I can see that now, but I could never see that before. My mentor and I have prayed for each and everything that we figured could be a need, and I mean each and every one of them plus a few we didn't even pray for—have all lined up.

~

BJ: Tell me about your mentor.

Paul: R is a very strong Christian, and our relationship has grown. And I know that just as him and I were matched up, it was what God had designed, because he was very strong in the Word. We set there and share about our personal life, but we are always sharing about our struggles and encouraging one another and we pray for each other every week. It's just a very, very strong spiritual relationship, which is what I needed—another man that understood where I was. R's just real with me, you know? He enjoys seeing all the things going on in my life, but him and I are just regular ol' pals every week. We laugh and cut up, and we cry about situations in our lives. He encourages me.

BJ: Will you stay in touch with him?

Paul: Oh yeah! And he's excited, too, that I'm not wandering off. That was one of the things that we talked about when I was telling him I might be moving. Even then, we would have stayed in touch by email and phone, but it's still not the same as being able to walk into a room with him and sitting down and talking. And he knows all the struggles that I have in my life. He keeps me honest with those, you know. Sometimes we'll be crying, and sometimes we'll be laughing, sometimes we cut up, but he's always there. To me, I couldn't have asked for a better mentor.

BJ: As everybody around here knows, you wrote the parole board to turn down a chance to be paroled early, in order to stay locked up for an additional year so you could complete the IFI program. There were IFI members who told you that you were a fool to turn down parole. Have those same people realized why you did it?

Paul: Most of the guys that were here with me in Group 2, before they left, have said that they realized I was just real and that I was just doing what God called me to do. And that God called each of us here for a reason and to deal with ourselves and what we had become. Especially one of them I remember, I mean he had very, very negative things to say the day we were talking about me staying during class. Then about a week before he left IFI, he said, "You know, I really understand you and appreciate what you did." And now when he calls in [to IFI] since I work in the office, I get to talk to a lot of the guys from time to time, we talk and he shares his struggles, and yet, at the end of our conversations we always end up with, "Hey, I love you." And to me, that's really neat, because that's what it's all about. It's staying in tune with God, and in tune with God's love, and not being afraid to tell another man, "Hey, I love you."

BJ: Had you ever done that before coming to prison?

Paul: Not really. Over all the years, I may have had a friend or two that I could have told them that I loved them. But now, it's almost, I mean, I love every guy that has gotten out of here. Even the ones I didn't necessarily like, I love them because I have God's love in my heart for them. That doesn't mean I always like the way they behave or what they tell me, but I know that I'm kind of like a little indicator to them of what God's love is like. Even though I may tell them they are crazy and that they need to straighten up today, I'm still going to be there for them tomorrow. I'm not going to let them down. And it's certainly not me, because if I did things the way I wanted to, sometimes I'd just write them off. I'd say, "Man I've got nothing for you no more." But I know that's not the way. God made it evident that he had a lot of love for me. You know, I turned my back on Him and run away from Him for a lot of years, and He was still there for me, so that's the least I can do.

～

BJ: Has your family noticed any changes in you?

Ben: My mother and my daughter really know me, and when they seen me in visitation they said they noticed a difference in me. They said I must have changed a lot because my conversation had changed and was real strong about God and things like that.

BJ: Tell me about Ben six months ago, and Ben today.

Ben: I think I've changed a whole lot. I've come a long way, but I'm not at the point where I want to be. I've learned to put God first in everything I do, in all the problems and tribulations that I go through. My friends couldn't understand a lot of the things that was going on here, like all the hugging, and people trying to help their brother out. And I had just never seen this before in other prisons. They show a lot of love here. People sharing personal things about their family and what's going on with their family and asking others to pray for them.

BJ: You haven't seen that before?

Ben: Oh, no. Through the power of prayer I've seen God answer prayer. And I've seen a lot of people come to IFI and give their lives over to Jesus Christ. In the scripture it says, I used to act like a child and talk like a child, and now I've put away childish things since I've become a man. And then it says, the old man has passed behold the new—increasing in Christ.

BJ: Tell me about the program here at IFI.

Ben: Well, I'd have to say that the best thing they done for me is to let me know about the Holy Bible. Through reading it, it strengthens you. Before coming here I didn't really know how to pray. I used to get on my knees and just say something, you know, like, "God, just look out for my family, don't worry about me, I done already messed my chance up." But I guess he was hearing my prayers and give me another chance by sending me to IFI. He sent me here to wake me up, and now I'm awoke. Now I'm trying to get where He has already gone—the gates of heaven.

BJ: You mentioned something earlier about trying to share your faith with others.

Ben: I be trying to witness to my father and my little brother too, trying to let them know about Christ and that He's good. Through Him, He'll make anything possible. I know that's right. And it's in the Bible, too. And I'm not all the way strong about the Bible, but I say, if you pick Jesus, you'll pick the best thing you've ever picked in your life. You know, every night I try to get a couple of guys that are younger, I ain't but twenty-four years old myself, and go into prayer. And I pray for their families and that touches their hearts to know that someone cares, because they're lonely just like I'm lonely, too.

IFI RECIDIVISTS: UP CLOSE AND PERSONAL

The descriptive narratives that follow are useful in identifying patterns and trends associated with a sample of eight IFI members who were unsuccessful after release from prison and ultimately returned to prison.

～

Wayne was paroled from TDCJ after completing fifteen months in the IFI program. He had served eight years of a thirteen-year sentence for burglary of a building with intent to commit theft. Wayne had served four previous prison sentences (three of these for robbery) prior to this most recent commitment. A warrant was issued nine months later for possession of cocaine, and Wayne's parole was subsequently revoked. According to his parole officer, he was mandated by the parole board to attend substance abuse treatment. Wayne had a long and even violent criminal history, and a series of institutional violations. He read at a fourth-grade level and had an IQ of 66. These elements placed Wayne in a high-risk group for reoffending. Even at IFI, there were documented cases of his anger and impulsiveness causing problems.

James was a mentor to Wayne and worked with him over the course of eight or nine months at the IFI prison program. James believed they had established a solid relationship during this time, reporting that they had "bonded for life." After release from prison, things were going well, and Wayne's mentoring relationship was progressing nicely. James reported that he met Wayne at the aftercare meetings on Tuesday or Thursday evenings. Furthermore, Wayne became a member of his mentor's church. James reported having contact with Wayne's parole officer. Mentor James told the parole officer that he had instructed Wayne to contact him at any time, day or night, and that he would take him to church.

After a period of time, Wayne began attending a different church located in his own neighborhood. Though it never seemed obvious to James that Wayne was using drugs, James remembered during the interview that Wayne had admitted using marijuana. Wayne justified his drug use by arguing that he was mad at his employer. James confronted and counseled Wayne, but he responded, "I don't care." Later, James saw Wayne carrying a six-pack of beer and confronted him about this. By this time Wayne was no longer attending church regularly.

Wayne initially lived at his sister's residence, but was asked to leave the residence after he and his brother-in-law "got into it." Wayne then moved across town into a bad neighborhood. Indeed, according to his mentor, his new girlfriend was anything but a positive influence in his life, enticing him into an unstable and drug-using lifestyle. Wayne's parole officer agreed that "challenges" at home were the beginning of his downfall. The parole officer also remembered that the other IFI parolees and Wayne's mentor James were praying for him during one of the evening parole meetings, when a number of his difficulties were discussed before the group. James stated that if Wayne had stayed in church and not moved, the outcome could have been different.

~

Kenny was released after completing eighteen months in IFI. He had served approximately eight years on a robbery conviction. Kenny has one previous prison commitment for robbery. Ten months after release, Kenny was rearrested on theft charges.

With regard to IFI, Kenny was an active participant in the program. He held a leadership position for ten months and was noted as a positive role model. He achieved quite a reputation during his stay in the IFI program; he was outgoing and very popular with the other program members. However, toward the end of his time in the IFI program, he became apathetic toward the program. Despite his popularity and initial enthusiasm, he never won the confidence of the entire IFI program staff and other inmate leaders within the program. For this reason, the program director decided that Kenny would not receive a graduation certificate despite the fact that he was one of the first to actually complete the entire eighteen-month program. The consensus seemed to be that he was a typical con who was never really sincere in his religious commitment. Chester began mentoring Kenny as a volunteer with the Kairos ministry. He felt their relationship only grew stronger and better during those thirteen months prior to Kenny's release. Chester stated that he believed his role as a mentor was "to be a friend and encouragement to Kenny, not to crack the whip; he would leave that to the IFI staff. We both enjoyed the time together and both looked forward to it."

Chester acknowledged that Kenny was quite smart, but that he was a "carnal Christian" and wanted to have feet standing in both worlds. In fact, Kenny admitted he wanted to live life on the high side and that he liked to party. Chester remembers Kenny saying, "Let's stay away from the spiritual stuff and just talk." Spiritually speaking, Chester said that Kenny wanted to keep things at arms' length. In fact, he said that when the IFI environment began to more intentionally resemble a church, "Kenny just checked out. It got too personal. If it had been me, I would have kicked him out of the program. Maybe I should have told him that."

Although Kenny seemed to being doing okay after his initial release, it didn't take long for things to turn bad. Initially, Kenny lived with his mother and was attending church, a men's Bible study and attended a few IFI parole meetings. But within two months, he had moved out, was living in a hotel, and was taking cocaine. Kenny and Chester talked by telephone virtually every day, and therefore Chester was very knowledgeable about Kenny's behavior. Kenny then tried to reconcile with his former wife and was living with her parents. This living arrangement didn't last too long as he moved back in with his mother, though that living situation didn't last either. He eventually moved to north Houston near Intercontinental Airport, thus separating him geographically from his mentor, who lived in Sugarland.

Kenny had a long history of both alcohol and drug abuse and was active in the drug recovery program while incarcerated. According to mentor Chester, Kenny wanted to live by his own abilities. He stated that Kenny's focus has always been on money more so than even his family.

～

Peter was released after completing eleven months in IFI. He was serving a seventeen-year prison sentence for a theft conviction. Peter has a long criminal history; it includes six previous prison sentences for convictions such as forgery, burglary, and possession of drugs. Peter had been out of prison for nineteen months when he was rearrested. He was caught selling drugs to an undercover cop and was subsequently charged with manufacturing/delivery of a controlled substance–cocaine.

Peter was interviewed at the Harris County Jail. He explained that he had a mentor, Gerald, but only for a short period at IFI. Peter stated that their interaction was very brief and they certainly did not establish any kind of a meaningful relationship. He never saw his mentor after leaving prison. The research team was unable to locate Gerald for an interview. Both telephone numbers listed for him were disconnected. Peter indicated that he attended church regularly for three months after leaving prison. He says transportation problems plus his work schedule at Church's Chicken caused him to begin to miss church—essentially cutting his church attendance in half. At this point Peter moved from the southwest to the southeast side of town, continued to live alone, and began attending a different church. Peter felt that it wasn't the same because, apparently, at the first church he attended, the pastor had taken a special interest in him. Peter never became a permanent member of this second church.

Peter claims he was let down by IFI since he was never given a real mentor, and he indicated that a close mentor would have helped him greatly. During the interview Peter stated he had tried to go out and do things on his own, and that was his biggest problem. Although he admits to making some mistakes, such as using drugs after his release from IFI, he was reluctant to accept full responsibility for the behavior that ultimately led to his arrest. Peter reported he is still doing Bible study in the Harris County Jail.

～

JR was released after completing twelve months in the IFI program. He had served seven years of a fifteen-year sentence for delivery of controlled substance–cocaine. He had served four previous prison sentences (auto theft, credit card abuse, theft, delivery of a controlled substance), and has accumulated some twenty institutional violations. Initially JR was noted for being quiet, but eventually he opened up to IFI counselors and became more involved in the program. He spoke highly about his family and expressed a desire to teach children that crime is not the way to go. Before release from prison, JR was described by the IFI program director as "having done everything that we have asked of him."

According to mentor Roger, he and JR had established a good mentoring relationship. Roger picked up JR every Sunday and took him to his Baptist church. This regular church attendance lasted from his release in April until June. Around this time JR moved out of his parents' house because he wanted to start doing things for himself. But, upon moving, JR left no new telephone number for Roger and thus began, by his own admission, distancing himself from his mentor.

By September, JR's boss had told him to clean up his act. In response, JR just quit. JR was now using drugs and after leaving a "dirty urine," his parole officer told him he should turn himself in. He didn't. His parole officer stated she "wasn't surprised," and tried to intervene on his behalf and did what she could to encourage JR to seek help. She even got him a bed at a drug treatment facility. Unfortunately, when JR finally agreed to come in, it was too late. He was arrested for possession of cocaine the evening prior to his entry to the treatment center.

When interviewed back in prison, JR stated that his mistakes were his own fault. He went on to say that the church was indeed helpful and that he was made to feel as though he was a part of the church. He also explained that his mentor was very important to him—in fact, even more important than the influence of his church. JR described his mentor, Roger, as someone who supported him and "stayed in the Word."

ᴗ

Frank was released on parole after completing twelve months in IFI. He served more than eight years of an eighteen-year sentence for forgery. Frank has a long criminal history including four previous prison commitments (two for forgery and two for burglary). According to his parole officer, Frank was initially reporting in regularly, but by December, four months after being released, he had started using drugs. He was ordered to complete an inpatient treatment but failed to continue attending classes after the program ended. Progress reports in his parole file indicate he was doing poorly and twice tested positive for cocaine use.

Frank's mentor, Bobby, has hired a number of parolees over the years and has provided transportation as well as financial support for these former inmates. Bobby stated that he saw Frank every day because he took him to and from work. Together, they were regularly attending services at Lakewood Church, weekly Bible studies (sometimes both Tuesday and Thursday nights), and IFI parole meetings. Bobby claims Frank was doing fine for a while, but then things began to change. First, Frank was not completely happy at Lakewood and started attending church elsewhere. Then Frank openly admitted to having two girlfriends, and bragged about the fact that neither of the women knew about the other relationship. Then his mentor began to notice a change in Frank's attitude and appearance; he started using excuses for missing church, IFI parole meetings, and Bible study. In addition, his clothing began to take on more of a street look. According to his parole officer, Frank was in complete denial in regard to his drug problem. Although he was doing very well at the beginning, she says he went down fast.

Bobby has helped many former prisoners and has seen other cases similar to Frank's. Like other former prisoners whom Bobby has employed and supported, there was certainly potential for a successful reentry into society. However, Bobby contends that many former prisoners fall prey to a common foe: idleness. He claims that unless former prisoners are occupied with constructive activities, such as work, church attendance, or volunteerism, they will eventually relapse in some way. When asked if the idleness could be replaced by regular church attendance and Bible study, mentor Bobby quickly responded in the negative, "These guys need to be occupied all the time. They can't handle free time. Church and Bible study only account for several hours out of the entire week." For Bobby, the key is constructive activities, and since it is impossible to be in church all the time, it is necessary to associate with positive role models, and often the best role models are found in the social networks that exist within congregations.

Bobby reported that he gave Frank many opportunities to make things right, but Frank never did. In addition to making excuses, Frank began to lie to his mentor. Eventually Bobby decided that his time would be better spent with other former prisoners. Bobby feels that things might have been different if he had been able to mentor Frank for a longer period of time before Frank left the prison because establishing a strong mentoring relationship is a paramount concern.

~

Sam was released from prison after completing only six months in the IFI program. He was arrested five months later on a new charge of forgery. Sam was interviewed back in prison. Sam indicated that he left prison without a mentor. He lived at home with his wife and daughter and attended church. He stated that he attended church weekly until August. His wife stated that Sam was attending church regularly when he first got out of prison, and would even attend when she could not. However, his adjustment to the free world was difficult because he was so impatient. Minor arguments or problems were difficult for him to handle.

Sam stated that problems at home caused him to quit attending church and go back to living on the streets. However, when asked about the problems at home, he was never clear as to what the struggles were about. When asked where he moved to after leaving home, he responded, "I was motel hopping." When asked about his church, he indicated that there was more of a spiritual feeling at IFI than the church he was attending in the free world. In other words, the church on the outside didn't measure up to the church behind the prison bars. He stated that nobody knew him at church and that he never really was "plugged in."

Sam stated that he left home, church, and his job all at the same time. When asked if he knew he was throwing it all away when he left, he responded, "Yes." He also stated that if he had stayed at IFI for the full eighteen months, he would have been much better off. His statement, "I didn't have anybody to turn to," is troubling since it appears he turned away from exactly the people who could help him most. According to his wife, "He didn't have support from a mentor. There were times he needed someone else besides me." She stated that Sam needed more patience, and that eventually he was just looking for an excuse to snap. She indicated a mentor could have made a difference. She further stated that he had a job at Holiday Cleaners, and she had even found him a truck to purchase. Unlike many of Sam's IFI colleagues on parole, money was not an issue as his family was quite stable financially.

Lessons Learned from IFI Recidivists

What distinguishes IFI recidivists from those IFI participants who managed to survive in society without recidivating? A number of characteristics emerge when reflecting on these IFI participants who were unsuccessful following their release from prison. First, as is clear from the accounts of recidivists presented above, the relationship between the mentor and the IFI participant is pivotal in prisoner reentry. Initially, a number of IFI participants enjoyed frequent contact with their mentor; however, the contact seemed to diminish over time as parolees changed jobs, residences, or phone numbers. This made it difficult for mentors to maintain regular contact. Mentors described the severe contrast between constant supervision on the inside and virtually no supervision on the outside. This contrast makes it difficult for parolees to adjust to life outside of prison. The diminishing role (or outright absence) of mentors seems to be a shortcoming shared by a number of IFI recidivists. The absence or lack of mentoring is critical because so many other features of postrelease success are based on the relationship between mentor and former prisoner. For example, though many prisoners struggled with and resisted accountability early in the IFI prison program, most came to recognize that accountability would be central to their long-term success during the aftercare phase. The diminishing role of mentors meant IFI participants were largely unaccountable for poor decision making. Without frequent supervision and contact with mentors, parolees have too much idle time. Simply stated, frequent contact between mentor and offender is vital to postrelease success. Conversely, infrequent contact is the first step on a path to ultimate postrelease failure.

Second, the failure to build and sustain consistent contact with churches seems to be a common feature. The social support network and positive role models that many had indicated would be critical to their postrelease success remained largely untapped resources. A number of mentors mentioned that the IFI member went to a different church than the one the mentor attended. Consequently, most mentors were not able to facilitate or build a strong relationship between the IFI participant and a congregation where the mentor was not known. Few IFI participants had a home church to return to or one willing to adopt them. Thus, few churches were able to provide the support network so essential for former prisoners to succeed in their transition back to society. There is little doubt that houses of worship can provide a number of the social supports essential to assist former prisoners in societal reintegration, but this requires that bridges of trust be built first, which was not typically the case for IFI recidivists.

Third, recidivists tend to isolate themselves from those most likely to provide them with assistance. While isolation reflected an intentional set of decisions for some, it was an unintentional process for others. For the former, instead of confiding in their mentors and gaining assistance with their struggles, by isolating themselves, recidivists were showing a lack of trust or fear associated with the discovery of their unacceptable behavior. For the latter, isolation was partially a by-product of erratic work schedules, housing problems, and access to transportation. Observations and interviews confirmed that as parolees experienced difficulties, there was an attempt to distance themselves from those most likely to hold them accountable for their behavior. Decreasing church attendance and Bible study was associated with reduced mentor contact and deterioration of the mentoring relationship. One reason for this is the fact that few mentors saw their role as holding parolees accountable and preferred to be seen as friends who supported rather than confronted inappropriate behavior.

Fourth, a number of the recidivists are either in denial about their current problems or have a pessimistic outlook on their situation and tend to blame their struggles on the IFI program, especially the inability of the IFI aftercare component to adequately provide for them. A number of recidivists minimize the issue of personal responsibility, a hallmark of the IFI program. These four factors not only are central to their return to criminal activity, but run counter to the five spiritual transformation themes discussed earlier. Rather than exhibiting attributes associated with spiritual transformation or rehabilitation, recidivists more closely resemble a return to the penitentiary mentality or prison code.

Interviews with and observations of IFI participants (pre- and postrelease), IFI staff, TDCJ employees, and mentors provide insights that help to explain the success as well as failure of IFI participants following release from prison. First, five spiritual transformation themes emerged from the ongoing interviews of IFI participants. While prisoners may identify a single point in time when they had a conversion experience, spiritual transformation is best viewed as an ongoing process shaped by the faith-based environment and program curriculum. Additionally, each of these spiritual transformation themes seems to be consistent with characteristics associated with offender rehabilitation. Stated differently, it would appear that markers of spiritual transformation and rehabilitation are quite similar and may well overlap. Indeed, markers of spiritual transformation and rehabilitation may be mutually reinforcing.

Second, mentoring matters for prisoners and especially ex-prisoners. Further, mentoring needs to be continuous throughout the period of incarceration. Mentors should be matched with inmates as soon as possible rather than waiting for a length of time in order to be eligible for a mentor. This is particularly true for ex-prisoners during reentry back to the community following release from prison. Finally, since mentors are natural role models for prisoners, it makes sense that mentors should also facilitate the spiritual development of prisoners and bolster the postrelease decision making of ex-prisoners.

Third, severing ties to a mentor makes the reentry process much more difficult to navigate successfully. If ex-prisoners fail to remain connected to mentors, they are much more likely to take a downward spiral typified by a lack of accountability, isolation, and, ultimately, recidivism. Fourth, failure to connect with congregations in an intentional way prevents IFI participants from receiving a host of important social and spiritual supports they were accustomed to receiving while in prison, thus making them prone to an increasingly fatalistic attitude, eventually leading to a return to criminal behavior. Finally, we need additional ethnographic research to be able to understand more fully the linkages between spiritual development and rehabilitation, and the ways in which both of these phenomena may be fostered in correctional institutions as well as the communities to which offenders will be returning.

## CHAPTER 8

Jailhouse Religion, Spiritual Transformation, and Long-Term Change

"Jailhouse religion"—the sudden desperate piety of an inmate who's up against it and hopes that God will somehow bail him out.[1]

I'm reminded of an inmate who spent 90 percent of his time in disciplinary confinement until he got "saved." The change in his life was so dramatic that the institution was never the same. He never got into another fight after that. He started writing people while he was in prison in order to make restitution.[2]

M OST OF US have heard stories of a drug addict or alcoholic who overcomes addiction as a result of a religious transformation. Likewise, we often hear stories of criminals and prisoners who have experienced dramatic turnarounds as a result of a spiritual conversion. For example, there is the notorious jewel thief, Jack Murphy (aka Murph the Surf), who stole the world's largest sapphire in 1964, the 563-carat Star of India. Murphy would become a Christian in 1974 as a result of an evangelistic prison ministry. He would subsequently lead Bible studies and mentor other inmates until his release from prison in 1986, and he has been involved in prison ministry since then. Years following his release from prison, when asked about his conversion to Christianity, he would recount, "I didn't get letters from the bartenders, the hoodlums and all the wise guys I hung around with. I got letters from Christians I didn't even know."[3]

Testimonials of conversions like Murphy's have been the subject of books, movies, and documentaries, and are readily accessible on the

Internet. For example, *The Cross and the Switchblade* is a book that chronicles the dramatic conversion of former gang member Nicky Cruz in New York City during the 1950s.[4] David Wilkerson, a minister, witnessed to Cruz and would be the key figure in his conversion to Christianity. Cruz would later become an evangelist, and he continues to share his testimony and preach around the world.[5] Shortly after the conversation of Nicky Cruz, Wilkerson would found Teen Challenge, and over the next several decades it would become the world's largest faith-based drug treatment program.[6]

The book *Born Again* details the conversion of Charles Colson, special counsel to President Richard Nixon from 1969 to 1973. The former Nixon aide was sentenced to prison in 1974 for his involvement in Watergate. Many observers, including those at publications like *Newsweek* and *Time*, dismissed his conversion as nothing more than an attempt at an early release from prison. But soon after his release from prison, Colson founded Prison Fellowship Ministries, a faith-based organization dedicated to serving prisoners, ex-prisoners, and their families. Colson still regularly ministers in prisons across the country and around the world, and Prison Fellowship has been active in prison ministry since 1976. Colson went on to receive the Templeton Prize for Progress in Religion in 1993. He donated the money from the prize (worth more than $1 million), as he does all speaking fees and royalties, to further the work of Prison Fellowship.

From convicted serial murderers Ted Bundy and Jeffrey Dahmer, to countless lesser-known people, there are many examples one could mention in a discussion of dramatic religious conversions or experiences of spiritual transformation among those who end up incarcerated. It should come as no surprise, therefore, that a number of individuals and groups dedicated to working with prisoners, offenders, and drug addicts are evangelical ministries whose work is based on the notion that a religious conversion is synonymous with reform or rehabilitation. In fact, for some faith-based groups or ministries, conversion is not only the first step—it is the only step necessary. In other words, if one accepts Jesus, then one's needs have been met, not only from an eternal, but a temporal perspective.

Though perhaps less prevalent now, this position is still very much pervasive among many faith-motivated volunteers in prison ministry.

For example, Champions for Life, founded in 1969 by former NFL player Bill Glass, is a Christian-based prison ministry that brings athletes, entertainers, and former prisoners into correctional facilities to present a very clear evangelistic message to the prisoners. The message is simple: accept Jesus and you can become a new person.[7] In fact, I recently had a candid conversation with the leadership of Champions for Life about this very subject. They were troubled by one of my earliest studies which found that born-again prisoners were just as likely to return to prison as other comparable prisoners. They did not understand how this could be possible if one really believes the Bible, and especially 2 Corinthians 5:17: "Therefore, if anyone is in Christ, he is a new creation; the old has gone, the new has come!" Knowing I was a Christian, they wanted to know how I could reconcile my findings with this particular scripture. The question raised by leaders of this prison ministry captures an additional bias I have observed among many other Christians and ministries. Some secular individuals and groups often will not admit or accept that religion has a legitimate role in public life, while some religious people believe that faith alone is sufficient for ongoing transformation and that meeting worldly needs is not critical to sustain belief. At the expense of society at large, this paradox contributes to faith-based approaches remaining peripheral rather central to our crime-fighting strategies.

In response to the question posed by members of Champions for Life, I explained that I agreed with this scripture, but that it did not change the fact that prisoners face numerous and formidable challenges when they return to society. Just because an inmate makes a profession of faith in prison does not change the fact that he or she will struggle to find stable employment, acceptable housing, adequate transportation, and supportive family members. Because of these as well as other reentry difficulties, it is only a matter of time before many ex-prisoners return to prison. I would go on to argue that many (and perhaps most) inmates who experience religious conversions in prison are either unable or unwilling once released from prison to connect to a local congregation. Because reentry is so difficult, the decision to bypass the church is a recipe for disaster—effectively separating former prisoners from the support they would absolutely have to have in order to live a law-abiding and productive life in the free world. Without connections to the church, ex-prisoners will not have a mentor to hold them accountable, and they will not have access to the vibrant networks of social support that exist in so many congregations. The networks can touch each of the areas that are problematic during the reentry back to society.[8]

Let me briefly return to the original question that an executive of Champions for Life asked me: how could I reconcile 2 Corinthians 5:17 with one of my published studies showing born-again inmates were just as likely to return to prison? My answer was painfully simple and direct. If the only difference between inmates who leave prison is that some are born-again Christians, it made sense to me that Christian inmates would have comparable recidivism rates. The conversion experience in and of itself is not enough to protect ex-prisoners from all manner of missteps they might take following release from prison. In-prison programs that provide highly structured instruction and mentoring are important to be sure, but they are only the start. Whatever instruction and mentoring inmates receive behind bars, they need significantly more support as ex-prisoners. Born-again Christian prisoners who are not the beneficiaries of this kind of support will most likely be re-arrested and returned to prison at similar rates as their nonreligious counterparts. Thus, these born-again ex-prisoners—new creations they may be—are just as likely to return to prison, though this time they will bring Jesus with them when they return.

I have interviewed hundreds of inmates over the years who are four- and even five-time losers (i.e., they have served four or five previous prison sentences). When asked about their faith background, many have indicated they became Christian during their first or second prison commitment. As many inmates have told me, they simply strayed from the truth and abandoned the commitments they made in prison and intended to keep after release. Though a tough pill to swallow, representatives from Champions for Life understood what I was saying, and perhaps reluctantly they agreed with me. I was certainly not trying to minimize their work or question their call to preach the gospel in prisons. They understood my point: unless other faith-based ministries on the outside of prisons are willing to do more to intentionally work with ex-prisoners, new converts would have a hard time making it in the free world. In essence, my position was that a conversion experience is really only the first step in a much longer journey. Spiritual transformation is an ongoing process that cannot be averted once an inmate leaves prison.

Take, for example, faith-based programs like Teen Challenge, the largest faith-based drug treatment program in the world. Teen Challenge follows something similar to a twelve-step program, but with the distinction that the first step is based on accepting Jesus Christ as one's Savior.[9] In other words, they recognize that many more steps are necessary to remain sober, but the nonnegotiable first step is faith in Jesus.

JAILHOUSE RELIGION

When people speak of jailhouse religion they are usually making a disparaging statement about those claiming to "find God" when they have hit rock bottom, and for many, that means prison. Most people (including prisoners) view the term "jailhouse religion" in a suspicious or even pejorative way. Charles "Tex" Watson, known as Charles Manson's right-hand man, and who has been serving a life sentence for murder since 1971, made the statement at the top of this chapter about jailhouse religion. Watson became a born-again Christian in 1975 and for quite some time has been an ordained minister. Watson recognized that such conversions tend to be tied to people in utter despair, and with absolutely no hope they turn to God as a last resort. Because these professions of faith are made out of sheer desperation, many people argue that prisoners simply do not mean it. Therefore, jailhouse conversions are meaningless. Further, even if we assume inmates who find God in prison really do mean it (i.e., they make a genuine profession of faith), many observers concede that they have serious doubts that such conversions will stick.

We know from research that most religious conversions are not of the dramatic type. Rather, they tend to take place over time, often in connection with friends or family, and are anything but dramatic.[10] This is not to say that most people would deny the reality of dramatic conversion experiences or even the possibility of a person being delivered from some addiction or other social problem. Rather, it is simply an acknowledgment that dramatic conversions more likely represent the exception rather than the rule. However, many prison ministries (and there are thousands of them) would likely claim just the opposite.

Unfortunately, to date, we do not have much empirical documentation of the prevalence of religious conversions, much less the role of conversions or spiritual transformations in influencing the behavioral change of inmates within correctional facilities,[11] or more importantly, following release from prison.[12] I published a dissertation that tracked, over a ten-year period, inmates released from a prison in Florida who reported having a "born again" experience.[13] The born-again ex-prisoners were just as likely to be reincarcerated as comparable inmates from the same prison who did not report having a religious conversion.[14] In light of this finding, can we argue that religious conversions are meaningless or that jailhouse religion is of little value? Let me explain why the answer is an emphatic no.

First, one study does not a literature make. Second, the results from this particular study are not generalizable. That is to say, we can only argue that for this particular Florida prison, having a born-again experience had no significant impact on recidivism during the ten-year study period in which this research took place. Obviously, it is difficult to know the sincerity of prisoners who make professions of faith. Many powerful testimonials would seem to indicate an authentic conversion, but it is difficult to know exactly how to document the sincerity of such religious experiences. For example, at the point of death in the prison infirmary, Charles "Tex" Watson describes a spiritual turning point this way:

> As I lay strapped on my back in the hospital, the words of the twenty-third Psalm—one I'd memorized as a child and read again in the Bible my mother had sent—began to run through my head: "The Lord is my shepherd; I shall not want. . . ." I repeated the whole Psalm, over and over, with a sudden clarity of memory. First it was a prayer; then it became the answer to the prayer. I was suddenly aware of another presence in the stark hospital cell, not exactly visible, but unmistakably, powerfully there. It was this new Christ I'd been reading about. There was no doubt of it; this Son of God was saying: "Come to Me . . ." and He was there. As the Psalm continued to flow through my mind it was as if He took me to Himself, held me, and filled me with a peace and a quiet that left me sure that everything was going to be all right, no matter what came next. Whether I lived or died, I had nothing to fear: "Yea,

though I walk through the valley of the shadow of death, I will fear no evil, for thou art with me." He was with me; I knew it and I could rest. It didn't matter anymore what happened—He would not desert me.[15]

Charles Watson has spent approximately thirty-five years sharing his faith with other prisoners. Without the possibility of parole, it would seem that Watson would have little, if anything, to gain by dedicating his life to prison ministry.

Many people remember the story of Karla Faye Tucker. She received the death penalty for the brutal murder of her friend Jerry Dean in 1983. After fourteen years on death row, Tucker was executed in 1998, in Huntsville, Texas. She had become an evangelical Christian in prison and would become a model inmate. Her acts of service became well known not only within the Texas Department of Criminal Justice, but around the country. Many prominent and powerful people would come to her aid in trying to convince then-governor George W. Bush to intervene and stop the execution.[16] During her incarceration Tucker met her victim's brother, Richard Thornton, and he would become a Christian as a result of her interaction with him. When asked if she had any last words before the lethal injection was administered, here is part of her statement:

> Yes sir, I would like to say to all of you —the Thornton family and Jerry Dean's family—that I am so sorry. I hope God will give you peace with this. . . . Everybody has been so good to me. I love all of you very much. I am going to be face to face with Jesus now. Warden Baggett, thank all of you so much. You have been so good to me. I love all of you very much. I will see you all when you get there. I will wait for you.

Recounting the last words of Karla Faye Tucker reminds me of conversations I have had over the years with prison chaplains who have worked specifically with death row inmates. In 1983, in search of suitable data for my dissertation, I met with William E. Counselman, chaplaincy services coordinator for the Florida Department of Corrections, in Tallahassee, Florida. Counselman had for many years been a death row chaplain at Florida State Prison in Starke, Florida, before taking an administrative post with the Florida Department of Corrections. When I asked him about his experiences of working with death row inmates, he indicated it had been a very difficult assignment. He shared with me that he had walked many men to the electric chair prior to May 1964.[17] In fact, he explained that executions for a good number of years were quite common and would receive very little media coverage. He related to me that many of the prisoners he worked with on death row would become Christians. And because many remained on death row for a number of years before the sentence was actually carried out, he was able to become a spiritual mentor to a number of these converts. Counselman asserted that the spiritual change he observed over time in many of these converts was truly remarkable. I remember Counselman stating, "Invariably, it was the condemned prisoner that ministered to me on that walk to the electric chair—instead of me ministering to them. They were prepared to die, but I wasn't prepared to see them die." Knowing that these prisoners were completely remorseful, that they had turned their lives over to God and were completely different people from the ones who had committed some awful act years earlier, made it all the more difficult for Chaplain Counselman.

A few years later, in 1988, I visited the Changi Prison in Singapore. I will never forget my shock when touring that facility. Built by the British in 1936, the prison was the most primitive I had ever seen.[18] One had the feeling a good gust wind of could blow the dilapidated facility down. It was hot and muggy in Singapore, and of course, there was no air conditioning in the prison. On my tour, I remember walking by a life-size photograph of a nude inmate who had recently been caned. Caning is a legal form of corporal punishment where inmates are beaten with canes (large, heavy, soaked rattan). The photograph showed blood flowing from a series of cuts running horizontally along the entire back, buttocks, and legs of the prisoner who was being disciplined. The photograph, of course, was intended to be a deterrent for future rule violators.

Shortly after my tour, I visited with the warden of the prison, and after offering me a cup of tea, the first thing he said was, "I know what you're thinking—you are thinking we have no human rights here in Singapore." What was I supposed to say to that? He was correct, of course.

That is exactly what I was thinking, but at the same time I did not want to offend him or appear to be an ungrateful visitor. I simply smiled and said something stupid like, "You know the prisoners here seem remarkably well-behaved." To which he smiled and replied, "Yes, I believe our recidivism rate is much lower than that found in the United States."

While at the prison I also met with Henry Khoo. Rev. Khoo had been the chaplain at Changi Prison for many years, and he shared with me how they handle religious services and programs for the inmates. Accommodating the diverse spiritual needs of inmates is not as simple as some might think. Among other things, Khoo shared with me his memories of walking inmates to the gallows. In Singapore, hanging is the method by which inmates receiving the death penalty are executed.[19] I remember Khoo telling me how vastly different it was to walk to the gallows with prisoners who had become Christians, as opposed to non-Christians. He stated that the non-Christians tended to be bitter and angry during that last walk, and that you could see the torment in their faces. For the Christians, however, the situation was completely different. He described Christians as being at complete peace before the hanging, a calmness that was obvious to anyone observing. In essence, they were ready to meet their maker. I remember vividly Rev. Khoo telling me of one instance while walking an inmate to the gallows, the chaplain was so distraught he could not hold in his emotions and began to weep openly. The prisoner could hear the chaplain crying behind him, and stopped and turned around and told the chaplain, "I'm ashamed of you, where's your faith? I'm going to be with Jesus in a few minutes. There's no need to cry." Khoo would tell me this was not an isolated case, and that many of the prisoners he walked to the gallows ended up ministering to him, rather the reverse.[20]

There can be no denying that we certainly need more solid research on the role of religion within the correctional setting, and especially more focused research on spiritual conversion in prison. Nonetheless, it would seem shortsighted—for reasons I will share momentarily—to argue that religious conversions in prison are meaningless, or to assume they will not stick.

First, let me be very clear about my position on religious conversions in prison. I do not believe that conversion experiences—no matter how dramatic—are *the* answer to prisoner reform, or for that matter, a host of other crime-related problems (e.g., delinquency, violence, substance abuse, prisoner reentry, and aftercare). At the same time I do believe that "finding God" or becoming a born-again Christian can play a critically important role as a starting point in the process of long-term change and reform. In other words, religious conversions play a necessary role, but these conversions, in isolation, are insufficient in reforming offenders and bringing about lasting change. That is to say, the key to sustainable behavioral change is the ongoing process of spiritual transformation. My statement that conversion experiences (e.g., becoming a born-again Christian) in isolation of other factors is insufficient for reforming offenders will no doubt be viewed as heresy among some devote believers. To invoke Oswald Chambers, "what we call the process—God calls the end."[21] The process of spiritual growth and development makes it possible to sustain a turning point that may have been initiated through a conversion. Let me explain.

In chapters 10 and 11, I discuss the many obstacles that prisoners face in returning to society. For many, it is only a matter of time before they break the law or violate a condition of their parole. Housing, employment, transportation, lack of life skills, and inability to handle stressful conditions are just some of the problems facing ex-prisoners. Former inmates who have had a conversion experience are not exempt from these obstacles. Indeed, unless ex-prisoners who happen to be born-again Christians get the social and spiritual support necessary to develop a deep and lasting religious commitment—mainly via congregations—they will likely fail in their effort to transition back to society. To deny this prospect one has to be completely naïve or unwilling to examine the facts.

SPIRITUAL TRANSFORMATION AND CHANGE OVER THE LIFE COURSE

Sheldon and Eleanor Glueck conducted one of the most well-known delinquency studies of all time. The Gluecks in 1950 published the classic book *Unraveling Juvenile Delinquency*, where they studied, among other things, five hundred troubled boys raised in Boston who had already been involved in delinquent behavior and had been put into reform school.[22] The Gluecks collected extensive records about the boys and tracked them through adolescence. Many years later, Robert Sampson and John Laub, two leading criminologists, would find all the original files from the Gluecks' research and would ultimately follow up with the original respondents, to see how they were doing now that they were around 60 years of age. Sampson and Laub found out that some of the troubled boys, as one might expect, ended up in trouble with the law for the rest of their lives.[23] Others, however, lived very normal lives and had no legal problems. In an important book, Sampson and Laub not only examined why troubled kids remained in trouble, but more important, they also focused on how so many of these troubled youth actually turned out well.[24]

The answers that Sampson and Laub put forward are consistent with a life-course perspective. They found that the troubled kids who would get straightened out experienced some sort of a turning point or event that was pivotal in bringing them out of a criminal lifestyle or path, and into a more traditional and law-abiding pattern of behavior. These turning points, for example, could be landing a job, getting married, or becoming a parent. For others, going into military service might prove to be a turning point by perhaps providing the discipline and structure they were lacking. Likewise, the demands and responsibility that tend to come with employment, marriage, or raising a family likely provided the stability and purpose that are part and parcel of looking out for others' welfare—all while staying out of trouble. In other words, life-course theory suggests that people can and do change. Just because a person starts out on the wrong track does not mean that he or she is destined to stay on the wrong track.

Essentially Sampson and Laub, as well as other life-course theorists, agree that having ties or bonds to social institutions (marriage, family, employment, etc.) significantly influences behavior over the course of a lifetime.[25] However, these theorists have had precious little to say about the factors that lead to the changes in ties or bonds. Stated differently, scholars have been reluctant to discuss how changes within the individual during adulthood may lead to the formation of these important social bonds.

In recent years, however, several scholars have acknowledged that changes in the individual must take place before that person is ready to develop ties and bonds to social institutions. In other words, the

individual must change if the bond is to form. According to Doris MacK-
enzie, "To get along with family, keep a job, support children, or form
strong, positive ties with other institutions, the person must change in
cognitive reasoning, views toward drug use, anti-social attitudes, reading level, or vocation skills. A focus on individual change is critical to
our understanding of what works in corrections."[26] Peggy Giordano and
her colleagues call this kind of change "cognitive transformation."[27] For
them, these cognitive transformations are essential before a person is
able to sustain a new way of life. These researchers suggest that religion
can be viewed not only as a source of external control over an individual's conduct but also as a catalyst for new definitions and a cognitive
blueprint for how one is to proceed as a changed individual.[28] This process of change is facilitated by faith or spirituality, whether through an
affiliation with a religious congregation, based more on personal spiritual experiences, or both. This process makes possible the development
of a new and more favorable identity to replace the old one associated
with any or all of the following: failure, violence, abuse, addiction, heart-
break, and guilt.[29]

This is why religious conversions and spiritual transformations are
important. These religious experiences are turning points or events in
the lives of offenders. These religious experiences allow offenders to
build a new foundation and to start their lives over. As discussed in
chapter 6, many born-again inmates are able for the first time to admit
to the crimes they have committed and get a new lease on life. As Shadd
Maruna argues, getting a chance to rewrite one's own narrative can be a
powerful and redemptive thing, giving ex-prisoners the hope and purpose they need to start a new and prosocial life, while coming to grips
with the antisocial life they have left behind.[30]

Along these same lines, a number of restorative justice programs are
interested in bringing crime victims and offenders face-to-face. These
programs, many of which are faith-based, exist in order to bring closure
and emotional healing to an experience that has never been reconciled.[31]
I remember interviewing a particular prisoner on multiple occasions,
Ron Flowers, a convicted murderer from Houston. Ron had become a
Christian in prison, but nonetheless maintained his innocence. Flowers
was convicted of shooting a teenage girl at gunpoint. The girl, Dee Dee

Washington, was in the car of another person who, unbeknownst to her, was attempting to purchase drugs. In police parlance, she was simply an innocent bystander—collateral damage.

Ron Flowers participated in a faith-based prison program and met a pastor of a church in Houston who did volunteer work at the prison. One day the minister mentioned working with prisoners at a nearby prison. Intrigued, one of the members, Arna Washington, a schoolteacher, asked the pastor if he had met or had heard of Ron Flowers. "That's the name of the man who killed my daughter fourteen years ago," she stated. The pastor replied, "He's in my group—would you like to meet him?" I doubt either the pastor or Mrs. Washington realized the mathematical long shot of Ron Flowers being in this small faith-based prison group. After all, Texas is home to more than one hundred thousand inmates in more than one hundred prisons.[32]

Mrs. Washington, did, in fact, want to meet Ron Flowers—the person she had come to hate for literally devastating her family. Not long after her daughter's murder, Mrs. Washington's husband and son also died. Though a devout Christian, Mrs. Washington was clearly bitter and had written letters to the Texas parole board in an effort to ensure that Flowers would stay in prison as long as possible. Now she would actually have the opportunity to meet him and ask the question she had been struggling with for fourteen years.

When the meeting took place, several unexpected things happened. The second they met face-to-face, Flowers, to his surprise, for the first time, confessed to the murder. Mrs. Washington then asked the question she had been waiting to ask: "Why did you shoot and kill my daughter?" Flowers explained he had been a crazed young teenager who was strung out on drugs, and he just started shooting and she happened to get shot. He went on to say, "I don't know if you can forgive me, but I'm sorry for what I have done." To Mrs. Washington's surprise, she heard herself saying, "I forgive you." Reflecting on that day, Mrs. Washington told me in one of our interviews, "That was the moment I got my life back. A huge load was lifted the instant I forgave him." The story does not end there. Mrs. Washington went on to develop a strong and lasting relationship with Ron Flowers. In her own words, she "would adopt him as [my] son." Ron got out of prison in 1998 and visited Mrs. Washington weekly. He sat with her in church on Sundays, and she played a crucial role in his successful transition back to society. Now happily married, Ron has been out of prison for more than a decade, has been employed at the same company for nine years, has a four-year-old son, and has a bright future. Ron recently told me his spiritual transformation is one that is still a work in progress, but it is something he continually seeks to deepen and mature.[33] Mrs. Washington died in 2007.

Though there are a number of significant aspects to this compelling story, perhaps the most significant for me was the impromptu admission of guilt by Flowers when confronted with Mrs. Washington. I would argue that his surprising admission of guilt, coupled with Mrs. Washington's decision to forgive him, represented a powerful turning point that changed Ron Flowers's life. This critical turning point, however, would not have happened had Ron not become a Christian through a faith-based prison program. For this reason, religious conversions are important. Becoming a born-again Christian may put into motion a sequence of events that become pivotal in dramatically changing a person's behavioral trajectory. The conversion itself is not necessarily enough, but it provides a bridge to other faith-motivated individuals and resources that could prove instrumental in having a tipping effect in one person's life.

Every year hundreds of thousands of prisoners participate in religious services and interact with faith-motivated volunteers and mentors. Many of these offenders have had religious conversions. In and of itself, this may not mean a great deal to criminologists, correctional practitioners, or policy makers. However, faith-based prison programs and, more importantly, faith-based reentry and aftercare programs have the potential to build upon these religious conversions. In the life course, conversions should not be viewed cynically as jailhouse religion, but rather as the opportunity to connect these converts to volunteers and faith-based networks that can facilitate and nurture spiritual transformation.

This is exactly why the most effective programs helping offenders are those that intentionally link spiritual transformation to other support networks, especially those that are faith-motivated and faith-friendly. Let me be clear: simply relying only on faith-based prison programs to reform prisoners and reduce crime would be a misguided policy recommendation. However, faith-based organizations, governmental agencies, and other social service providers need to think strategically about partnerships and mutual accountability in order to produce results that reduce recidivism and protect the public safety. The next three chapters elaborate on why these religious connections are important and how we can be intentional about developing them.

## CHAPTER 9

Why Religion Matters

A S WE HAVE seen from the current systematic review of the research
literature (chapter 5), clear and compelling empirical evidence
exists that religiosity is linked to reductions in crime.[1] In short, we know
that religion matters in consequential and beneficial ways when it comes
to crime, but researchers have spent far less time explaining *why* religion
matters. There are several reasons for this oversight. The first reason is
a partially valid one in that many of the relevant studies on religion and
crime simply do not have the data necessary to definitively answer the
why-religion-matters question. Consequently, though many scholars
now acknowledge the link between religion and crime reduction, most
tend to be vague regarding thoughtful explanations of this relationship.
On the other hand, in light of the empirical evidence to the contrary,
some scholars are still ambiguous about the role of religion. Worse,
many researchers, practitioners, and decision makers continue to ignore
religion in spite of a growing literature suggesting its relevance. This is
exactly why the late David B. Larson in a number of his publications so
often referred to religion as the "forgotten factor".

The other reason so many researchers are reluctant to answer why
religion matters is that to do so would be tantamount to endorsing the
power of religion as a force for good. In light of the fact that social
scientists tend not to be a very religious group,[2] recognizing the importance of religion or offering explanations of the role of religion or faith
itself to reduce crime might taint one's reputation within the academy.
That is to say, one could seriously run the risk of being labeled a religious person, and being labeled "religious" would certainly not be a
good thing—especially for younger academics seeking to secure tenure
and promotion, as evidenced by my own experience as described in

chapter 1. Further, an assumption held by many within the academic community is that being religious prevents one from being objective when it comes to the study of religion. By extension, then, we should only seriously trust the results of totally secular scholars when it comes to objective research on religion. This is, of course, nonsense, and yet another form of the last acceptable prejudice outlined in chapter 1. This point may explain why some scholars go out of their way to keep their faith a completely private matter.[3] A couple of personal examples of this form of discrimination help illustrate this point.

Following the election of George W. Bush and the launch of the Office of Faith-Based and Community Initiatives in 2001, I was invited along with several other scholars to write a white paper on religion and crime for the National Institute of Justice (NIJ), the research arm of the Department of Justice. These white papers were commissioned in order to help brief the NIJ program officers and staff on the state of the field as well as identify fruitful areas of research that might be considered for future NIJ solicitations for research.[4] Put differently, NIJ was admitting it was one of the many culprits in treating religion as the forgotten factor. The commissioning of these white papers was an effort on the part of the NIJ to get up to speed on the subject since it was obvious this topic would be a priority during the Bush administration.

During the presentations of our white papers at NIJ, one of the other scholars indicated that should NIJ decide to fund a major research project on religion and crime, it would be wise to select someone known not to be religious—thereby ensuring an unbiased assessment. The remark was greeted with a positive response; most of the NIJ program officers in attendance obviously agreed with this assessment. As a religious person I was deeply offended by the statement. Even though I have published as much or more than any other scholar in the country on this topic, NIJ representatives were essentially agreeing they would not want someone like me doing this research. Once again, the last acceptable prejudice reared its ugly head.

In my opinion, an outstanding scholar who happens to be religious is anything but a liability, and can actually bring added value to research on religion. Drawing upon my own religious experiences has helped me immensely over the years in selecting the most appropriate research design, by identifying the best measures of religiousness, or making decisions on particular data analysis strategies. A completely irreligious person, one not having a religious background at all, would seem to me to be at a methodological disadvantage. Without any experience to draw upon, he or she may not think to do the analysis in the most appropriate way, and may potentially miss what otherwise might have been an important finding.

One more example is in order to illustrate the bias I have observed against research on religion. I once submitted an article on religion and crime to one of the top journals in the field of criminology.[5] After several months I received a letter from the editor informing me that the journal had received two positive reviews and one negative review of my article. On the basis of these three anonymous reviews, the editor invited me to revise and resubmit the manuscript to the journal. For the nonacademic reading this chapter, receiving a revise and resubmit is generally good news, especially if the reviewers are clear about the revisions necessary in order for the article to get published. I painstakingly incorporated each of the suggestions and modifications that the reviewers requested. Because the revision was done with such detail and care, I was confident the paper would now be accepted. After several months I received a letter from the editor indicating the paper had been rejected. I was really surprised about this news since the revisions addressed very clearly every single concern of the reviewers, and the revised paper was much better than the original manuscript, which two of the reviewers had already indicated they liked. I was so baffled I decided to call the editor to discuss his decision to reject—something I had never done before nor have I done since. The editor was very forthright in the conversation and suggested that two of the three reviewers were indeed very positive about the revised paper, but the third reviewer, who happened to be a "heavyweight" in the field, remained very negative. The editor went on to quote this third reviewer as saying, "There is something wrong about this paper, I don't know what it is, I can't put my finger on it, but something is not right." Though I did not say it to the editor, I remember thinking to myself, *How bizarre. He read the paper and could not determine what was wrong with it.* Since no research is perfect, reviewers normally have little problem pointing out numerous shortcomings when reviewing manuscripts, especially papers they do not like. Without specifying any particular criticism, this reviewer had cast a strong vote against the paper being published. Ordinarily, the editor told me, he would have ignored such a review, but since this person happened to be a heavyweight within the field, he decided to go along with his recommendation.

I then asked the editor if he would consider another alternative. Would he be willing to consider publishing my article in the journal, but let this third reviewer publish a response to my article? This approach would give the reviewer the opportunity to level whatever criticism he might have about the research in front of the entire journal readership. But I would then be given the opportunity to write a rebuttal to his critique of my article. The editor paused for a moment and then said, "I like this idea. Let me talk to him and get right back to you." I received a call the next day from the journal editor, who indicated that the negative reviewer had decided to drop his opposition to the article and that the paper would be published in the journal without any additional changes. What the reviewer had said in private, he was unwilling, of course, to state in public. When backed into the corner, this heavyweight refused to take me on in what would have been a very public exchange—which reinforces my contention of hostility among many academics toward research on religion, especially when the findings are not what they want to hear. Invoking my mentor, David B. Larson, one more time is appropriate in this context. Larson told me to expect to receive FLRs anytime I submitted an article for publication that dealt with religion—especially when the results were positive. When asked what he meant by FLR, Larson said, "An FLR is a funny looking review—a review that makes little sense and not only reflects the bias of the reviewer, but how uncomfortable they are with the findings."

I have been asked on many occasions if things have changed for the better within the academy since I was a young professor. I guess I would have to say yes, but with a cautionary note. It is better in that social science journals have now published many empirical studies on the role of religion. The research evidence on the link between religion and crime reduction is solid and speaks for itself. In fact, there are sections at the major professional meetings in criminology and criminal justice, as well as corrections, that specifically address the role of religion. These developments are positive, to be sure. We still need, however, for serious research on religion to be a funding priority not only for private foundations but also for federal agencies seeking to reduce crime and delinquency.

SUMMARIZING THE LINK BETWEEN RELIGION AND CRIME REDUCTION

As stated before, decades of research document that religiosity or religious commitment is associated with reductions in delinquent behavior and deviant activities.[6] In fact, the effect of religion remains significant even in the absence of other factors in the surrounding community that might normally prevent illegal behavior. For example, studies have demonstrated that high-risk youth were much less likely to be involved in crime and delinquent behavior if they regularly attended church.[7] Similarly, research has found that highly religious low-income youth from high-crime areas are less likely to use drugs than less religious youth in these same disadvantaged communities. Indeed, highly religious teens living in communities recognized as crime "hot spots" were also less likely to use drugs than less religious teens from middle-class suburban communities or "good places."[8] There is also evidence that religious involvement may lower the risks of a broad range of delinquent behaviors, including both minor and serious forms of criminal behavior.[9] Research also shows that religious involvement may have a cumulative effect throughout adolescence and may significantly lessen the risk of later adult criminality.[10] In other words, uninterrupted and regular church attendance may further inoculate or insulate youth from crime and delinquency. Further, studies have demonstrated that religion can be used as a tool to help prevent high-risk urban youths from engaging in delinquent behavior.[11]

Youth who attend church frequently are less likely to engage in a variety of delinquent behaviors, including drug use, skipping school, fighting, and violent and nonviolent crimes.[12] Indeed, youth exposure to religious and spiritual activities is a powerful inhibitor of juvenile delinquency and youth violence. But why does religiosity or religiousness help reduce the likelihood of criminal activity? What are the factors explaining why at-risk youth from disadvantaged communities who regularly attend church are less likely to violate the law? In the rest of this chapter I shed light on why religion matters.

RELIGION PROTECTS FROM HARM

Many reasonable explanations are available for how religious beliefs and practices may ultimately influence behavior. To review all such explanations would go beyond the scope of this chapter, but it is important to list a few. We know that certain factors put youth at risk for being involved in crime or delinquency; having an incarcerated parent, being raised in poverty, or poor academic performance and dropping out of school are just a few. The opposite is also true; some protective factors are known to buffer or shield youth from crime. Being raised in an intact home, doing well in school, and, more recently, increasing levels of religiosity represent just some of the important factors that are known to insulate youth from crime and delinquency. Taken together, many of these risk as well as protective factors resonate with commonsense explanations for deviant activity (or the lack thereof).

Discovering religion as a protective factor is one thing, but explaining why religion is protective is a different matter. Study after study documents that regular church attendance is associated with lower levels of delinquent or criminal behavior, including drug and alcohol use among youth and adolescents, and a wide range of illegal behaviors ranging from minor to serious forms of criminal behavior.[13] Regardless of the sample, the data set utilized, or other study differences, church attendance tends to be an important factor linked to lower levels of deviant behavior.[14] Simply put, increasing church attendance is associated with lower levels of deviance. Decreasing church attendance, on the other hand, is significantly related to higher levels of crime or delinquency. To understand why church attendance is so consequential, we need to understand what about regular attendance is so beneficial.

When people attend churches they tend to get connected to different networks of people. Whether through classes, retreats, small groups, mission trips, church-sponsored volunteer work, or any number of related group functions, these activities connect people to multiple networks of social support that have the potential to be meaningful. Harvard scholar Robert Putnam suggests that churches are enormous repositories of goodwill.

> Houses of worship build and sustain more social capital—and social capital of more varied forms—than any other type of

institution in America. Churches, synagogues, mosques, and other houses of worship provide a vibrant institutional base for civic good works and a training ground for civic entrepreneurs. Nearly half of America's stock of social capital is religious or religiously affiliated, whether measured by association memberships, philanthropy, or volunteering.[15]

I agree with Putnam's rather profound assessment of the influence of congregations in America.[16] Houses of worship can become an effective training ground for good works and civic engagement. More recently, Putnam argues that people with religious affiliations are more satisfied with their lives, mainly because they attend religious services more frequently and construct social networks with people who share their faith and religious experience, thus building a strong sense of belonging to a community of religious faith.[17] So compelling are these faith-based networks, Putnam argues, that they generate unique effects which cannot be explained in any other way. That is to say, these faith-infused networks of support—in and of themselves—are powerful independent predictors of beneficial outcomes.[18]

It makes sense, therefore, that an adolescent's involvement in religious practices and related activities may become an important vehicle for fostering the development of and integration into personal networks that provide social and emotional support. When such personal networks become embedded in neighborhoods, and these networks overlap with other networks (e.g., friends living in the same neighborhood who attend the same church), one can expect such networks not only to constrain but also to protect an adolescent from the effects of living a high-crime community.[19] In other words, an adolescent's integration into a neighborhood-based religious network actually weakens the effects of other factors that might otherwise influence inappropriate adolescent behavior. Thus, the religious network buffers or shields him or her from the harmful effects of unhelpful peers or other negative influences. In addition, individual religiosity can "insulate" the adolescent against behaviors such as illicit drug use.[20]

It makes sense, therefore, that those who regularly attend church and participate in religious activities are much more likely to internalize values modeled and taught in such settings. These faith-filled networks encourage appropriate behavior and emphasize concern for others' welfare. Such processes are likely to contribute to the acquisition of positive attributes that give participants a greater sense of empathy toward others, which in turn makes them less likely to commit acts that harm others. Indeed, recent research confirms that religiosity can help youth and adults to be resilient (i.e., they bend, but don't break) even in the midst of poverty, unemployment, and other social ills. Religion is important because it provides the wherewithal for people to be resilient in spite of negative influences of decaying communities. Communities of faith are known to provide instruction and the teaching of religious beliefs and values that, if internalized, help youth as well as adults to make good decisions.

Preliminary evidence suggests that youth who have continued religious participation in congregations throughout the adolescent period may be the beneficiary of a cumulative religiosity effect that lessens the risk of future illicit drug use.[21] Even more revealing, church-attending youth from disadvantaged communities are less likely to use illicit drugs than youth from suburban communities who attend church less frequently or not at all.[22] In a similar vein, preliminary research has examined intergenerational religious influence and finds that parental religious devotion can protect youth from delinquency.[23] Taken together, these findings suggest that the effect of church attendance is compelling in and of itself. Through the networks of support they provided, the learning of self-control through the teaching of moral beliefs, or the condemning of inappropriate behavior, regular church attendance fosters each of these possibilities.

Additional research documents that religion can be used as a tool to help prevent especially difficult populations, like urban youths raised in poverty, from engaging in delinquent behavior.[24] For example, youth living in poverty tracts in urban environments, or what criminologists call disadvantaged communities, are at elevated risk for a number of problem behaviors, including poor school performance, drug use, and other delinquent activities. However, youth from these same disorganized communities who participate in religious activities are significantly less likely to be involved in deviant activities. In other words, youth from bad places can still turn out to be good kids if religious beliefs and practices are regular and important in their lives. In this way, religiously committed youth are resilient to and protected from the negative consequences of living in impoverished communities.[25]

Whereas criminologists have tended to focus on the effects of community disadvantage on predisposing youth to delinquent behavior, we are now beginning to understand the effects that religion or religious institutions may play in providing communities of "advantage." Using data from the Social and Health Assessment, Pearce and associates investigated the relationship between exposure to violence and later problem behavior. They found that several measures of religiosity reduced the effect of exposure to violence and victimization on delinquency. The authors found that youth exposed to high levels of violence and who reported higher levels of religious practices reported less of an increase in conduct problems over time. Additionally, youth experiencing high levels of victimization but also indicating higher levels of religiousness were less likely to report an increase in conduct problems.[26] As a result, a growing body of research has focused on how protective factors reduce involvement in delinquency.[27]

The fact that these findings hold even in disadvantaged communities provides additional evidence of the connection between religiousness and resilience. Stated differently, the role of religion and religious institutions is especially critical in communities where crime and delinquency are most prevalent. For example, research has shown the African American church likely plays a key role in reducing crime among black youth from urban communities.[28] Therefore, the African American church is an important protective factor, though scholars and policy experts rarely recognize it as a vital agency of local social control. It would be a mistake to continue to overlook the important role these religious congregations play in the lives of so many disadvantaged youth.[29] In summary, the protective effects of religiosity seem to counter the impact of a wide variety of risk factors that otherwise make delinquency and substance use more likely. An important study by Evans and colleagues found that religious activities reduced the likelihood of adult criminality as measured by a broad range of criminal acts. Further, the finding did not depend on social or religious contexts.[30]

If religion is important, can it help individuals already involved in deviant or illegal behavior? In other words, is it possible that participation in specific kinds of religious activity can help steer one back to a course of less deviant behavior and, more important, away from potential career criminal paths? As discussed in chapter 7, the developmental/ life course perspectives help us understand the role that religious experiences can play as critical turning points in the life course that change behavioral trajectories from bad to good.[31] Preliminary research suggests that religion can be an antidote to reverse previous behavior. For example, preliminary empirical studies addressing faith-based approaches to prison treatment have shown that inmates who regularly participate in volunteer-led Bible studies or who complete a faith-based program are less likely to commit institutional infractions,[32] or to commit new crimes following release from prison.[33] In the first major evaluation study of a faith-based prison. I found that inmates completing the InnerChange Freedom Initiative, an eighteen- to twenty-four-month-long faith-based prison program operated by Prison Fellowship (a Christian prison ministry), were significantly less likely to be arrested than a matched group of prisoners not receiving this religious intervention (8 percent vs. 20 percent, respectively) during a two-year postrelease period.[34] Similar results were reported in a study comparing former prisoners in two Brazil prisons—one a faith-based prison program[35] and the other a model prison based on a vocational model in Brazil.[36]

In sum, a review of the relevant research on religion and deviant behavior indicates that, in general, higher levels of religious involvement are associated with lower rates of crime and delinquency. The empirical evidence demonstrates that those who are most involved in religious activities are less likely to commit criminal or delinquent acts. Thus, aided by several systematic reviews of the literature, it is fair to state that religiosity is now beginning to be acknowledged as a key protective factor that buffers or shields youth from criminal and delinquency outcomes.

RELIGION PROMOTES THE GOOD

Criminologists have for several centuries studied factors thought to be linked to the causes of crime and delinquency. Books, journals, and thousands of studies have been dedicated to examining the many characteristics of offenders and communities, as well as the antecedents to criminal behavior, in order to predict more accurately future criminal or delinquent behavior. Quite naturally, a great deal of criminological research can best be understood as attempting to answer these two central questions: *Why do people commit crime?* and *How can we prevent it?* As a result, voluminous research literatures have emerged that examine the deleterious effects of poverty and disadvantage, lack of education, and unemployment, to mention just a few, in causing or contributing to crime and deviant behavior. Indeed, many criminology course curricula in academic institutions are literally devoted to the study of crime causation.

Social scientists and criminologists have much less often asked another equally important question: *Why is it that people do not commit crime?* Social control theorists like Travis Hirschi provided a unique and important perspective, arguing for some very important reasons that people do not commit crime or engage in delinquent behavior.[37] Religion, therefore, is but one of many factors that control theorists argue "bond" an individual to society and conventional or normative behavior. These bonds help youth to be resilient and to avoid delinquent paths in spite of characteristics and factors that would otherwise seem to predict a deviant behavioral trajectory. But we now pose another equally important though understudied question, "Why is it that people do good things?"

Less commonly acknowledged by researchers is the contribution of religious belief and practice in fostering positive or normative behavior. I argue here that it is at least as important to understand why people turn into good citizens as to understand why they go bad. In essence, we have probably spent too much time asking why people do bad things, but not enough time asking why people do good things or exhibit prosocial behavior. For example, in addition to documenting the protective factor that religion can play, scholars have also discovered that at-risk youth from disadvantaged communities who exhibit higher levels of religiousness are not only less likely to commit crimes than their disadvantaged counterparts, they are also more likely to stay in school, make better grades, and find and retain steady employment.[38]

Clearly, not enough scholarship has focused on the prosocial side of the equation. Scholars need to do a much better job of documenting the factors and conditions that motivate, cause, support, and sustain positive or prosocial behavior. When discussing prosocial behavior, much more is involved than merely obeying the law and desisting from criminal behavior. We need to know why people do admirable things such as supporting charities, doing volunteer work, returning lost valuables, or participating in different kinds of civic activities.

A number of studies have been published in recent years documenting the relationship between increasing religiosity and higher levels of prosocial behavior. This body of research consistently finds that religious commitment is a source for promoting or enhancing beneficial outcomes like well-being;[39] hope, meaning, and purpose;[40] self-esteem;[41] and even educational attainment.[42] Indeed, the more actively religious are more likely to give to charities (both religious and nonreligious) and to volunteer time for civic purposes.[43] The review of a large number of studies across multiple disciplines, with diverse samples and methodologies, leaves one with the robust conclusion that the empirically documented effect of religion on physical and mental health outcomes is remarkably positive.[44] Studies also suggest that being involved in or exposed to altruistic or prosocial activities and attitudes—something that is central to the mission of many churches and other faith-based organizations—appears to reduce the risk of youth violence.

Based on an objective assessment of the research literature, we know that religious congregations and other measures of religiousness can have a significant buffering or protective effect that lessens the likelihood of delinquent or criminal behavior among youth as well as adults. In a separate review of the research literature we also document that increasing measures of religiosity are associated with an array of prosocial outcomes. In this way, religion not only protects from deleterious outcomes like crime and delinquency, but it also promotes prosocial or beneficial outcomes that are considered normative and necessary for a productive society.

It is safe to say that religious involvement helps many learn prosocial behavior (i.e., actions that emphasize concern for others' welfare). These prosocial skills may instill a greater sense of empathy toward others and thus lessen the likelihood of committing acts that harm others. Similarly, once individuals become involved in deviant behavior, participation in religious activities may help steer them back to a course of less deviant behavior and away from potential career criminal paths.[45] Religiosity is now beginning to be acknowledged as a key protective factor that not only buffers or protects from harmful outcomes but also serves as a variable promoting prosocial behavior.[46] If congregations can be viewed as institutions dedicated to improving the plight of at-risk populations, it may be that faith- and community-based organizations will be recognized for being key factors in helping ex-prisoners transition to society.

CONCLUSION

Research is beginning to help us understand the importance of religious influences in protecting people from harmful outcomes as well as promoting beneficial and prosocial outcomes. This beneficial relationship is not simply a function of religion's constraining function or what it discourages—opposing drug use or delinquent behavior—but also through what it encourages: promoting behaviors that can enhance purpose, well-being, or educational attainment. Yet religion measures are not routinely included in research examining important social outcomes. It is time for researchers and federal funding agencies to discontinue the pattern of overlooking this important line of policy-relevant research. New research will allow us to more fully understand the ways in which religion directly and indirectly impacts crime and delinquency, as well as various prosocial outcomes. Indeed, a better understanding of the mechanisms associated with prosocial behavior will assist in the development of future prevention and intervention strategies. Unraveling the role of religiosity, religious institutions and congregations, as well as religious practices and beliefs, in promoting prosocial behavior should be a priority for academic researchers as well as federal and private sources of funding.

It is time for secularists and governmental leaders to recognize that churches, synagogues, mosques, inner-city blessing stations, and other houses of worship collectively represent one of the few prosocial institutions that remain within close proximity of most adolescents, their families, and their peers. Research is beginning to confirm that these religious institutions can play an important role in promoting the health and well-being of those they serve. As policy makers consider strategies to reduce delinquency, gang activity, and crime, it is essential for such deliberations to seriously and intentionally consider the role of religion and religious institutions in implementing, developing, and sustaining multifaceted approaches. Many faith-based organizations never seek government funding for the delivery of social services, a decision that should be fully respected. However, many other faith-based groups, especially those located in some of our most disadvantaged communities, are ready and willing to work with the government and secular groups in playing a more intentional role in combating any number of social ills. However, many of these groups still feel marginalized by the federal government. It is necessary for local, state, and federal authorities to pursue actively the involvement of faith-motivated individuals and organizations. From after-school programs for disadvantaged youth to public/private partnerships that bring together secular and sacred groups to tackle social problems like mentoring at-risk youth and the prisoner reentry crisis, any strategy will be needlessly incomplete unless the power of religion and religious communities is integrally involved.

## CHAPTER 10

Prisoner Reentry and Aftercare

*America is the land of the second chance—and when the gates of
the prison open, the path ahead should lead to a better life.*[1]

As long as prisons have existed, ex-prisoners have had difficulty
in transitioning back to society. What is different today is the sheer
magnitude of prisoners leaving prisons and returning to American communities each year. In less than three decades, the U.S. prison population
has increased by 482 percent.[2] Approximately two thousand prisoners
are being released from prisons each day, a trend that is expected to continue into the foreseeable future. The increase in the number of prisoners returning to communities across the country has created a national
debate about how best to handle one of the most vexing dilemmas in
correctional history.[3]

A number of well-known correctional initiatives have been implemented over the years to help manage the difficult adjustment period
when prisoners transition back to society. Halfway houses, community
corrections programs, intensive supervision, and community reintegration programs represent but a few of the various postrelease efforts
designed to make the transition back to society less difficult for ex-
prisoners.[4] In spite of these efforts, the likelihood of a former prisoner
succeeding in the community has not improved. About two-thirds of
all offenders released from prison are rearrested within three years of
their release.[5] As a result of the difficulty in effectively managing large
numbers of returning prisoners, concern is growing that the increasing number of ex-prisoners returning to communities all across the
country will become a major threat to public safety. In a Department of

Justice–sponsored report, leading experts agree that the successful reintegration of former prisoners is one of the most formidable challenges
facing society today.[6]

PRISONER REENTRY OBSTACLES

For a number of reasons, ex-prisoners face myriad challenges in remaining crime-free. First, former inmates have a difficult time finding and
keeping jobs when they leave prison. Second, many inmates leave prison
still very much in need of substance abuse treatment as well as other
forms of mental health counseling. Third, most are returning to disadvantaged communities and neighborhoods where poverty and crime
are especially concentrated. Finally, ex-prisoners do not have the education, skills, or positive social supports to assist them during this difficult transition period. Most do not have the benefit of returning to
a strong marriage or mentors to hold them accountable and provide
positive role models. As a result, many ex-prisoners commit new crimes
or violate the terms of parole in the first days, weeks, or months after
release. In fact, during the period of time immediately following release
from prison, deaths among former prisoners are more than 12 times
the average for the general population. Further, the death rate for drug
overdose among ex-prisoners is 129 times the death rate for comparable
citizens.[7] Prisoner reentry, therefore, is a very dangerous time for both
ex-prisoners and the public at-large.

Most correctional experts agree that any comprehensive reentry
strategy must include the following components: close community
supervision, access to substance abuse treatment, mental health services, educational programs, vocational training, and job placement.
Additionally, these services need to be coordinated and well resourced.
However, funding such a plan would place a significant financial burden
on correctional budgets already regarded by many as too high. In an era
when many jurisdictions are being asked to do more with less, the likelihood of significantly expanding educational, vocational, and counseling
programs in correctional environments is unlikely to be viewed as a high
public policy priority.

In spite of this recognition, most policy recommendations tend to place the responsibility of a comprehensive prisoner reentry plan solely at the feet of government. Though often overlooked by government leaders, policy makers, practitioners, and especially academics, the role of religious volunteers, religious programs, and faith-based organizations may be particularly consequential for ex-prisoners facing so many different obstacles. This oversight is unfortunate since numerous theoretical perspectives, published papers, common sense, and even recent federally sponsored prisoner reentry experiments suggest that communities of faith have the potential to be powerful allies in confronting the reentry crisis. This chapter reviews research documenting the role of religion in prisoner reentry. It concludes with a recommendation for a public-private model that prioritizes the central role of faith-based individuals, communities, and intermediary organizations in building and sustaining a comprehensive approach to prisoner reentry. Finally, I argue why any prisoner reentry plan including only a marginal rather than a central role for the faith factor cannot succeed.

THE RELEVANCE OF RELIGION FOR PRISONS AND PRISONER REENTRY

The evolution of the American correctional system is one that has been accompanied by the constant influence of religion and religious workers. Terms like "corrections," "penitentiary," "reformation," "restoration," and "solitary confinement" can be traced to religious origins.[8] The role of religion in prisons is important not only in a historical sense but it also continues to be prominent and pervasive in correctional institutions today. Faith-motivated volunteers in prisons are as likely to be involved in life-skills training or instruction in GED programs as they are to conduct Bible studies or lead worship services. In this way, religious volunteers have played and continue to play a vital role in the vast majority of American correctional institutions. Indeed, beyond work, education, or vocational training, religious activities attract more participants than any other type of personal enhancement program offered inside a prison.[9] Religion might be consequential for prisoners and ex-prisoners in many ways.[10] However, where correctional decision makers and policy stakeholders are concerned, the one overriding outcome is whether an intervention reduces the likelihood of recidivism (re-arrest and reincarceration).

In the mid-1990s, Prison Fellowship (PF), a nonprofit religious ministry to prisoners, commissioned research to determine the effects of faith-based interventions on prisoner recidivism. Utilizing a quasi-experimental design, the study examined the influence of religious programs on prisoner adjustment (i.e., institutional infractions or rule violations) and recidivism rates (i.e., postrelease arrests) in two matched groups of inmates from four adult prisons in New York State.[11] One group had participated in programs sponsored by PF; the second group had no involvement with PF programs. Researchers found that after controlling for level of involvement in PF-sponsored programs, inmates who were most active in Bible studies were significantly less likely to be arrested during the one-year follow-up period.[12] A second study was conducted with an additional seven years of follow-up data and document that after dividing the sample into groups of high and low levels of participation in Bible studies, high participants were less likely to be re-arrested two and three years after release from prison.[13] The study also concluded that more research is necessary to determine how religion might be related to offender rehabilitation, inmate adjustment, and prisoner reentry. This small but growing body of research indicates that participation in religious programs and activities can contribute to positive inmate adjustment while in prison, as well as reduce the likelihood of recidivism following release from prison.[14]

An overarching implication of this relatively new body of research is that religious volunteers and faith-based programs have the potential to play a significant role in how one thinks about prison management, safety, and offender rehabilitation. For example, preliminary research suggests that faith-based dorms and housing units have the potential to significantly counter the negative and often debilitating prison culture that permeates so many correctional institutions.[15]

A six-year evaluation of a faith-based prison program called the InnerChange Freedom Initiative (reported in detail in chapter 5) found that inmates completing the program were significantly less likely than a matched group of offenders[16] to be re-arrested (17 percent vs. 35 percent) or reincarcerated (8 percent vs. 20 percent) during a two-year follow-up period. The study revealed a stark contrast between the areas of the prison controlled by the faith-based program as opposed to those areas housing prisoners from the general population. The general population was typified by the presence of a distinct prison code of behavior that often condones rule breaking and other inappropriate behaviors. Not surprisingly, traditional prison culture often works to undermine the very premises on which a rehabilitation model is based.[17]

In contrast, the faith-based side of the prison was typified by educational classes, study, work, worship services, little free time, and the absence of television sets. Further, the faith-based program enjoyed an atmosphere promoting forgiveness, honesty, and personal accountability. Faith-based efforts like InnerChange and Kairos (another faith-based prison program) are designed to discourage antisocial and destructive behavior and to encourage transparency, contrition, and spiritual transformation—all of which run counter to the pervasive prison code. Preliminary research lends at least initial support to the notion that faith-based dorms or units can create an environment conducive to effective treatment and to rehabilitation programs more generally. In this way, faith-based interventions have the potential to enhance the achievement of a secular goal and civic good: lower recidivism.

HARNESSING HUMAN AND SPIRITUAL CAPITAL
FOR PRISONER REENTRY

President George W. Bush signed an Executive Order in January 2001, establishing the White House Office of Faith-Based and Community Initiatives.[18] Over the next several years, Centers of Faith-Based and Community Initiatives in eleven federal agencies were created through a series of Executive Orders.[19] In his executive orders and speeches on the initiative, Bush acknowledged the long tradition of faith-based and community organizations helping Americans, especially those confronting serious disadvantages. Bush was also convinced that the federal government had not been a very good partner to faith- and community-based groups working to target serious social problems. Further, President Bush believed the federal government for far too long had made it difficult for faith-based and community groups to compete for funds on an equal standing with secular nonprofit service providers. The 2001 White House report *Unlevel Playing Field* systematically reviewed federal funding and identified the barriers that stand in the way of effective government partnerships with faith- and community-based organizations.[20] The report, for example, found that the Office of Justice Programs at the Department of Justice estimated it would award in fiscal year 2001 about 0.3 percent of its total discretionary grant funds—one-third of 1 percent—to faith-based organizations ($1.9 million of $626.7 million).

Since 2001 considerable progress has been made in alleviating obstacles (e.g., prior to 2001 references to faith-based groups were virtually absent from federal funding announcements covering social service delivery or demonstration projects) that have prevented faith-based and community organizations from seeking grants to build capacity and thereby strengthen outreach to underserved populations, including prisoners and ex-ex-prisoners. Since 2001 conferences for faith- and community-based groups have been offered in all regions of the United States in order to identify the federal funding processes. Indeed, no American president devoted more funding, resources, and attention to the plight of ex-prisoners and their families than did Bush. First as a governor and then as president, Bush consistently favored public-private partnerships whose mission was to assist offenders, prisoners, ex-prisoners, and their children. Although Bush indicated that the government has a very clear role to play when it comes to prisoner reentry, he was equally clear that government is not equipped to provide the mentoring, care, and social supports that are essential for any effective and holistic plan for prisoner reentry.

Stated differently, government cannot effectively address the prisoner reentry crisis by itself. The alternative is also true: faith-based organizations and individuals cannot effectively address the prisoner reentry problem by themselves. In fact, sacred and secular partnerships represent our best hope for developing an effective prisoner reentry strategy.

In the concluding chapter of their book *Prisoner Reentry and Crime in America*, Jeremy Travis and Christy Visher ask two important questions:

> Is it possible to imagine a world in which the agencies of the justice system—corrections, police, courts, and parole—work together with other public and private institutions—housing providers, workforce development agencies, drug treatment providers, foster care agencies, and churches and other

faith institutions—to systematically reduce the risk of failure around the time of reentry? . . . What would such a strategy look like?[21]

As a result of President Bush's interest in prisoner reentry, two major prisoner reentry initiatives have provided some preliminary and positive answers to these two important questions. A third and related initiative, commonly referred to as the Second Chance Act, has also been passed in Congress.[22]

Ready4Work

In 2003 the U.S. Department of Labor launched Ready4Work, a three-year pilot program to address the needs of ex-prisoners through faith-based and community-based organizations. Ready4Work placed an emphasis on job training, job placement, case management, mentoring, and other aftercare services. Community and faith-based organizations were selected to provide services to adult ex-offenders in eleven cities.[23]

Ready4Work purposely targeted participants with a high probability of recidivism:[24] ex-prisoners in Ready4Work had extensive criminal histories, and half had been previously arrested five or more times.[25] Once individuals entered the program, they were eligible for services lasting up to one year. Participants were also matched with mentors in one-to-one or group mentoring relationships. Job placement specialists helped participants find jobs, and case managers continued to provide assistance after participants were employed.

The Ready4Work pilot ended in 2006, and results indicate a total of 4,482 former prisoners enrolled in Ready4Work. Of these ex-prisoners, 97 percent received case management services, 86 percent received employment services, and 63 percent received mentoring services. Ready4Work sites placed 2,543 participants (57 percent) into jobs, with 63 percent retaining jobs for three consecutive months after placement.[26]

Public/Private Ventures (PPV), an action-based research, public policy, and program development organization, oversees the Ready4Work demonstration project as an intermediary. P/PV reports that only 2.5 percent of Ready4Work participants were reincarcerated within six months, and 6.9 percent were reincarcerated at the one-year postrelease mark. While not a randomized design, the preliminary findings are impressive.

Over 60 percent of Ready4Work participants received mentoring as part of their services. We know that mentoring matters for youth, but this study demonstrated that mentoring affects outcomes for Ready-4Work participants. Ready4Work participants who met with a mentor remained in the program longer, were twice as likely to obtain a job, and were more likely to stay employed than participants who did not meet with a mentor.[27] P/PV researchers conclude that "while mentoring alone is not enough, supportive relationships—which can be fostered through mentoring programs—should be considered a core component of any reentry strategy."[28]

Ready4Work gives us an important initial snapshot of what is possible when an intermediary brings together public and private partnerships to address prisoner reentry in a comprehensive and coordinated strategy. Early results from Ready4Work support the notion that a comprehensive prisoner reentry plan is possible and without a massive expansion of the existing criminal justice system. As far as federal projects go, the Ready4Work initiative in eleven cities represents a major demonstration project. Additionally, Ready4Work has helped to highlight the work of faith- and community-based groups addressing prisoner reentry, such as Exodus Transitional Community in Harlem; Word of Hope Ministries in Milwaukee; and the Safer Foundation of Chicago.

The President's Prisoner Reentry Initiative

The Prisoner Reentry Initiative (PRI) was announced by President Bush in 2004, and grew out of the Department of Labor's Ready4Work project. PRI was designed to further test the proposition that prisoner reentry could be effectively accomplished with a comprehensive strategy that is designed to draw heavily from partnerships with community and faith-based groups. The PRI helps to connect former prisoners with faith-motivated groups as well as secular community-based organizations willing to help ex-prisoners locate employment, and to stay out of trouble by following prosocial paths. Thirty PRI grantees across the country provided mentoring, employment, and other transitional services to thousands of ex-inmates.

PRI sites began serving program participants in the spring of 2006 and like Ready4Work, early results are promising. These early outcomes, however, are very preliminary, and they are not based on a randomized design with strict controls. A total of 10,361 PRI participants had been enrolled as of November 2007, and about 6,000 participants have been placed into jobs. Participants' one-year postrelease recidivism rate is currently 20 percent. Though very early, these initial findings are very positive.

As can be seen in appendix C, nine of the thirty PRI grants went to faith-based organizations. Twenty-one grants went to community-based organizations, and all but three of these secular organizations report working with faith-based organizations. Indeed, collaborations with faith-based organizations appear to be equally important for faith-based as well as community-based PRI recipients. These alliances confirm the premise that sacred and secular partnerships can be critical in establishing a network of social supports necessary for comprehensive and coordinated prisoner reentry.

KEYS TO A HOLISTIC PRISONER REENTRY PLAN—
OVERCOMING PREJUDICE

Any prisoner reentry plan that is comprehensive and able to reach scale will require a massive influx of new people and programs that do not currently exist in most jurisdictions. Since the government alone cannot provide these programs, faith- and community-based groups represent a critical piece of the reentry puzzle that has yet to be tapped in any systematic fashion. The reasons for this lack of cooperation can be reduced to the word *prejudice*. On the one hand, most faith-based organizations tend to believe the government and secular institutions such as universities and academic researchers are prejudiced against them. Instances where agencies of the government have tried to curtail the work of those who feel called to minister to offenders are always present. Additionally, most secular universities do not have a reputation for being particularly faith-friendly. Ditto for academics, and especially those within the social and behavioral sciences—the disciplines most likely to study the effectiveness of any program. These concerns are not without merit as research has confirmed the academy contains far fewer religious people than the population at large.[29] Additionally, research confirms a significant antievangelical Christian bias among university professors.[30] Consequently, a degree of distrust is present toward outsiders among faith-motivated individuals and ministries.

On the other hand, secular organizations and governmental entities worry about the motives and qualifications of faith-based individuals and groups that aspire to provide various kinds of social services. These concerns are not unwarranted. Clearly, security should always be the primary concern of any prison worker, and not all religious volunteers understand or are sympathetic to this overarching purpose. Proper training for volunteers does not take place instantly. Because many offenders have been in and out of prison for years, they are capable of manipulative behavior that could easily compromise security and put lives in jeopardy. Too many religious workers do not take the concerns of custodial staff seriously, which potentially further exacerbates any preexisting distrust.

I believe any comprehensive prisoner reentry plan is sustainable only if partnerships between sacred and secular as well as national and community groups are encouraged and embraced, rather than discouraged and viewed with distrust. A healthy atmosphere of mutual respect must replace the suspicion that still too often typifies relations between public and private organizations as well as between secular and religious groups—entities that share similar social service missions even if their approach is vastly different.

For example, religious individuals and faith-based groups need to recognize that ongoing training regarding correctional issues is something to be coveted rather than merely tolerated—a feature I have commonly observed over the last twenty years of conducting correctional research on religion. Because volunteers often see only one side of the prisoner, some do not appreciate the need for serious training. Religious volunteers should be required to undergo basic training regarding custodial and security issues before being allowed to do volunteer work. Further, ongoing training for religious volunteers should be endorsed as well as widely promoted by faith-based organizations. This is especially true for faith-motivated volunteers who are interested in mentoring prisoners and ex-prisoners.

Faith-based groups need to understand that accountability, assessment, and evaluation of their efforts—something that will surely follow if these groups partner with government—are extremely useful tools for improving service delivery. Overstating program effectiveness without empirical evidence has often been a problem for many religious volunteers and faith-based organizations. If faith-based efforts are to be considered seriously, then religious volunteers need to understand that faith-based programs, like others, should be objectively evaluated. This kind of faith-based accountability will go a long way in improving relationships with other private and public groups whose confidence faith-based groups must have in order to establish a comprehensive and coordinated response to prisoner reentry.

The Role of Volunteerism in Prisoner Reentry

We know that lack of housing, employment, transportation, counseling, and mentoring are substantial obstacles that make the transition from prison to society so difficult for ex-prisoners. Tackling these problems obviously requires a great deal of new human and financial resources as well as the participation of key community leaders. Thus, any comprehensive strategy for confronting the problems of prisoner reentry requires an infusion of an unprecedented number of new volunteers who have or can develop strategic alliances focused on each of the problems ex-prisoners encounter.

Instead of leading a Bible study in prison, many religious volunteers need to consider developing strategies to improve the housing and employment conditions for ex-offenders already living in the community as well as prisoners who will eventually be returning home. One cannot overemphasize the importance of mentoring relationships that are established in prison and carry over to the community. Research confirms that mentoring matters—for kids as well as for adults. The real problem is that we have a severe shortage of mentors, especially for prisoners and ex-prisoners. This is precisely why communities of faith, by far America's most volunteer-rich organizations, are uniquely positioned to assist in alleviating the mentoring deficit.[31] Tragically, almost all the seven hundred thousand people leaving prison this year will do so without the benefit of a mentor. Remarkably, communities have not been approached in any systematic or meaningful way on a national or even statewide scale to provide these mentors. And it is still very much an empirical question whether congregations will respond to this great challenge of mentoring prisoners and ex-prisoners. Effectively impacting prisoner reentry requires a paradigm shift for many within America's houses of worship.

Another way in which faith-motivated individuals can assist prisoner reentry efforts is by agreeing to undergo necessary training to specifically assist parole and other community-based correctional personnel. Ultimately, a comprehensive prisoner reentry plan requires very large numbers of committed and trained volunteers (e.g., probation and parole) who agree to bring to bear their varied networks of social and spiritual support to correctional, governmental, and secular entities committed to prisoner reentry and aftercare. Without a comprehensive approach that coordinates public and private, secular and sacred partnerships, prisoner reentry support will remain fragmented and poorly resourced, and continue to be a national crisis. There is great promise if government and faith-based groups collaborate in meaningful partnerships to successfully address prisoner reentry problems.

Organizations such as Big Brothers and Big Sisters of America (BBBS), one of the largest mentoring organization in the world, have developed immensely successful strategies for recruiting mentors. In the last eight or nine years alone, BBBS has more than doubled the number of children served.[32] Along with many other grantees, BBBS has led the Mentoring Children of Prisoners (MCP) efforts nationally. It took BBBS ninety-five years to make 120,000 matches; there are currently 250 MCP programs in forty-eight states partnering with more than six thousand churches to serve at least one hundred thousand children.[33] Conversations with Rev. Dr. W. Wilson Goode, who has directed the amazing growth of Amachi, reveal the foundational role of congregations in recruiting mentors. The Amachi experience confirms what we already knew from previous research—when people are asked to volunteer, many will do just that. A comprehensive plan for prisoner reentry that draws heavily on volunteers needs to develop strategies for recruiting mentors, though this effort will certainly look different than either the BBBS or Amachi models. Indeed, attracting mentors for adults is significantly more difficult than attracting mentors for a child.

The vast majority of the many thousands of correctional volunteers tend to come from religious congregations. There is no other source that is more volunteer-rich than America's houses of worship,[34] and there are approximately 375,000 congregations in the United States.[35] Religious congregations not only mobilize volunteer labor for the church itself, but also are feeder systems for many other nonprofit and voluntary organizations. Further, religious volunteers do not necessarily choose between volunteering for the church or a secular organization; many do both.[36] Surveys have consistently found a positive association between religious affiliation and attendance and charitable behavior—in terms of both financial giving and volunteering.[37] Harvard University scholar Robert Putnam echoes this finding when he observes,

> houses of worship build and sustain more social capital—and social capital of more varied forms—than any other type of institution in America. Churches, synagogues, mosques, and other houses of worship provide a vibrant institutional base for civic good works and a training ground for civic entrepreneurs. Roughly speaking, nearly half of America's stock of social capital is religious or religiously affiliated, whether measured by association memberships, philanthropy, or volunteering.[38]

Though research confirms that volunteers respond if approached with the right message, simply attracting large numbers of volunteers is not enough. The coordination and mobilization of volunteers and organizations are equally important.

FAITH-BASED PRISONER REENTRY

As important as volunteer work within correctional facilities might be, it does not change the fact that most religious volunteers and organizations largely tend to overlook prisoner reentry and aftercare. Why this oversight? I would argue that compared to reentry and aftercare, prison ministry is a much easier task to pursue. Although it may sound counterintuitive, prisons provide a much safer and easier service opportunity for volunteers working with offenders. Prisoners tend to be very appreciative of the time and attention they receive from outside visitors, and these exchanges tend to be overwhelmingly positive and nonthreatening for volunteers. Because the prison environment tends to be controlled and heavily monitored, prison ministry can be viewed as safe and easy. After completing a quick Bible study or mentoring session, volunteers can be on their way in an hour or two. This may have a great deal to do with the prevalence of prison ministries and why they can be found in many if not most U.S. congregations, and why thousands of religious volunteers visit prisons every day.

For these same reasons, I would argue that faith-based organizations disproportionately opt for in-prison ministry as opposed to out-of-prison ministry and the delivery of services to ex-prisoners. Prisoner reentry is anything but easy or safe to confront. For example, Prison Fellowship Ministries (PF), the largest faith-based prison ministry in the United States, has always recognized that prisoner reentry and aftercare are vitally important, but for many years their efforts were only marginally involved in reentry and aftercare. This oversight has been acknowledged by PF leadership as well as the intention of prioritizing a new emphasis and focus on prisoner reentry and aftercare.[39] Indeed, Prison Fellowship would soon thereafter launch Out4Life, a major initiative designed to remedy this imbalance by significantly expanding PF's reentry and aftercare emphasis.[40]

Out4Life: Working Together to Give Ex-Prisoners a Second Chance

Out4Life argues that we all have a stake in increasing the ability of more than seven hundred thousand inmates released each year from prisons to successfully return to their families and communities. Out4Life—mobilized by Prison Fellowship—engages stakeholders in a national reentry network to help make this happen. Out4Life works to

1. Generate awareness of the needs and obstacles facing newly released prisoners and the urgency to address those needs.
2. Pull together government agencies, businesses, churches and faith-

based organizations, and civic groups in a collaborative effort to help ex-prisoners successfully reintegrate into society.

3. Identify and offer best practices that prove effective in restoring formerly incarcerated men and women to their families and to society.
4. Build regional and state coalitions and support existing coalitions to help offer a comprehensive array of services and support to returning prisoners.
5. Network all of these coalitions to change lives and reduce recidivism throughout the nation.

Out4Life was launched in Louisiana in 2008 and Arkansas in 2009, and in 2010 in the following states: Arizona, Georgia, Michigan, Minnesota, Ohio, Oregon, Tennessee, Texas, and Virginia. Out4Life seeks to build a national reentry and aftercare movement by supporting three distinct stages of action: reentry conferences, establishing coalitions, and building a national network.

Reentry conferences build awareness by bringing together representatives from government, community, and churches to discuss the needs and the potential of returning prisoners. Through plenary talks and workshops, these conferences provide a platform for addressing barriers to reintegration as well as the opportunity to identify strategies for overcoming these barriers, and to begin the process of cultivating collaborative relationships.

Out4Life Coalitions include agencies, faith-based organizations, businesses, community organizations, and other social service providers who reach out to formerly incarcerated men and women with much-needed resources and ongoing support. These regional and state-level collaborative teams offer diverse services that may include mentoring, support groups, housing assistance, job placement, educational opportunities, counseling, and other supportive services.

The Out4Life National Network seeks to link all of these regional and statewide coalitions together to maximize the exchange of information and the shared use of best practices for successful reentry. Prisoner reentry and aftercare are formidable problems for every community in the country. Consequently, it is essential to build a national network that pays attention not only to urban centers where so many offenders will be returning, but also to small and rural communities that have their own unique set of challenges.

In terms of prisoner reentry and aftercare, Ready4Work, the Prisoner Reentry Initiative, and Out4Life represent the most positive developments in the last two decades. Led by Prison Fellowship, Out4Life is critical on a number of fronts. First, it corrects an oversight common to prison ministry for many decades, namely, the disproportionate emphasis on faith-motivated volunteerism in prisons rather than communities. Out4Life seeks to bring a whole new generation of volunteers—and the vast network of services these volunteers can systematically tap into—to bear on the needs of reentry and aftercare. Second, Out4Life acknowledges that government programs as well as faith-based efforts in isolation of each other are insufficient to adequately address prisoner reentry and aftercare. Stated differently, the solution to reentry and aftercare cannot be achieved by faith or government alone. Thus, Out4Life is all about coalition building and networking in an effort to build and sustain the necessary capacity to achieve what otherwise will be an unattainable civic good. By intentionally focusing on reentry and aftercare by highlighting best practices, and supporting public/private as well as sacred/secular collaborations, Out4Life has the potential to represent a serious paradigm shift for the field of corrections and our only hope for a viable and scalable solution.

CONCLUSION

Since prisoner reentry is a problem facing communities all across the United States, the ultimate goal of any plan should be to establish a model that is not only effective in a particular area, but also that can be effective on a larger scale in multiple communities. Isolated success is one thing; success at a statewide level is quite another. For example, while not a prisoner reentry program, Amachi Texas is a unique public-private partnership designed to provide mentors for children of prisoners and reach scale throughout the state of Texas.[41] What has been missing until recently is a prisoner reentry model or template that links all the nonnegotiable elements of reentry together in a way that can be replicated and sustained in cost-effective ways in local communities, in regions, or statewide. We are in need of a plan where coordination and collaboration are central, where the goals of the reentry model are realistically achievable, where the specific elements of the plan are replicable in any community, and finally, where the plan is affordable and does not add new costs to already overburdened correctional budgets.

The role of the government in reentry and aftercare is important, even core, but it cannot be all-encompassing. The criminal justice system should be viewed as a key partner among other public and private partners collaborating with the many reentry initiatives being led in the community and coordinated through intermediaries. Ready4Work and PRI provide initial evidence that sacred and secular groups as well as national and community government institutions can work together to address comprehensive prisoner reentry in a scalable way. In order to replicate these experiences, the government needs to continue to welcome and accommodate religious and community-based volunteers and groups. For far too long, government has viewed faith-based groups with suspicion and distrust, rather than as volunteers who, motivated by faith, have made a substantial impact for good. Observers are interested in seeing if the government will continue to support reentry initiatives that partner with religious organizations.

Additionally, faith- and community-based intermediaries need to bring much-needed expertise in coordinating and training volunteers as well as organizations in the areas of employment, housing, education, and counseling. Although many volunteers have their hearts in the right place, most do not have the training or understanding necessary to work with offenders in correctional settings or in the free world. If these shortcomings can be met, sacred and secular partnerships can play a catalytic role in a truly comprehensive and scalable approach to prisoner reentry.

In general, policy makers are reluctant to support correctional policies that endorse or appear to favor offender treatment, job training, and counseling for ex-prisoners and their families in the community. Such efforts can easily be interpreted as taking a soft-on-crime approach. Even though one might argue that a prisoner reentry plan including such programs has the potential to significantly reduce recidivism and thus improve public safety, policy makers tend to be unwilling to defend such programs publicly. Not surprisingly, law-and-order crime policies have consistently trumped those favoring offender treatment models.[42] This is why any effective prisoner reentry plan will have to draw heavily from faith-motivated volunteers, groups, and intermediary organizations to make it possible to provide the necessary support to effectively manage the unprecedented number of prisoners returning to our communities each year. Governmental partnerships with faith-based groups hold the key to a truly holistic prisoner reentry plan that not only reduces recidivism and promotes public safety, but also can be replicated in communities across the country.

Not by Faith Alone: The Need for Intermediaries

THE FIRST FEW chapters of this book addressed the ways in which faith-based approaches to crime prevention are making a difference. For example, the TenPoint Coalition showed how it was possible for clergy and inner-city congregations to partner with police and local authorities to significantly lower youth crime and gang violence in troubled neighborhoods in Boston. Indeed, Boston police officials have often credited the role of clergy and local congregations for being the catalyst for the dramatic reductions in youth homicides known as the Boston Miracle.

The Amachi experiment in Philadelphia documented that large numbers of faith-motivated volunteers could be attracted from congregations in order to mentor children of prisoners. Additionally, Amachi proved that the nation's leading mentoring organization, Big Brothers and Big Sisters, could intentionally partner with faith-based organizations—in this case, predominantly African American churches in the city of Philadelphia—and other secular organizations to pair up in record-breaking numbers faith-motivated volunteer mentors with children of prisoners.

Subsequent chapters provided preliminary research showing how spiritual transformation can be central to offender rehabilitation. For example, my evaluation study of the InnerChange Freedom Initiative documented that a faith-based prison program facilitated inmate rehabilitation as well as reductions in recidivism for former prisoners following release from prison. Finally, systematic reviews of published research consistently recognize that religiosity is a key protective factor that shields youth from harmful influences as well as helping youth to be resilient when raised in high-risk environments. These studies show what any sensible person would have expected: that religious people commit fewer crimes. In sum, the best available data confirms that the faith factor has a significant and beneficial influence on youth and adults.

Likewise, faith-based organizations (FBOs) have proven they can partner with the federal government and other groups to successfully implement two separate national prisoner reentry projects. Similarly, Out4Life,[1] a prisoner reentry program sponsored by Prison Fellowship Ministries, is quickly spreading in many different states and by all accounts holds great potential for bringing together faith-based organizations, volunteers, and government agencies in partnerships to address prisoner reentry.[2] Though rarely recognized by scholars, FBOs have proven they can play a significant role in helping to build coalitions and networks, especially faith-based networks, to provide the necessary supports to help ex-prisoners become gainfully employed and lead crime-free and productive lives.

Recognizing that religiosity or the faith factor is linked to reductions in crime and delinquency is an important though largely ignored development. Perhaps even less noticed is the fact that research consistently documents that religiosity is linked to prosocial or positive behavior. Stated differently, increasing religiosity tends to be associated with increasing hope, meaning, and purpose.[3] Religious people are more likely to volunteer, give to charities—both religious and secular—and to be civically engaged.[4] There is also growing empirical evidence that religious commitment positively influences academic achievement in youth, especially minority youth.[5] These findings, taken together, represent a powerful acknowledgment that the faith factor is undeniably important for the functioning of a healthy civil society.

THE PARADOX

We have a substantial body of evidence documenting that America is a religious country and that religion is good for America. At the same time, American society has many deeply entrenched social maladies. How do we reconcile the fact that serious social problems are pervasive in America, and yet, as they say, there's a church on almost every street corner? This apparent contradiction continues to frustrate many religious as well as nonreligious observers. It would be easy to argue—as many devoutly religious people regularly do—that America is losing its religion, and ever-increasing social problems are the consequence of our rapid secular downward spiral. This line of thinking suggests that America's social ills have simply filled the vacuum left by an ineffective or irrelevant church and an increasingly irreligious culture. This rhetoric plays well in many pulpits across the country. The problem with this "explanation" is its simple inaccuracy on multiple levels.[6]

Often fed by bad data and dubious thought leaders, many well-intentioned ministers unwittingly pass along misinformation to their congregants on a regular basis, perpetuating false and misleading information. For example, there is not one empirical study published in a reputable journal supporting the claim that we are one generation away from a godless youth society. Similarly, no credible studies show that divorce is now more prevalent among churchgoing evangelicals than those who are unchurched. Nonetheless, accusations such as these are common fodder for sermons and are accepted at face value as empirical facts by people sitting in pews across the country. Thankfully, Bradley Wright, a scholar at the University of Connecticut, has published an entire book on this subject and completely shatters many of the myths congregants are regularly fed by misinformed clergy.[7]

How then do we reconcile the fact that on the one hand religion tends to be vibrant and stable (and not in decline),[8] while at the same time social problems tend to flourish in America? First, it is wrong to think that if society was religious enough our social problems would disappear. Even though substantial space in scripture is dedicated to the imperative of looking out for the poor and the priority of ministering to the "least of these," was it not Jesus who declared the poor would always exist in society?[9] The reality is that social problems are the product of multiple factors, and such multifaceted problems tend to require multifaceted solutions. Similarly, the challenges facing ex-prisoners, for example, require more than simply introducing prisoners to faith. This is not to suggest that spiritual interventions are not important; they clearly are. However, a conversion experience that happens as an isolated event and is not nurtured or connected to other needed supports is unlikely to transform a life or change a person's long-term behavioral trajectory. Simply put, spiritual interventions must be part of a more comprehensive strategy. Though this observation should be obvious, for many religious volunteers and workers it is not.[10] The reason is that most volunteers tend to be evangelical Christians, and churches these volunteers come from tend to take a very simplistic, shortsighted view of the problem. In other words, most people are taught in churches that prisoners need Jesus, but are not told they need housing, transportation, counseling, life skills, and ongoing mentoring, or that the church should be willing to enthusiastically embrace and support this population.

NOT BY FAITH ALONE

Though the next statement will surely offend many believers, based on decades of empirical evidence it is undeniable: serious social problems (e.g., poverty, crime, homelessness, etc.) cannot be solved through faith-based efforts alone. Likewise, we know the government cannot solve these same social ills. These two realities, unfortunately, are not always obvious to religious and secular observers. For some, the solution is more religion. For others, the answer is more government. Based on objective evaluation of the data, it is increasingly obvious that faith-based organizations have the potential to be essential allies with government and other social service providers in combating many of the most difficult challenges facing contemporary society.

Faith-based organizations are already located in the poorest and most distressed communities within our cities. Indeed, the only social service organizations that remain active in high-poverty areas often tend to be churches and FBOs. Consequently, houses of worship and FBOs are widely acknowledged to be some of the few organizations that have not abandoned many of our most disadvantaged communities. The American public recognizes the good work that clergy and religious leaders accomplish. Consider a recent Rasmussen poll which found that 72 percent of Americans view members of Congress unfavorably, while 74 percent view pastors and religious leaders favorably.[11] Only small business owners had a higher favorable rating (89 percent) than religious leaders. Even in the wake of highly public scandals in the church, Americans overwhelmingly like the clergy. People in the pews know from experience they can turn to clergy and religious leaders in times of need, when their kids are on drugs, when they have lost a job, or when they have experienced some personal loss.

It should also be obvious that collaborations between faith-based groups and the government may well extend resources the government has available to help communities that tend to be difficult to reach. In addition, research confirms that these houses of worship and communities of faith can have a significant and stabilizing influence in urban communities where decay and poverty tend to be especially concentrated.[12] The problem is that government and religious organizations do not have an outstanding track record for forging partnerships with each other. As described in chapter 2, the federal government, by its own admission, has often discriminated against religious groups that provide social services.[13] Not surprisingly, many devoutly religious people and faith-based groups are suspicious of the government and are reluctant to partner with an entity they do not trust.

Having conducted research on these topics since the mid-1980s, and having observed firsthand both government and faith-based responses to crime, I am convinced our only hope for effectively facing problems like prisoner reentry is through a series of private/public, sacred/secular partnerships. But this will require being devoted to improving outcomes in the delivery of social services by connecting church and faith-based resources with innovative, collaborative initiatives among social service providers. These innovative collaborations must first start at the local level, but eventually must take place at regional and state-wide levels.

We humans have physical, mental, emotional, and spiritual aspects to our lives. Thus, effective social service delivery systems need to find new ways to address the whole person, utilizing all available community resources, including the often untapped resources of churches and other faith-based organizations. In the face of economic and budget crises, secular agencies and faith-based groups need new, cost-effective ways to collaborate with each other in order to develop and implement holistic assistance plans for distressed individuals. We must recognize that partnerships among secular and sacred groups represent our only real hope for providing the holistic interventions necessary to achieve effective results that are replicable and scalable in communities across the country. The leads us to the next big question: how do we make these partnerships happen?

THE NEED FOR INTERMEDIARIES

What exactly is an intermediary, and what roles does one play? Drawing from the field of education, here's a helpful definition of an intermediary:

> Intermediaries are organizations that occupy the space in between at least two other parties. Intermediary organizations primarily function to mediate or to manage change in both those parties. Intermediary organizations operate independently of these two parties and provide distinct value beyond what the parties alone would be able to develop or to amass by themselves. At the same time, intermediary organizations depend on those parties to perform their essential functions.[14]

Without faith-based or community organizations serving as intermediaries to bridge the gap between disadvantaged populations and the resources they need, high-risk groups will likely remain beyond effective reach and service. On the other hand, with the help of individuals and groups that come from the very communities being served, at-risk populations are not only reached, but relationships are developed in a way that increases the likelihood of positive results. For example, in 2006 the research center I direct at Baylor University became an intermediary between the federal government and small faith-based and community organizations in an unusual pilot project. We received a grant titled the Faith and Community Technical Support (FACTS) project, funded by the Violence Against Women Office (OVW), within the U.S. Department of Justice. This grant was an excellent example of how government agencies like OVW and faith- as well as community-based organizations can partner to improve services to disadvantaged populations—in this case, victims of domestic violence in rural and isolated communities with limited access to social services.

Domestic violence is a serious problem that takes place in communities across the country, but the geographical isolation of many people living in extremely rural communities presents even greater challenges for the safety of battered women and their families. In fact, in many of these isolated jurisdictions, churches and faith-based organizations are some of the only viable institutions that (1) remain connected in an intentional way to many local residents and especially those from low-income families, and (2) have the capacity and desire to provide a variety of social services to those in need.

To partner with these agencies in an effort to extend services and assist families in crisis simply makes good sense in terms of public policy, and to fail to do so would be a tragic missed opportunity to collaborate and provide effective ways to protect and serve needy populations.[15] Small grants provided through the FACTS project to both community and faith-based groups allowed them to build capacity and to extend service outreach. This comment from a shelter director at one of the thirty-nine sub-grantees in our project confirms how they benefited from working with an intermediary through the FACTS project:

> When Cindy first came to the shelter, she had totally given up on herself. Cindy had lost everything, her job, apartment, car, and her children had moved away. On top of all the negatives created by the domestic violence, she had begun to try to forget her sorrows through the use of alcohol. Realizing there was no other way, she checked herself into a rehab program where she found out about the Safe Passage domestic violence shelter. Thanks to the assistance provided through the FACTS grant, and the services provided through the shelter, she is using her skills and working at a job, making a sustainable living. She has been able to reacquire her car, find an apartment, and is reestablishing contact with her children. She has refrained from the use of alcohol and is making friends in the area. Without meeting the economic barriers such as rental and utility deposits, Cindy may have been stuck in a homeless shelter for an extended period of time, making the likelihood of her success questionable at best.

Without this kind of assistance, there is a strong likelihood that small grassroots groups will ultimately fail.[16] According to Mike Doyle, executive director of the Cornerstone Assistance Network, a faith-based intermediary organization in Fort Worth, failure to develop a sound organization will cause even successful programs to suffer if not surrender to financial and reporting pressures. Intermediaries can play a key role in coordinating the efforts of fragmented community and faith-based organizations.[17] Too often these small groups operate in relative isolation from each other and as a result are not able to build or sustain capacity. Rather than working in isolation, influential and well-networked intermediaries are uniquely positioned to play a key role in coordinating resources locally and beyond. Organizations like the United Way provide an outstanding example of how organizations through targeted mission statements can have substantial and scalable influence.[18]

Intermediaries are essential to comprehensive and coordinated plans that recruit large numbers of skilled and trained volunteers, while developing private and public partnerships in order to confront an array of social problems from youth violence to prisoner reentry. Further, intermediaries are suited to interact with governmental entities while drawing upon the substantial human capital of volunteers, as well as the social and spiritual capital of individuals and organizations in the private sector. Indeed, the Compassion Capital Fund, Baylor University's Faith and Community Technical Support Project, as well as the Latino Coalition for Faith and Community Initiatives, Public/Private Ventures, Cornerstone Assistance Network, and Nueva Esperanza, are but a few examples of intermediaries that have succeeded at local and national levels.

As discussed in chapter 9, developing a truly comprehensive prisoner reentry plan is difficult because there are so many different challenges complicating an ex-prisoner's ability to successfully transition back to society. Focusing on housing without giving proper consideration to employment is a recipe for failure. Likewise, concentrating on transportation without giving consideration to mentoring and other social supports is likely to be unsuccessful. Any comprehensive prisoner reentry plan must be able to coordinate all the major obstacles to successful reentry. Ready4Work and the PRI have provided a very preliminary, but positive glimpse of a multifaceted reentry plan that owes much to the contribution of intermediary organizations to coordinate such efforts.

In the case of Ready4Work, Public/Private Ventures oversaw the demonstration project as a national intermediary. PRI utilized a different approach by essentially funding community- and faith-based organizations to serve as local intermediaries coordinating reentry efforts. In recent years the federal government has begun to utilize intermediaries to help faith- and community-based organizations build capacity, strengthen programs, and improve the delivery of social services. In this way, intermediaries are strategic in building bridges and alliances in order to address immense social problems.[19] Perhaps the best recent example is the Compassion Capital Fund (CCF), established by Congress in 2002, which provides funds to be distributed by the U.S. Department of Health and Human Services to intermediary organizations to provide training, technical, and financial assistance to faith- and community-based organizations.

The role of faith- and community-based intermediaries in social service provision is still relatively new and underdeveloped. This is unfortunate, since intermediary organizations may be the most important element underutilized in building successful prisoner reentry models that are intentional about working with volunteers, especially volunteers who come from religious congregations. Intermediaries can be a bridge, for example, between ex-prisoners and the many social service providers and various governmental agencies, as can be seen in Figure 1. Intermediaries can coordinate prisoner reentry efforts of community- and faith-based organizations, volunteers, social service providers, mentors, and parole officers. Additionally, intermediaries can serve many important roles by providing (1) management and oversight to groups and organizations; (2) technical assistance to agencies, groups, and ministries; (3) ongoing training to strengthen capacity and sustainability; and (4) structure and tools necessary to make partnering groups accountable for achieving outcomes (e.g., recidivism reduction).

As illustrated in Figure 1, the left side of the model shows the traditional approach to prisoner reentry. The right side of the model represents recent prisoner reentry efforts where intermediaries have been involved. It is easy to see how reentry can be much more effectively addressed when drawing upon the varied network of resources that the intermediary coordinates and monitors.

Any effective prisoner reentry plan has to draw heavily from faith-motivated volunteers and groups, and intermediary organizations can make it possible to provide the necessary support to manage effectively the unprecedented number of prisoners returning to our communities each year. Governmental partnerships with faith-based groups hold the key to a truly holistic prisoner reentry plan that not only reduces

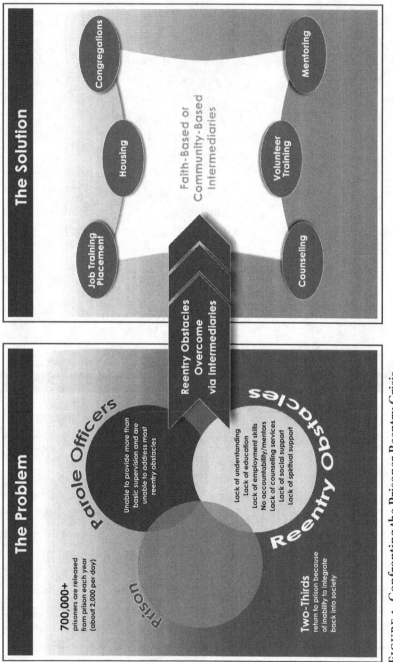

FIGURE 1. Confronting the Prisoner Reentry Crisis

recidivism and promotes public safety but can be replicated in communities across the country.

CAPACITY BUILDING

Beau Egert described the connection between capacity building and the desire to increase and improve faith based and community organizations (FBCOs) collaborations for the Texas-based OneStar Foundation's Compassion Capital Fund project:

> We recognized that in order to serve our role of encouraging and developing more government collaborations, we needed to raise the level of organizational competency and sophistication of FBCOs in the state. The state of Texas, particularly through its human services and workforce development agencies, had a history of engaging FBCOs, so we already had strong networks among those organizations. However, many of those collaborations were nonfinancial and related to FBCOs coordinating their efforts with local human service agencies. The CCF project provided the tools for many of these community-serving organizations to be able to engage in more formal collaborations as well.

Intermediaries are an important strategy to level the playing field by assisting organizations in being more productive and enhancing important community resources. This is especially true for undersized and underfunded organizations that tend to have relatively less management, reporting, and fiscal capacity, but are anxious nevertheless to partner with government programs. In this way, intermediaries serve as a bridge—putting their administrative and fiscal strengths at the service of small organizations—absorbing much of the load of government duties and providing training, technical assistance, and encouragement to the sub-organizations so that they can successfully take part in the government program. Intermediaries enhance as well as make possible more extensive involvement in government programs and greater access to government resources. This is especially true of organizations that are too small or too limited in capacity to readily partner with government on their own. For any small organization, the scale and bureaucracy of government can be daunting. Intermediaries are not so large; they tend to have a solid community reputation; they are private, not government; and they may be faith-based themselves.

Intermediaries can also serve as a buffer between government and faith-based organizations. Some faith-based organizations are very comfortable working with public programs and their restrictions. Others, though, are leery, put off by secular talk, and take the absence of religious symbols and artifacts as a sign of hostility to religion. For example, I have had a number of individuals and faith-based groups ask me if they must get rid of their Bibles if they receive a grant from the government. One person even asked me if they could still say "God bless you" if someone sneezed at the office.

Effective intermediaries can build the capacity of FBCOs and thus improve the likelihood they will be strong partners in coordinated collaborations. For example, intermediaries can help small faith-based organizations to develop much-needed program skills such as case management, data collection, reporting of outcomes, and more. One leader of a faith-based group had this to say about working with an intermediary:

> At the onset of the grant, none of our sub-grantees had the knowledge or capability to collect the data or track outcomes necessary for a federal labor grant. Without the technical assistance and hands-on support of the intermediary, the sub-grantees would have been overwhelmed by the reports required with no systematic way of finding instruction or assistance. . . . The intermediary was a key element to our success.

Capacity-building services not only improve effectiveness but also help sustain and grow the organization; they thereby assist in not only serving more clients but also serving in more effective ways. Once FBOs improve and mature, they tend to become more optimistic about sustainability as a result of their capacity-building efforts.

IRON SHARPENS IRON

William Wubbenhorst and I have recently published a case study on the role of intermediaries in Workforce Development.[20] We found that the experience of working with faith-based and community organizations gave the Workforce Investment Board (WIB) grantees a new appreciation for the type of role that FBCOs can play in local workforce systems. One WIB administrator described this lesson best by acknowledging that more work is needed to define and refine roles and responsibilities, and by recognizing the various special-needs populations that WIBs could not serve without the help of these FBCOs:

> The FBCOs can have an important role in workforce development if we can clearly define the role and responsibilities of each party and address the challenges facing each other. Each party should understand its own strengths and weaknesses and be allowed to build upon them to meet the needs of the targeted populations. The FBCOs can fill several gaps in service that are currently encountered by the hard-to-serve groups we serve. . . . These groups have special needs that can only be met by entities such as faith-based and community organizations.

FBCOs not only assisted WIBs in reaching these special-needs people, but also changed the perception of government services itself, as described by one WIB employee:

> Working with the FBCOs has helped in dispelling some of the misconceptions regarding government agencies as uncaring and aloof. Partnerships with FBCOs have helped in bringing in a new target population that would not have occurred were it not for the new FBCOs partnerships.

One government employee described the "more-than-expected" level of effort required to get FBCOs up to speed on the projects as definitely worth it in the end:

> The successes here really have to do with overcoming the challenge of building capacity while delivering services. FBCOs are built for collaboration and coordination and were hungry for learning and building. I see this as the greatest success, as it

leads to creating new services and enhancing existing services for the populations they serve. When the FBCO initiative first came out, many folks didn't believe that faith-based organizations should receive federal funds. I was skeptical but gave it a shot. This project proved that the idea worked.

To summarize, intermediaries are critical to addressing social problems like youth violence or prisoner reentry. Intermediaries serve many important roles, including management and oversight to groups and organizations that need accountability. Additionally, through ongoing technical assistance to agencies, groups, and ministries, intermediaries have the potential to improve the effectiveness of these groups. Further, intermediaries have the ability to provide ongoing training to strengthen the capacity and sustainability of these faith-based and community organizations. Finally, intermediaries can provide the structure and tools necessary to facilitate connecting these much-needed partnerships and networks for achieving outcomes. We need faith to be sure, but without intermediaries we will not be able to realize the full potential of faith-motivated individuals and groups to combat crime, delinquency, offender rehabilitation, and prisoner reentry.

The annual cost of crime to society is as much as $1 trillion or more. Economists are helping us understand that the real costs and impact of crime are significantly higher than previously understood. Economists are also correct to suggest that programs or interventions designed to reduce crime, if found to be effective, can save taxpayers a great deal of money.

Not only are faith-based approaches beginning to show promise when it comes to the issue of effectiveness, but they are cost-efficient since so much of the work is completed by faith-motivated volunteers. In fact, a number of faith-based organizations are adopting programs that are completely or almost completely staffed by volunteers. Congregations, more than any other institution in America, are volunteer-rich organizations able to leverage millions of talented people to feed these faith-based efforts. *More God, Less Crime* recognizes and documents how faith-based approaches are already making a difference in confronting difficult-to-solve social problems from delinquency, crime, offender reform, and prisoner reentry. If we only consider the costs and benefits from a purely economic perspective, then we can no longer afford to discount faith-based approaches to crime reduction. Imagine what might be possible if we can overcome the last acceptable prejudice that continues to deter the building of partnerships and networks of support where sacred and secular efforts come together in addressing and solving many of our current crime-related problems.

Acknowledgements

THE DESIRE to write this book has been coming into focus for at least a decade, but it took the encouragement of many to make it a reality. I am grateful to the Achelis and Bodman Foundations as well as the Bradley Foundation for their generous funding to initiate this project. I wish to thank Stephen G. Post and the Institute for Research on Unlimited Love, for providing key support in completing this book. I am also appreciative to the John M. Templeton Foundation not only for supporting a number of my studies on religion and crime, but also for its ongoing role in supporting research at the intersection of religion and science. I am greatly indebted to Susan Arellano, editor-in-chief at Templeton Press, for her thoughtful insights and guidance in writing a book that communicates academic research in an accessible manner.

I want to thank John J. DiIulio Jr., my former colleague at the University of Pennsylvania, who told me I was born to write *More God, Less Crime*. I also want to thank Luis Tellez, Robert P. George, and colleagues at the Witherspoon Institute for their able assistance and encouragement.

I wish to thank the following staff members from the Baylor Institute for Studies of Religion (ISR) for their gracious assistance: Frances Malone, Cameron Andrews, Lauren Allen, Daniel Jang, and Fiona Bond. I would also like to acknowledge a number of ISR scholars and friends with whom I have carried on numerous discussions that helped to inform the contents of this book. These include Rodney Stark, Jay Hein, Sung Joon Jang, Jeff Levin, Philip Jenkins, Thomas Kidd, Ronald Akers, Jerry Pattengale, Tony Gill, Gerald McDermott, Jeff Ulmer, and Rebble Johnson.

My hope is that this book will be a source of encouragement to the thousands of volunteers whose efforts are now helping us to reconsider how best to approach problems of crime and justice in a more holistic and effective way. I am optimistic the book will be a catalyst for meaningful discussions and eventual partnerships between sacred and secular individuals and groups. This is a task that will make both sides uneasy—as it should—but nonetheless represents our best hope for viable solutions to our crime-related problems.

Finally, I thank my family. My parents, Bob and Betty Johnson, have always been such a great example to me and their support has been constant. Elton and Betty Taylor, my in-laws, have also been extremely supportive. Most especially I want to thank my wife, Jackie Johnson, for believing in the importance of this book. She has been an endless and relentless source of encouragement. I would not have completed the book without her and I gratefully dedicate the book to her. I am also grateful to our children, Jeremy, Daché, and Courtney, for not only having to listen to more religion and crime discussions than anyone should have to suffer, but for providing thoughtful feedback along the way.

Table 3 References

Adamcyzk, Amy, and Ian Palmer. 2008. Religion and initiation into marijuana use: The deterring role of religious friends. *Journal of Drug Issues* 38: 717–42.

Adelekan, Moruf L., Olatunji A. Abiodun, et al. 1993. Psychosocial correlates of alcohol, tobacco and cannabis use: Findings from a Nigerian university. *Drug and Alcohol Dependence* 33: 247–57.

Adlaf, Edward M., and Reginald G. Smart. 1985. Drug use and religious affiliation, feelings and behaviour. *British Journal of Addiction* 80: 163–71.

Albrecht, Stan L., Bruce A. Chadwick, and David S. Alcorn. 1977. Religiosity and deviance—application of an attitude-behavior contingent consistency model. *Journal for the Scientific Study of Religion* 16: 263–74.

Albrecht, Stan L., Cheryl Amey, and Michael K. Miller. 1996. Patterns of substance abuse among rural black adolescents. *Journal of Drug Issues* 26: 751–78.

Alford, Geary S., Roger A. Keohler, and James Leonard. 1991. Alcoholics Anonymous–Narcotics Anonymous model inpatient treatment of chemically dependent adolescents: A 2-year outcome study. *Journal of Studies on Alcohol and Drugs* 52: 118–26.

Allen, Donald E., and Harjit S. Sandhu. 1967. A comparative study of delinquents and non-delinquents: Family affect, religion, and personal income. *Delinquency: Family, Religion, Income* 46: 263–69.

Amey, Cheryl H., Stan L. Albrecht, and Michael K. Miller. 1996. Racial differences in adolescent drug use: The impact of religion. *Substance Use & Misuse* 31: 1311–32.

Amoateng, Acheampong Yaw, and Stephen J. Bahr. 1986. Religion, family, and adolescent drug use. *Sociological Perspectives* 29: 53–76.

Bahr, Stephen J., and John P. Hoffman. 2008. Religiosity, peers, and adolescent drug use. *Journal of Drug Issues,* 743–70.

Bahr, Stephen J., Ricky D. Hawks, and Gabe Wang. 1993. Family and religious influences on adolescent substance abuse. *Youth and Society* 24: 443–65.

Bahr, Stephen J., Suzanne L. Maughan, Anastasios C. Marcos, and Bingdao Li. 1998. Family, religiosity, and the risk of adolescent drug use. *Journal of Marriage and the Family* 60: 979–92.

Barnes, Grace M., Michael P. Farrell, and Sarbani Banerjee. 1994. Family influences on alcohol abuse and other problem behaviors among black and white adolescents in a general population sample. *Journal of Research on Adolescence* 4: 183–201.

Barrett, Mark E., D. Dwayne Simpson, and Wayne E. K. Lehman. 1988. Behavioral changes of adolescents in drug abuse intervention programs. *Journal of Clinical Psychology* 44: 461–73.

Bell, Rick, Henry Wechsler, and Lloyd D. Johnston. 1997. Correlates of college student marijuana use: Results of a US national survey. *Society for the Study of Addiction to Alcohol and Other Drugs* 92: 571–81.

Benda, Brent B. 1994. Testing competing theoretical concepts: Adolescent alcohol consumption. *Deviant Behavior: An Interdisciplinary Journal* 15: 375–96.

Benda, Brent B. 1995. The effect of religion on adolescent delinquency revisited. *Journal of Research in Crime and Delinquency* 32: 446–65.

Benda, Brent B., and Robert Flynn Corwyn. 1997a. Religion and delinquency: The relationship after considering family and peer influences. *Journal for the Scientific Study of Religion* 36: 81–92.

Benda, Brent B. 1997b. An examination of a reciprocal relationship between religiosity and different forms of delinquency within a theoretical model. *Journal of Research in Crime and Delinquency* 34: 163–87.

Benda, Brent B. 1999. Theoretical model with reciprocal effects of youthful crime and drug use. *Journal of Social Service Research* 25: 77–106.

Benda, Brent B., and Robert Flynn Corwyn. 2000a. A theoretical model of religiosity and drug use with reciprocal relationships: A test using structural equation modeling. *Journal of Social Service Research* 26: 43–67.

Benda, Brent B., and Nancy J. Toombs. 2000b. Religiosity and violence. Are they related after considering the strongest predictors? *Journal of Criminal Justice* 28: 483–96.

Benda, Brent B., and Robert Flynn Corwyn. 2001. Are the effects of religion on crime mediated, moderated, and misrepresented by inappropriate measures? *Journal of Social Service Research* 27: 57–86.

Benda, Brent B., and Nancy J. Toombs. 2002. The effects of religiosity on drug use among inmates in boot camp: Testing a theoretical model with reciprocal relationships. *Journal of Offender Rehabilitation* 35: 161–83.

Benda, Brent B., Sandra K. Pope, and Kelly J. Kelleher. 2006. Church attendance or religiousness: Their relationship to adolescents' use of alcohol, other drugs, and delinquency. *Alcoholism Treatment Quarterly* 24: 75–87.

Benson, Peter L., and Michael J. Donahue. 1989. Ten-year trends in at-risk behaviors: A national study of black adolescents. *Journal of Adolescent Research* 4: 125–39.

Bjarnason, Thoroddur, Thorolfur Thorlindsson, Inga D. Sigfusdottir, and Michael R. Welch. 2005. Familial and religious influences on adolescent alcohol use: A multi-level study of students and school communities. *Social Forces* 84: 375–90.

Bliss, Stephen K., and Cynthia L. Crown. 1994. Concern for appropriateness, religiosity, and gender as predictors of alcohol and marijuana use. *Social Behavior and Personality* 22: 227–38.

Bowker, Lee H. 1974. Student drug use and the perceived peer drug environment. *International Journal of the Addictions* 9: 851–61.

Brizer, D. A. 1993. Religiosity and drug abuse among psychiatric inpatients. *American Journal of Drug and Alcohol Abuse* 19: 337–45.

Brook, Judith S., Martin Whiteman, Ann Scovell Gordon, and David W. Brook. 1984. Paternal determinants of female adolescent's marijuana use. *Developmental Psychology* 20: 1032–43.

Brown, Tamara L., Gregory S. Parks, Rick S. Zimmerman, and Clarenda M. Phillips. 2001. The role of religion in predicting adolescent alcohol use and problem drinking. *Journal of Studies on Alcohol* 62: 696–705.

Brown, Tony N., John Schulenberg, Jerald G. Bachman, Patrick M. O'Malley, and Lloyd D. Johnston. 2001. Are risk and protective factors for substance use consistent across historical time? National data from the high school classes of 1976 through 1997. *Prevention Science* 2: 29–43.

Brownfield, David, and Ann Marie Sorenson. 1991. Religion and drug use among adolescents: A social support conceptualization and interpretation. *Deviant Behavior* 12: 259–76.

Burkett, Steven R., and Mervin White. 1974. Hellfire and delinquency: Another look. *Journal for the Scientific Study of Religion* 13: 455–62.

Burkett, Steven R. 1977. Religion, parental influence, and adolescent alcohol and marijuana use. *Journal of Drug Issues* 7: 263–73.

Burkett, Steven R. 1980. Religiosity, beliefs, normative standards and adolescent drinking. *Journal of Studies on Alcohol* 41: 662–71.

Burkett, Steven R., and Bruce O. Warren. 1987. Religiosity, peer associations, and adolescent marijuana use: A panel study of underlying causal structures. *Criminology* 25: 109–31.

Burkett, Steven R. 1993. Perceived parents' religiosity, friends' drinking, and hellfire: A panel study of adolescent drinking. *Review of Religious Research* 35: 134–54.

Cancellaro, L. A., D. B. Larson, and W. P. Wilson. 1982. Religious life of narcotic addicts. *Southern Medical Journal* 75: 1166–68.

Caputo, Richard K. 2004. Parent religiosity, family processes, and adolescent outcomes. *Journal of Contemporary Social Services* 85: 495–510.

Caputo, Richard K. 2005. Religiousness and adolescent behaviors: A comparison of boys and girls. *Journal of Religion & Spirituality* 24: 39–67.

Carlucci, Kathleen, Jay Genova, Fran Rubackin, Randi Rubackin, and Wesley A. Kayson. 1993. Effects of sex, religion, and amount of alcohol consumption on self-reported drinking-related problem behaviors. *Psychosocial Reports* 72: 983–87.

Carr-Saunders, A. M., H. Mannheim, and E. C. Rhodes. 1944. *Young Offenders*. New York: Macmillan.

Cecero, John J., and Adam L. Fried. 2005. Parental rejection and religiosity: Differential predictors of mood and substance use. *Research in the Social Scientific Study of Religion* 16: 185–206.

Chadwick, Bruce A., and Brent L. Top. 1993. Religiosity and delinquency among LDS adolescents. *Journal for the Scientific Study of Religion* 32: 51–67.

Chandy, Joseph M., Robert W. Bloom, and Michael D. Resnick. 1996. History of sexual abuse and parental alcohol misuse: Risk, outcomes, and protective factors in adolescents. *Child and Adolescent Social Work Journal* 13: 411–32.

Chawla, Neharika, Clayton Neighbors, Melissa A. Lewis, Christine M. Lee, and Mary E. Larimer. 2007. Attitudes and perceived approval of drinking as mediators of the relationship between the importance of religion and alcohol use. *Journal of Studies on Alcohol and Drugs* 68: 410–18.

Chen, Chuan-Yu, Catherine M. Dormitzer, J. Bejarano, and James C. Anthony. 2004. Religiosity and the earliest stages of adolescent drug involvement in seven countries of Latin America. *American Journal of Epidemiology* 159: 1180–88.

Christo, G., and C. Franey. 1995. Drug users' spiritual beliefs, locus of control and the disease concept in relation to Narcotics Anonymous attendance and six-month outcomes. *Drug and Alcohol Dependence* 38: 51–56.

Chu, Doris C. 2007. Religiosity and desistance from drug use. *Criminal Justice and Behavior* 34: 661–79.

Cisin, I. H., and D. Cahalan. 1968. Comparison of abstainers and heavy drinkers in a national survey. *Psychiatric Research Reports* 24: 10–21.

Clark, David C., Steven R. Daughtery, D. C. Baldwin, and P. H. Hughes. 1992. Assessment of drug involvement: Applications to a sample of physicians in training. *British Journal of Addiction* 87: 1649–62.

Clear, Todd, and Melvina Sumter. 2002. Prisoners, prison, and religion: Religion and adjustment to prison. *Journal of Offender Rehabilitation* 35: 127–59.

Cochran, John K. 1989. The effect of religiosity on secular and ascetic deviance. *Sociological Focus* 4: 293–306.

Cochran, John K. 1991. The effects of religiosity on adolescent self-reported frequency of drug and alcohol use. *Journal of Drug Issues* 22: 91–104.

Cochran, John K. 1993. The variable effects of religiosity and denomination on adolescent self-reported alcohol use by beverage type. *Journal of Drug Issues* 33: 479–91.

Cochran, John K., and Ronald K. Akers. 1989. Beyond hellfire: An explanation of the variable effects of religiosity on adolescent marijuana and alcohol use. *Journal of Research in Crime and Delinquency* 25: 198–225.

Cochran, John K., Peter B. Wood, and Bruce J. Arneklev. 1994. Is the religiosity-delinquency relationship spurious? A test of arousal and social-control theories. *Journal of Research in Crime and Delinquency* 31: 92–123.

Cohen, Patricia, and Judith Brook. 1987. Family factors related to the persistence of psychopathology in childhood and adolescence. *Psychiatry* 50: 332–45.

Coleman, Sandra, Doreene Kaplan, and Robert Downing. 1986. Life cycle and loss: The spiritual vacuum of heroin addiction. *Family Process* 25: 5–23.

Cook, Christopher H., Deborah Goddard, and Rachel Westall. 1997. Knowledge and experience of drug use amongst church affiliated young people. *Drug and Alcohol Dependence* 46: 9–17.

Coombs, Robert H., David K. Wellisch, and Fawzy I. Fawzy. 1985. Drinking patterns and problems among female children and adolescents: A comparison of abstainers, past users, and current users. *American Journal of Drug and Alcohol Abuse* 11: 315–48.

Crano, William D., Jason T. Siegel, Eusebio M. Alvaro, Andrew Lac, and Vanessa Hemovich. 2008. The at-risk adolescent marijuana non-user: Expanding the standard distinction. *Prevention Science* 9: 129–37.

Cretacci, Michael A. 2003. Religion and social control: An application of a modified social bond on violence. *College of Health and Human Sciences* 28: 254–77.

Cronin, Christopher. 1995. Religiosity, religious affiliation, and alcohol and drug use among American college students living in Germany. *Interdisciplinary Journal of the Addictions* 30: 231–38.

Dennis, Kimya Nuru. 2005. The impact of religiosity on deviance and criminal activity in youth and young adults. *Research in Race and Ethnic Relations* 12: 93–130.

Desmond, D. P., and J. F. Maddux. 1981. Religious programs and careers of chronic heroin users. *American Journal of Drug and Alcohol Abuse* 8: 71–83.

Desmond, Scott A., Sarah E. Soper, David J. Purpura, and Elizabeth Smith. 2009. Religiosity, moral beliefs, and delinquency: Does the effect of religiosity on delinquency depend on moral beliefs? *Sociological Spectrum* 29: 51–71.

Dudley, Roger L., Patricia B. Mutch, and Robert J. Cruise. 1987. Religious factors and drug usage among Seventh-Day Adventist youth in North America. *Journal for the Scientific Study of Religion* 26: 218–33.

Dunn, Michael S. 2005. The relationship between religiosity, employment, and political beliefs on substance use among high school seniors. *Journal of Drug and Alcohol Education* 49: 43–88.

Elifson, Kirk W., David M. Peterson, and C. Kirk Hadaway. 1983. Religiosity and delinquency. *Criminology* 21: 505–27.

Ellis, Lee. 2002. Denominational differences in self-reported delinquency. *Journal of Offender Rehabilitation* 35: 185–98.

Ellis, Lee, and Robert Thompson. 1989. Relating religion, crime, and arousal and boredom. *Sociology and Social Research* 73: 132–39.

Ellison, Christopher G., John P. Bartkowski, and Kristin L. Anderson. 1999. Are there religious variations in domestic violence? *Journal of Family Issues* 20: 87–113.

Ellison, Christopher G., Jenny A. Trinitapoli, Kristin L. Anderson, and Byron R. Johnson. 2007. Religion and domestic violence: An examination of variations by race and ethnicity. *Violence Against Women* 13: 1094–112.

Ellison, Christopher G., and Kristin L. Anderson. 2001. Religious involvement and domestic violence among U.S. couples. *Journal for the Scientific Study of Religion*: 40: 269–86.

Engs, Ruth C. 1980. The drug-use patterns of helping-profession students in Brisbane, Australia. *Drug and Alcohol Dependence* 6: 231–46.

Engs, Ruth C., Beth A. Diebold, and David J. Hanson. 1996. The drinking patterns and problems of a national sample of college students. *Journal of Alcohol and Drug Education* 41: 13–33.

Engs, Ruth C., and Kenneth Mullen. 1999. The effect of religion and religiosity on drug use among a selected sample of post secondary students in Scotland. *Addiction Research* 7: 149–70.

Evans, T. David, Francis T. Cullen, R. Gregory Dunaway, and Velmer

S. Burton. 1995. Religion and crime reexamined: The impact of religion, secular controls, and social ecology on adult criminality. *Criminology* 33: 195–224.

Evans, T. David, Francis T. Cullen, Velmer S. Burton Jr., R. Gregory Dunaway, Gary L. Payne, and Sesha R. Kethineni. 1996. Religion, social bonds, and delinquency. *Deviant Behavior: An Interdisciplinary Journal* 17: 43–70.

Fernquist, Robert M. 1995. A research note on the association between religion and delinquency. *Deviant Behavior: An Interdisciplinary Journal* 16: 169–75.

Forliti, John E., and Peter L. Benson. 1986. Young adolescents: A national study. *Religious Education* 81: 199–224.

Forthun, Larry F., Nancy J. Bell, Charles W. Peek, and Sheh-Wei Sun. 1999. Religiosity, sensation seeking, and alcohol/drug use in denominational and gender contexts. *Journal of Drug Issues* 29: 75–90.

Foshee, Vangie A., and Bryan R. Hollinger. 1996. Maternal religiosity, adolescent social bonding, and adolescent alcohol use. *Journal of Early Adolescence* 16: 451–68.

Francis, Leslie J., and Kenneth Mullen. 1993. Religiosity and attitudes towards drug use among 13–15 year olds in England. *Addiction* 88: 665–72.

Francis, Leslie J. 1994. Denominational identity, church attendance and drinking behavior among adults in England. *Journal of Alcohol and Drug Education* 39: 27–33.

Fraser, Graeme S. 1967. Parent-adolescent relationships and delinquent behavior: A cross-national comparison. *Sociological Quarterly* 8: 505–13.

Free, Marvin D., Jr. 1992. Religious affiliation, religiosity, and impulsive and intentional deviance. *Sociological Focus* 25: 77–91.

Free, Marvin D., Jr. 1993. Stages of drug use: A social control perspective. *Youth and Society* 25: 251–71.

Free, Marvin D., Jr. 1994. Religiosity, religious conservatism, bonds to school, and juvenile delinquency among three categories of drug users. *Deviant Behavior* 15: 151–70.

Freeman, Richard B. 1986. Who escapes? The relation of churchgoing and other background factors to the socioeconomic performance of black male youth from inner-city tracts. In *The Black Youth*

Employment Crisis, ed. Richard B. Freeman, Harry J. Holzer. Chicago: University of Chicago Press, 353–76.

Galen, Luke W., and William M. Rogers. 2004. Religiosity, alcohol expectancies, drinking motives and their interaction in the prediction of drinking among college students. *Journal of Studies on Alcohol* 65: 469–76.

Gannon, Thomas M. 1967. Religious control and delinquent behavior. *Sociology and Social Research* 51: 18–31.

Gardner, J. M., C. A. Powell, and S. M. Grantham-McGregor. 2007. Determinants of aggression and prosocial behavior among Jamaican schoolboys. *West Indian Medical Journal* 56: 34–41.

Garis, Dalton. 1998. Poverty, single-parent households, and youth at-risk behavior: An empirical study. *Journal of Economic Issues* 32: 1079–81.

Grasmick, H. G., R. Burskin, and J. Cochran. 1991a. Render unto Caesar what is Caesar's: Religiosity and taxpayers' inclinations to cheat. *Sociological Quarterly* 32: 251–66.

Grasmick, Harold G., Karyl Kinsey, and John K. Cochran. 1991b. Denomination, religiosity and compliance with the law: A study of adults. *Journal for the Scientific Study of Religion* 30: 99–107.

Grunbaum, Jo Anne, Susan Tortolero, Nancy Weller, and Phyllis Gingiss. 2000. Cultural, social, and intrapersonal factors associated with substance abuse among alternative high school students. *Addictive Behaviors* 25: 145–51.

Guinn, Robert. 1975. Characteristics of drug use among Mexican-American students. *Journal of Drug Education* 5: 235–40.

Hadaway, C. Kirk, Kirk W. Elifson, and David M. Petersen. 1984. Religious involvement and drug use among urban adolescents. *Journal for the Scientific Study of Religion* 23: 109–28.

Hamil-Luker, Jenifer, Kenneth C. Land, and Judith Blau. 2004. Diverse trajectories of cocaine use through early adulthood among rebellious and socially conforming youth. *Social Science Research* 33: 300–321.

Hammermeister, Jon, Matt Flint, Julia Havens, and Margaret Peterson. 2001. Psychosocial and health related characteristics of religious well-being. *Psychosocial Reports* 89: 589–94.

Hansell, Stephen, and David Mechanic. 1990. Parent and peer effects on adolescent health behavior. In Klaus Hurrelmann and Friedrich Losel (eds.) *Health Hazards in Adolescence*. New York: Aldine de Gruyter, 43–65.

Hanson, David J., and Ruth C. Engs. 1987. Religion and collegiate drinking problems over time. *Psychology* 24: 10–12.

Hardert, Ronald A., and Timothy J. Dowd. 1994. Alcohol and marijuana use among high school and college students in Phoenix, Arizona: A test of Kandel's Socialization Theory. *International Journal of the Addictions* 29: 887–912.

Hardesty, Patrick H., and Kathleen M. Kirby. 1995. Relation between family religiousness and drug use within adolescent peer groups. *Educational and Counseling Psychology* 10: 421–30.

Harris, Mark A. 2003. Religiosity and perceived future ascetic deviance and delinquency among Mormon adolescents: Testing the "This-Wordly" Supernatural Sanctions Thesis. *Sociological Inquiry* 73: 28–51.

Hater, John J., B. Krisna Singh, and D. Dwayne Simpson. 1984. Influence of family and religion on long-term outcomes among opioid addicts. In Barry Stimmel (ed.) *Cultural and Sociological Aspects of Alcoholism and Substance Abuse.* Binghamton, NY: Haworth Press, Inc., 29–40.

Hawks, Ricky D., Stephen J. Bahr, and Gabe Wang. 1994. Adolescent substance use and codependence. *Journal of Studies on Alcohol* 55: 261–68.

Hays, Ron D., Alan W. Stacy, Keith F. Widaman, M. Robin DiMatteo, and Ralph Downey. 1986. Multistage path models of adolescent alcohol and drug use: A reanalysis. *Journal of Drug Issues* 16: 357–69.

Hays, Ron D., and Joseph P. Revetto. 1990. Peer cluster theory and adolescent drug use: A reanalysis. *Journal of Drug Education* 20: 191–98.

Heath A. C., P. A. F. Madden, J. D. Grant, T. L. McLaughlin, A. A. Todorov, and K. K. Bucholz. 1999. Resiliency factors protecting against teenage alcohol use and smoking: Influences of religion, religious involvement and values, and ethnicity in the Missouri Adolescent Female Twin Study. *Twin Research* 2: 145–55.

Hercik, J. 2004. *Navigating a New Horizon: Promising Pathways to Prisoner Reintegration.* Fairfax, VA: Caliber Associates.

Herrenkohl, Todd I., Emiko A. Tajima, Stephen D. Whitney, and Bu Huang. 2005. Protection against antisocial behavior in children exposed to physically abusive discipline. *Journal of Adolescent Health* 36: 457–65.

Higgins, Paul C., and Gary L. Albrecht. 1977. Hellfire and delinquency revisited. *Social Forces* 55: 952–58.

Hill, Karl G., James C. Howell, J. David Hawkins, and Sara R. Battin-Pearson. 1999. Childhood risk factors for adolescent gang membership: Results from the Seattle Social Development Project. *Journal of Research in Crime and Delinquency* 36: 300–322.

Hillman, Stephen B., and Jacqueline M. Haskin. 2000. Personality and drug abstention in adolescents. *Psychological Reports* 87: 1023–26.

Hirschi, Travis. 1969. *Causes of Delinquency.* Berkeley: University of California Press.

Hodge, David R., Paul Cardenas, and Harry Montoya. 2001. Substance use: Spirituality and religious participation as protective factors among rural youths. *Social Work Research* 25: 153–61.

Humphrey, John A., Paul Leslie, and Jean Brittain. 1989. Religious participation, southern university women, and abstinence. *Deviant Behavior* 10: 145–55.

Hundleby, John D., Richard A. Carpenter, R. A. J. Ross, and G. William Mercer. 1982. Adolescent drug use and other behaviors. *Journal of Child Psychology* 23: 61–68.

Hundleby, John D. 1987. Adolescent drug use in a behavioral matrix: A confirmation and comparison of the sexes. *Addictive Behaviors* 12: 103–12.

Isralowitz, Richard E. 1990. Religious values and beliefs and place of residence as predictors of alcohol use among Chinese college students in Singapore. *International Journal of the Addictions* 25: 515–29.

Jang, Sung Joon, and Byron R. Johnson. 2001. Neighborhood disorder, individual religiosity, and adolescent use of illicit drugs: A test of multilevel hypotheses. *Criminology* 39: 109–44.

Jang, Sung Joon, and Byron R. Johnson. 2003. Strain, negative emotions, and deviant coping among African Americans: A test of general strain theory. *Journal of Quantitative Criminology* 19: 79–105.

Jang, Sung Joon, and Byron Johnson. 2004. Explaining religious effects on distress among African Americans. *Journal for the Scientific Study of Religion* 43: 230–60.

Jang, Sung Joon, and Byron R. Johnson. 2005. Gender, religiosity, and reactions to strain among African Americans. *Sociological Quarterly* 46: 323–57.

Jang, Sung Joon. 2007. Gender differences in strain, negative emotions, and coping behaviors: A general strain theory approach. *Justice Quarterly* 24: 523–53.

Jang, Sung Joon, Christopher D. Bader, and Byron R. Johnson. 2008. The cumulative advantage of religiosity in preventing drug use. *Journal of Drug Issues* 38: 771–98.

Jang, Sung Joon, and Byron R. Johnson. 2010. Religion, race, and drug use among American youth. *Interdisciplinary Journal of Research on Religion* 6: 1–25.

Jessor, Richard, Shirley L. Jessor, and John Finney. 1973. A social psychology or marijuana use: Longitudinal studies of high school and college youth. *Journal of Personality and Social Psychology* 26: 1–15.

Jessor, R., and S. L. Jessor. 1977. *Problem Behavior and Psychosocial Development: A Longitudinal Study of Youth.* New York: Academic Press.

Jessor, Richard, James A. Chase, and John E. Donovan. 1980. Psychosocial correlates of marijuana use and problem drinking in a national sample of adolescents. *American Journal of Public Health* 70: 604–13.

Jeynes, William H. 2006. Adolescent religious commitment and their consumption of marijuana, cocaine, and alcohol. *Journal of Health and Social Policy* 21: 1–20.

Johnson, Richard E., Anastacios C. Marcos, and Stephen J. Bahr. 1987. The role of peers in the complex etiology of adolescent drug use. *Criminology* 25: 323–40.

Johnson, B. R., D. B. Larson, and T. Pitts. 1997. Religious programming, institutional adjustment and recidivism among former inmates in Prison Fellowship programs. *Justice Quarterly* 14: 145–66.

Johnson, Byron R., David B. Larson, Spencer D. Li, and Sung J. Jang. 2000a. Escaping from the crime of inner cities: Church attendance and religious salience among disadvantaged youth. *Justice Quarterly* 17: 377–91.

Johnson, Byron R., Sung Joon Jang, Spence D. Li, and David Larson. 2000b. The "invisible institution" and black youth crime: The church as an agency of local social control. *Journal of Youth and Adolescence* 29: 479–98.

Johnson, Byron R. and Sung Joon Jang. 2001a. Neighborhood disorder, individual religiosity, and adolescent drug use: A test of multilevel hypotheses, *Criminology* 39:501–35.

Johnson, Byron R., Sung Joon Jang, David B. Larson, and Spencer D. Li. 2001b. Does adolescent religious commitment matter? A reexamination of the effects of religiosity on delinquency. *Journal of Research in Crime and Delinquency* 38: 22–44.

Johnson, Byron R., and Marc V. Siegel. 2002. The great escape: How religion alters the delinquent behavior of high-risk adolescents, ISR Research Report, Institute for Studies of Religion, Baylor University. http://www.isreligion.org/publications/reports/.

Johnson, Byron R. 2003. The InnerChange Freedom Initiative: A preliminary evaluation of a faith-based prison program. ISR Research Report, Institute for Studies of Religion, Baylor University. http://www.isreligion.org/publications/reports/.

Johnson, Byron R. 2004. Religious programs and recidivism among former inmates in prison fellowship programs: A long-term follow-up study. *Justice Quarterly* 21: 329–54.

Jones, Kim A., and Brent B. Benda. 2004. Alcohol use among adolescents with non-residential fathers: A study of assets and deficits. *Alcoholism Treatment Quarterly* 22: 3–25.

Junger, Marianne, and Wim Polder. 1993. Religiosity, religious climate, and delinquency among ethnic groups in the Netherlands. *British Journal of Criminology* 33: 416–35.

Kandel, Denise B., Donald Treiman, Richard Faust, and Eric Single. 1976. Adolescent involvement in legal and illegal drug use: A multiple classification analysis. *Social Forces* 55: 438–58.

Kandel, Denise B. 1982. Epidemiological and psychosocial perspectives on adolescent drug use. *Journal of the American Academy of Child Psychiatry* 21: 328–42.

Kandel, Denise B. 1986. Risk factors for delinquency and illicit drug use from adolescent to young adulthood. *Journal of Drug Issues* 16: 67–90.

Kerley, Kent R., Todd L. Matthews, and Troy C. Blanchard. 2005a. Religiosity, religious participation, and negative prison behaviors. *Journal for the Scientific Study of Religion* 44: 443–57.

Kerley, Kent R., Todd L. Matthews, and Jeffrey T. Schulz. 2005b. Participation in operation starting line experience of negative emotions, and incidence of negative behavior. *International Journal of Offender Therapy and Comparative Criminology* 49: 410–26.

Kerley, Kent R., Marisa C. Allison, and Rachelle D. Graham. 2006. Investigating the impact of religiosity on emotional and behavioral coping in prison. *Journal of Crime and Justice* 29: 71–96.

Kerley, Kent R., and Heith Copes. 2009. "Keepin' my mind right": Identity maintenance and religious social support in the prison context. *International Journal of Offender Therapy and Comparative Criminology* 53: 228–44.

Kvaraceus, William C. 1944. Delinquent behavior and church attendance. *Sociology and Social Research* 28: 284–89.

Lee, Jerry W., Gail T. Rice, and V. Bailey Gillespie. 1997. Family worship patterns and their correlation with adolescent behavior and beliefs. *Journal for the Scientific Study of Religion* 36: 372–81.

Lee, Matthew R., and John P. Bartkowski. 2004. Love thy neighbor? Moral communities, civic engagement, and juvenile homicide in rural areas. *Social Forces* 82: 1001–35.

Leigh, Janis, Sarah Bowen, and G. Allan Marlatt. 2005. Spirituality, mindfulness and substance abuse. *Addictive Behaviors* 30: 1335–41.

Linville, Deanna C., and Angela J. Huebner. 2005. The analysis of extracurricular activities and their relationship to youth violence. *Journal of Youth and Adolescence* 34: 483–92.

Litchfield, Allen W., Darwin L. Thomas, and Bing Dao Li. 1997. Dimensions of religiosity as mediators of the relations between parenting and adolescent deviant behavior. *Journal of Adolescent Research* 12: 199–226.

Lo, Celia C., and Gerald Globetti. 1993. Black college students' drinking patterns: The roles of family religious affiliation and parental guidance during the first drinking experience. *Sociological Spectrum* 13: 343–63.

Long, Kathleen Ann, and Robert J. Boik. 1993. Predicting alcohol use in rural children: A longitudinal study. *Nursing Research* 42: 79–86.

Longest, Kyle C., and Stephen Vaisey. 2008. Control or conviction: Religion and adolescent initiation of marijuana use. *Journal of Drug Issues* 38: 689–715.

Longshore, Douglas, Eunice Chang, Shih-chao Hsieh, and Nena Messina. 2004. Self-control and social bonds: A combined control perspective on deviance. *Crime and Delinquency* 50: 542–64.

Lorch, Barbara R., and Robert H. Hughes. 1985. Religion and youth substance abuse. *Journal of Religion and Health* 24: 197–208.

MacDonald, John M., Alex R. Piquero, Robert F. Valois, and Keith J. Zullig. 2005. The relationship between satisfaction, risk-taking behaviors, and youth violence. *Journal of Interpersonal Violence* 20: 1495–1518.

Mainous, Rosalie O., Arch G. Mainous, Catherine A. Martin, Michael J. Oler, and Amy S. Haney. 2001. The importance of fulfilling unmet needs of rural and urban adolescents with substance abuse. *Journal of Child and Adolescent Psychiatric Nursing* 14: 32–40.

Marcos, Anastasios C., Stephen J. Bahr, and Richard E. Johnson. 1986. Test of a bonding/association theory of adolescent drug use. *Social Forces* 65: 135–61.

Mason, W. Alex, and Michael Windle. 2001. Family, religious, school and peer influences on adolescent alcohol use: A longitudinal study. *Journal on Studies of Alcohol* 62: 44–53.

Mason W. Alex, and Michael Windle. 2002. A longitudinal study of the effects of religiosity on adolescent alcohol use and alcohol-related problems. *Journal of Adolescent Research* 17: 346–63.

Mauss, A. L. 1959. Anticipatory socialization toward college as a factor in adolescent marijuana use. *Social Problems* 16: 357–64.

McIntosh, William Alex, Starla D. Fitch, J. Branton Wilson, and Kenneth L. Nyberg. 1981. The effects of mainstream religious social controls on adolescent drug use in rural areas. *Review of Religious Research* 23: 54–75.

McLuckie, Benjamin F., Margaret Zahn, and Robert A. Wilson. 1975. Religious correlates of teenage drug use. *Journal of Drug Issues* 5: 129–39.

Merrill, Ray M., Richard D. Salazar, and Nichole W. Gardner. 2001. Relationship between family religiosity and drug use behavior among youth. *Social Behavior and Personality* 29: 347–58.

Merrill, Ray M., Jeffrey A. Folsom, and Susan S. Christopherson. 2005. The influence of family religiosity on adolescent substance use according to religious preference. *Society for Personality Research* 33: 821–36.

Middleton, Russell, and Snell Putney. 1962. Religion, normative standards, and behavior. *Sociometry* 25: 141–52.

Miller, Lisa, Mark Davies, and Steven Greenwald. 2000. Religiosity and substance use and abuse among adolescents in the National Comorbidity Survey. *Journal of the American Academy of Child Adolescent Psychiatry* 39: 1190–97.

Miller, Lisa, Myrna Weissman, Merav Gur, and Phil Adams. 2001. Religiousness and substance use in children of opiate addicts. *Journal of Substance Abuse* 13: 323–36.

Mitchell, Jim, Richard A. Dodder, and Terry D. Norris. 1990. Neutralization and delinquency: A comparison by sex and ethnicity. *Adolescence* 25: 487–97.

Montgomery, Alice, and Leslie J. Francis. 1996. Relationship between personal prayer and school-related attitudes among 11- to 16-year-old girls. *Psychological Reports* 78: 787–93.

Moon, Hyukjun. 2000. Prevalence of adolescent behavior problems, smoking, and delinquency. *Journal of Korean Home Economics Association English Edition* 1: 37–58.

Moore, Michael, and Shoshana Weiss. 1995. Reasons for non-drinking among Israeli adolescents of four religions. *Drug and Alcohol Dependence* 38: 45–50.

Morris, Ronald J., and Ralph W. Hood Jr. 1981. The generalizability and specificity of intrinsic/extrinsic orientation. *Review of Religious Research* 22: 245–54.

Mullen, Kenneth, and Leslie J. Francis. 2001. Religiosity and attitudes towards drug use among Dutch school children. *Journal of Alcohol and Drug Education* 41: 16–25.

Muller, Chandra, and Christopher G. Ellison. 2001. Religious involvement, social capital, and adolescents' academic progress: Evidence from the national education longitudinal study of 1988. *Sociological Focus* 34: 155–83.

Nelsen, Hart M., and James F. Rooney. 1982. Fire and brimstone, lager and pot: Religious involvement and substance use. *Sociological Analysis* 43: 247–56.

Newcomb, Michael D., Ebrahim Maddahian, and P. M. Bentler. 1986. Risk factors for drug use among adolescents: Concurrent and longitudinal analyses. *American Journal of Public Health* 76: 525–31.

Newman, Ian M., Duane F. Shell, Tiandong Li, and Saranya Innadda.

2006. Buddhism and adolescent alcohol use in Thailand. *Substance Use and Misuse* 41: 1789–1800.

Nonnemaker, James M., Clea A. McNeely, and Robert William Blum. 2003. Public and private domains of religiosity and adolescent health risk behaviors: Evidence from the National Longitudinal Study of Adolescent Health. *Social Science and Medicine* 57: 2049–54.

O'Connor, Thomas P., and Michael Perreyclear. 2002. Prison religion in action and its influence on offender rehabilitation. *Journal of Offender Rehabilitation* 35: 11–33.

Oetting, E. R., and Fred Beauvais. 1987. Peer cluster theory, socialization characteristics, and adolescent drug use: A path analysis. *Journal of Counseling Psychology* 34: 205–13.

Oleckno, William A., and Michael J. Blacconiere. 1991. Relationship of religiosity to wellness and other health-related behaviors and outcomes. *Psychological Reports* 68: 819–26.

Onofrio, Brian M., Lenn Murrelle, Lindon J. Eaves, Michael E. McCullough, Jessica L. Landis, and Hermine H. Maes. 1999. Adolescent religiousness and its influence on substance use: Preliminary findings from the Mid-Atlantic School Age Twin Study. *Twin Research* 2: 156–68.

Parfrey, P. S. 1976. The effect of religious factors on intoxicant use. *Scandinavian Journal of Sociological Medicine* 4: 135–40.

Park, J. Y., G. P. Danko, S. Y. Wong, A. J. Weatherspoon, and R. C. Johnson. 1998. Religious affiliation, religious involvement, and alcohol use in Korea. *Cultural Diversity and Mental Health* 4: 291–96.

Park, Hae-Seong, Lauri Ashton, Tammi Causey, and Sung Seek Moon. 1999. The impact of religious proscriptiveness on alcohol use among high school students. *Journal of Alcohol and Drug Education* 44: 34–46.

Parsai, Monica, Flavio F. Marsiglia, and Stephen Kulis. 2008. Parental monitoring, religious involvement and drug use among Latino and non-Latino youth in the southwestern United States. *British Journal of Social Work* 38: 1–15.

Patock-Peckham, Julie A., Geoffrey T. Hutchinson, Jeewon Cheong, and Craig T. Nagoshi. 1998. Effect of religion and religiosity on alcohol use in a college student sample. *Department of Psychology* 49: 81–88.

Pearce, Lisa D., and Dana L. Haynie. 2004. Intergenerational religious dynamics and adolescent delinquency. *Social Forces* 82: 1553–72.

Pearce, Michelle J., Stephanie M. Jones, Mary E. Schwab-Stone, and Vladislav Ruchkin. 2003. The protective effects of religiousness and parent involvement on the development of conduct problems among youth exposed to violence. *Child Development* 74: 1682–96.

Peek, Charles W., Evans W. Curry, and H. Paul Chalfant. 1985. Religiosity and delinquency over time: Deviance deterrence and deviance amplification. *Social Science Quarterly* 66: 120–31.

Perkins, H. Wesley. 1985. Religious traditions, parents, and peers as determinants of alcohol and drug use among college students. *Review of Religious Research* 27: 15–31.

Perkins, H. Wesley. 1987. Parental religion and alcohol use problems as intergenerational predictors of problem drinking among college youth. *Journal for the Scientific Study of Religion* 26: 340–57.

Pettersson, Thorleif. 1991. Religion and criminality: Structural relationships between church involvement and crime rates in contemporary Sweden. *Journal for the Scientific Study of Religion* 30: 279–91.

Petts, Richard, and Chris Knoester. 2007. Parents' religious heterogamy and children's well-being. *Journal for the Scientific Study of Religion* 46: 373–89.

Petts, Richard J. 2009. Family and Religious characteristics' influence on delinquency trajectories from adolescence to young adulthood. *American Sociological Review* 74:465–83.

Piko, Bettina, and Kevin M. Fitzpatrick. 2004. Substance use, religiosity, and other protective factors among Hungarian adolescents. *Addictive Behaviors* 29: 1095–1107.

Piquero, Nicole Leeper, and Miriam D. Sealock. 2000. Generalizing general strain theory: An examination of an offending population. *Justice Quarterly* 17: 449–84.

Pirkle, Erin C., and Linda Richter. 2006. Personality, attitudinal and behavioral risk profiles of young female binge drinkers and smokers. *Journal of Adolescent Health* 38: 44–54.

Powell, Kathleen B. 1997. Correlates of violent and nonviolent behaviors among vulnerable inner-city youths. *Family Community Health* 20: 38–47.

Preston, James D. 2005. Religiosity and adolescent drinking behavior. *Sociological Quarterly* 10: 372–83.

Pullen, L., M. A. Modrcin-Talbott, W. R. West, and R. Muenchen. 1999. Spiritual high vs. high on spirits: Is religiosity related to adolescent alcohol and drug use? *Journal of Psychiatric and Mental Health Nursing* 6: 3–8.

Regnerus, Mark D. 2003a. Moral communities and adolescent delinquency: Religious contexts and community social control. *Sociological Quarterly* 44: 523–54.

Regnerus, Mark D., and Glen H. Elder. 2003b. Staying on track in school: Religious influences in high-and low-risk settings. *Journal for the Scientific Study of Religion* 42: 633–49.

Regnerus, Mark D. 2003c. Moral communities and adolescent delinquency: Religious contexts and community social control. *Sociological Quarterly* 44: 523–54.

Regnerus, Mark D., and Glen H. Elder. 2003d. Religion and vulnerability among low-risk adolescents. *Social Science Research* 32: 633–58.

Resnick, Michael D., Peter S. Bearman, Robert William Blum, et al. 1997. Protecting adolescents from harm: Findings from the National Longitudinal Study on Adolescent Health. *Journal of the American Medical Association* 278: 823–32.

Rhodes, Albert Lewis, and Albert J. Reiss. 1970. The "Religious Factor" and delinquent behavior. *Journal of Research in Crime and Delinquency* 7: 83–98.

Ritt-Olson, Anamara, Joel Milam, Jennifer B. Unger, et al., 2004. The protective influence of spirituality and "Health-as-a-Value" against monthly substance use among adolescents varying in risk. *Journal of Adolescent Health* 34: 192–99.

Rohrbaugh, John, and Richard Jessor. 1975. Religiosity in youth: A personal control against deviant behavior. *Journal of Personality* 43: 136–55.

Ross, Lee E. 1994. Religion and deviance: Exploring the impact of social control elements. *Sociological Spectrum* 14: 65–86.

Schiff, Miriam. 2006. Living in the shadow of terrorism: Psychological distress and alcohol use among religious and non-religious adolescents in Jerusalem. *Social Science and Medicine* 62: 2301–12.

Schlegel, Ronald P., and Margaret D. Sanborn. 1979. Religious affiliation and adolescent drinking. *Journal of Studies on Alcohol* 40: 693–703.

Scholl, M. E., and J. Becker. 1964. A comparison of religious beliefs of delinquent and non-delinquent protestant adolescent boys. *Religious Education* 59: 250–53.

Schulenberg, John, Jerald G. Bachman, Patrick M. O'Malley, and Lloyd D. Johnston. 1994. High school educational success and subsequent substance use: A panel analysis following adolescents into young adulthood. *Journal of Health and Social Behavior* 35: 45–62.

Simons, Leslie Gordon, Ronald L. Simons, and Rand D. Conger. 2004. Identifying the mechanisms whereby family religiosity influences the probability of adolescent antisocial behavior. *Journal of Comparative Family Studies* 25: 547–63.

Singh, B. K. 1979. Correlates of attitudes toward euthanasia. *Social Biology* 26: 247–54.

Sinha, Jill W., Ram A. Cnaan, and Richard W. Gelles. 2007. Adolescent risk behaviors and religion: Findings from a national study. *Journal of Adolescence* 30: 231–49.

Sloane, Douglas M., and Raymond H. Potvin. 1986. Religion and delinquency: Cutting through the maze. *Social Forces* 65: 87–105.

Smith, Christian, Michael Emerson, Sally Gallagher, Paul Kennedy, and David Sikkink. 1998. *American Evangelicalism: Embattled and Thriving*. Chicago: University of Chicago Press.

Sorenson, Ann Marie. 1995. Adolescent drug use and a general theory of crime: An analysis of a theoretical integration. *Canadian Journal of Criminology* 37: 19–37.

Stark, Rodney, Lori Kent, and Daniel P. Doyle. 1982. Religion and delinquency: The ecology of a lost relationship. *Journal of Research in Crime and Delinquency* 19: 4–24.

Stark, Rodney. 1996. Religion as context: Hellfire and delinquency one more time. *Sociology of Religion* 57: 163–73.

Steinman, Kenneth J., and Marc A. Zimmerman. 2004. Religious activity and risk behavior among African American adolescents: Concurrent and developmental effects. *American Journal of Community Psychology* 33: 151–61.

Steinman, Kenneth J., Amy K. Ferketich, and Timothy Sahr. 2008. The dose-response relationship of adolescent religious activity and substance use: Variation across demographic groups. *Health Education and Behavior* 35: 22–43.

Stewart, Chris. 2001. The influence of spirituality on substance use of college students. *Journal of Drug Education* 21: 343–51.

Stewart, Chris, and J. M. Bolland. 2002. Parental style as a possible mediator of the relationship between religiosity and substance use in African-American adolescents. *Journal of Ethnicity in Substance Abuse* 1: 63–81.

Stylianou, Stelios. 2004. The role of religiosity in the opposition to drug use. *International Journal of Offender Therapy and Comparative Criminology* 48: 429–48.

Sussman, Steve, Silvana Skara, Paride de Calice, Beth Hoffman, and Clyde W. Dent. 2005. Spirituality as a 1-year predictor of violence perpetration and drug use among youth at continuation high schools. *Journal of Applied Social Psychology* 35: 80–99.

Sussman, Steve, Silvana Skara, Yaneth Rodriguez, and Palav Pokhrel. 2006. Non drug use– and drug use–specific spirituality as one-year predictors of drug use among high-risk youth. *Substance Use and Misuse* 41: 1801–16.

Taub, Diane E. 1990. A social bonding-drug progression model of amphetamine use among young women. *American Journal of Drug and Alcohol Abuse* 16: 77–95.

Templin, Daniel P., and Michael J. Martin. 1999. The relationship between religious orientation, gender, and drinking patterns among Catholic college students. *College Student Journal* 33: 488–96.

Tenant-Clark, C. M., J. J. Fritz, and F. Beauvasis. 1989. Occult participation: Its impact on adolescent development. *Adolescence* 24: 757–72.

Tibbetts, Stephen G., and Joshua N. Whittimore. 2002. The interactive effects of low self-control and commitment to school on substance abuse among college students. *Psychological Reports* 90: 327–37.

Tittle, Charles R., and Michael R. Welch. 1983. Religiosity and deviance: Toward a contingency theory of constraining effects. *Social Forces* 61: 653–82.

Travers, John F., and Russell G. Davis. 1961. A study of religious motivation and delinquency. *Journal of Educational Sociology* 34: 205–20.

Trawick, Michelle. 2006. Crime and community heterogeneity: Race, ethnicity, and religion. *Applied Economic Letters* 13: 341–45.

Turner, Carol J., and Robert J. Willis. 1979. The relationship between self-reported religiosity and drug use by college students. *Journal of Drug Education* 9: 67–78.

Turner, Norma Haston, Gina Yvonne Ramirez, John C. Higginbotham, Kyriakos Markides, Alice C. Wygant and Sandra Black. 1994. Tri-ethnic alcohol use and religion, family, and gender. *Journal of Religion and Health* 33: 341–52.

Vakalahi, Halaevalu F. 2002. Family-based predictors of adolescent substance use. *Journal of Child and Adolescent Substance Abuse* 11: 1–15.

Valliant, George E., and Eva S. Milofsky. 1982. Natural history of male alcoholism. *Archives of General Psychiatry* 39: 127–33.

Van den Bree, Marianne B. M., Michelle D. Whimer, and Wallace B. Pickworth. 2004. Predictors of smoking development in a population-based sample of adolescents: A prospective study. *Journal of Adolescent Health* 35: 172–81.

Veach, Tracey L., and John N. Chappel. 1992. Measuring spiritual health: A preliminary study. *Substance Abuse* 13: 139–47.

Vener, Arthur M., Mary Margaret Zaenglein, and Cyrus Stewart. 2003. Traditional religious orthodoxy, respect for authority and nonconformity in adolescence. *Adolescence* 12: 43–56.

Walker, Carmella, Michael G. Ainette, Thomas A. Wills, and Don Mendoza. 2007. Religiosity and substance use: Test of an indirect-effect model in early and middle adolescence. *Psychology of Addictive Behavior* 21: 84–96.

Wallace, John M., and Jerald G. Bachman. 1991. Explaining racial/ethnic differences in adolescent drug use: The impact of background and lifestyle. *Social Problems* 38: 333–55.

Wallace, John M., and Tyrone A. Forman. 1998. Religion's role in promoting health and reducing risk among American youth. *Health Education & Behavior* 25: 721–41.

Wallace, John M., Tony N. Brown, Jerald G. Bachman, and Thomas A. Laveist. 2003. The influence of race and religion on abstinence from alcohol, cigarettes and marijuana among adolescents. *Journal of Studies on Alcohol* 64: 843–48.

Wallace, John M., Ryoko Yamaguchi, Jerald G. Bachman, Patrick M. O'Malley, John E. Schulenberg, and Lloyd D. Johnston. 2007.

Religiosity and adolescent substance use: The role of individual and contextual influences. *Social Problems* 54: 308–27.

Walsh, Anthony. 1995. Parental attachment, drug use, and facultative sexual strategies. *Social Biology* 42: 95–107.

Wattenberg, William W. 1950. Church attendance and juvenile misconduct. *Sociology and Social Research* 34: 195–202.

Wechsler, Henry, and Mary McFadden. 1979. Drinking among college students in New England: Extent, social correlates and consequences of alcohol use. *Journal of Studies on Alcohol* 40: 969–96.

Wechsler, Henry, George W. Dowdall, Andrea Davenport, and Sonia Castillo. 1995. Correlates of college student binge drinking. *American Journal of Public Health* 85: 921–26.

Weill, J., and B. Le Bourhis. 1994. Factors predicative of alcohol consumption in a representative sample of French male teenagers: A five-year prospective study. *Drug and Alcohol Dependence* 35: 45–50.

Welch, Michael, Charles Tittle, and Harold Grasmick. 2006. Christian religiosity, self-control, and social conformity. *Social Forces* 84: 1605–23.

White, Helene R., Charles B. Fleming, Min Jung Kim, Richard F. Catalano, and Barbara H. McMorris. 2008. Identifying two potential mechanisms for changes in alcohol use among college-attending and non-college-attending emerging adults. *Developmental Psychology* 44: 1625–39.

Wickerstrom, David Lee, and J. Roland Fleck. 1983. Missionary children: Correlates of self-esteem and dependency. *Journal of Psychology and Theology* 11: 226–35.

Wills, Thomas Ashby, Alison M. Yaeger, and James M. Sandy. 2003. Buffering effect of religiosity for adolescent substance use. *Psychology of Addictive Behaviors* 17: 24–31.

Windle, Michael, Eun Young Mun, and Rebecca C. Windle. 2005. Adolescent-to-young adulthood heavy drinking trajectories and their prospective predictors. *Journal of Studies on Alcohol* 66: 313–22.

Wright, Derek, and Edwin Cox. 1971. Changes in moral belief among sixth-form boys and girls over a seven-year period in relation to religious belief, age and sex difference. *British Journal of Sociology and Clinical Psychology* 10: 332–41.

Yarnold, Barbara M., and Valerie Patterson. 1995. Factors correlated with adolescents' use of crack in public schools. *Psychological Reports* 76: 467–74.

Young, Mark C., John Gartner, Thomas O'Connor, David Larson, and Kevin N. Wright. 1995. Long-term recidivism among federal inmates trained as volunteer prison ministers. *Journal of Offender Rehabilitation* 22: 97–118.

Youniss, James, Miranda Yates, and Yang Su. 1997. Social integration: Community service and marijuana use in high school seniors. *Journal of Adolescent Research* 12: 245–62.

Zhang, Jie, and Thomas E. Darwin. 1994. Modernization theory revisited: A cross-cultural study of adolescent conformity to significant others in mainland China, Taiwan, and the USA. *Adolescence* 29: 885–903.

Zimmerman, Marc A., and Kenneth I. Maton. 1992. Life-style and substance use among male African-American urban adolescents: A cluster analytic approach. *American Journal of Community Psychology* 20: 121–38.

IFI Selection Criteria

S INCE IFI IS a Christian-based program, many have assumed the program is open only to inmates with a Christian background. This is not the case, as inmates from various faith traditions (or no faith tradition) both applied to and were selected for participation in the program. Candidates simply needed to volunteer in order to participate and recognize that the program is pervasively Christian. In order to be eligible for consideration, inmates within the TDCJ population had to be between sixteen and twenty-four months from release on mandatory supervision or parole.[1] Only men were considered for the program, and candidates had to be able to speak English.[2] Sex offenders were excluded from consideration, as were inmates with significant medical problems. Adherence to the sex offender exclusion was strictly enforced, though offenders with fairly pronounced medical problems were admitted into the program.[3]

The final two criteria (county to which the offender is slated to return following release from prison and custody status) drastically reduced the selection pool and created complications for the IFI program before it could even get started. Eligibility dictated that prisoners must be returning to Houston or an adjacent county. Both TDCJ and PF surmised that it was in the best interest of the future participant as well as the IFI program to limit the pool of potential participants to those who were from Houston. Because the Carol Vance Unit is located just outside of Houston, where volunteers, mentors, and aftercare services are based, it was logically expected that offenders would fare better after release from prison if they were returning to family and other aftercare services in Houston. This criterion alone drastically reduced the size of the potential selection pool.[4]

The last criterion was even more restricting: prisoners had to have a minimum-out custody status in order to be considered for the IFI program. "Minimum-out" custody refers to "a designator used to identify those minimum custody offenders who have been approved to work outside the security perimeter with minimal supervision."[5] Minimum custody is reserved for prisoners who have been able to have their custody level reduced over time by exhibiting good institutional behavior or by not violating institutional rules. TDCJ policy stipulates that prisoners cannot work outside of the prison without minimum-out custody status.[6] Prerelease facilities throughout the TDCJ system rely heavily on inmates with minimum-out custody because of the cost savings associated with having them do work for the prison outside of the institution proper.

Since work and community service are important features of the IFI program and participants in Phase II have the opportunity to regularly work in a group outside of the prison in the community or what prisoners call the "free world," it was critical for IFI to require a minimum-out custody criteria. Prisoners with minimum-in custody status were not allowed to work outside the prison.[7] Since prisoners with minimum-in custody levels are far more prevalent than prisoners with minimum-out custody, there simply was an insufficient pool of eligible prisoners from which to draw. This dilemma caused both TDCJ and PF to make several critical concessions at the outset regarding the IFI selection criteria, namely, to consider prisoners with minimum-in status. To prevent misunderstandings about selection it should be noted that minimum-custody status is not determined by offense severity, but rather upon an inmate's institutional track record.

A MATCHED DESIGN

Initial plans between TDCJ and PF called for sending eligible cohorts of twenty-five to thirty-five prisoners every four months to the IFI program. The plans also called for eventually capping the IFI population at two hundred. These IFI projections certainly seemed reasonable to all the relevant parties, especially considering the total inmate population in TDCJ in 1997 was over 138,000 and climbed to over 151,000 in 2000. The research team proposed and both TDCJ and PF agreed to the process of randomly assigning inmates from the pool of eligible applicants to participation in the IFI program. It was believed that there would be a sufficient selection pool meeting all the criteria and allowing for random assignment to IFI. The control group would be those individuals who applied, met the criteria, and were selected for admission, but were randomly assigned to some other prerelease facility.

However, the initial selection process did not yield enough inmates to fill the twenty-five- to thirty-five-member cohort or group. This obstacle made random assignment impossible.[8] TDCJ subsequently agreed to consider those applicants to IFI who had minimum-in status, if there was a high probability of reducing their custody status to minimum-out during the first phase of the program. This process increased the number of prisoners eligible for IFI. Though this concession increased the pool size enough to send full cohorts to the program, it did not allow the luxury of assigning participants randomly to IFI or other prerelease facilities, as virtually every eligible prisoner meeting all other selection criteria was sent to the IFI program.

Comparison groups were thus selected from the records of inmates released during the evaluation period that met program selection criteria but did not enter the program.[9] As seen in Table 9, a total of 1,754 inmates were identified as the matched comparison group for this study. These inmates met IFI selection criteria but did not participate in the program. A second comparison group of 1,083 inmates was screened as eligible for the program but they did not volunteer or were not selected for program participation. A third comparison group of 560 inmates actually volunteered for the IFI program but did not participate, either because they were not classified as minimum-out custody, their remaining sentence length was either too short or too long to be considered, or they were not returning to the Houston area following release.

The comparison groups were matched with IFI participants based on the following characteristics: race, age, offense type, and salient factor risk score.[10] As Table 10 shows, the comparison groups are generally similar to those prisoners in the IFI group in regard to race, age, offense, and risk characteristics. This risk score is based on factors associated with recidivism and consequently categorizes offenders into three categories for risk of recidivating. The IFI participants and comparison groups have similar distributions by risk score.

TABLE 9. IFI and Comparison Group Descriptions

GROUP	DESCRIPTION	POPULATION
IFI Group	Prisoners who met the selection criteria and entered the program between April 1997 and January 1999, and were released from prison prior to September 1, 2000.	n=177
Match Group	Prisoners selected from the records of inmates released during the evaluation period that met program selection criteria but did not enter the program.	n=1,754
Screened Group	Prisoners selected from the records of inmates released during the evaluation period that met program selection criteria and were screened as eligible but did not volunteer or were not selected for program participation.	n=1,083
Volunteer Group	Prisoners selected from the records of inmates released during the evaluation period that actually volunteered for the IFI program, but did not participate either because they did not have a minimum-out custody classification, their remaining sentence was not within the required length (18–30 months) to be considered, or they were not planning to return to the Houston area following area.	n=560

Since none of the comparison groups include prisoners actually entering the program, we decided to identify a fourth comparison group of prisoners actually admitted to IFI, but who received early parole and thus left prison before completing the program. These early releasees make for a more appropriate comparison group since they were actually participants in IFI and removed from the program for strictly external reasons beyond the control of those administering program or those participating in the program. This comparison group provides another vehicle for estimating if IFI completion is associated with a program effect.

TABLE 10. Demographic Characteristics of IFI and Comparison Groups

CHARACTERISTICS OF OFFENDERS	COMPARISON GROUPS			
	IFI Participants	Match Group	Screened but Did Not Enter	Volunteered but Did Not Enter
Race/Ethnicity				
African American	67%	62%	49%	66%
Hispanic	16%	12%	31%	15%
Anglo	18%	26%	20%	19%
Age Group				
≤ 35	48%	48%	48%	56%
> 35	52%	52%	52%	44%
Offense Type				
Violent	12%	10%	18%	11%
Property	36%	34%	36%	38%
Drug	50%	53%	45%	48%
Risk Score				
High Risk	31%	33%	34%	32%
Medium Risk	54%	50%	50%	52%
Low Risk	15%	17%	17%	17%
Sample Size	177	1,754	1,083	560

IFI Participants—The Study Group

This study tracks the two-year postrelease recidivism rates for those prisoners who entered the IFI program from April 1997 through January 1999, and were released from prison prior to September 1, 2000. To allow for a two-year recidivism window or tracking period, IFI participants included in the study were those who had the potential to be out of prison for at least two years by September 1, 2002. A total of 177 IFI participants met these requirements and thus formed the basis of the study group.

In order to avoid confusion, however, about what it does or does not mean to be part of the study group, we need to make several observations. First, a two-year recidivism study like the current one actually means that, at a minimum, all offenders in the study have had the opportunity to be on release from prison for at least two years. Second, this does not mean that all 177 were out of prison for two years. Some, in fact, were arrested within days of release, and some were incarcerated within several months of release. Conversely, almost half of the study group (n=85) was released from prison prior to September 1999, and a substantial number of these (n=34) was released before September 1998, meaning that a significant number of prisoners had the potential to be on release from IFI for as much as three or four years.

Selection Bias

In the absence of conducting a study with randomly assigned cases to both experimental and control groups, we cannot eliminate all lists of selection bias. Acknowledging that we cannot refute the existence of selection bias, we need to address a number of the most obvious related concerns.

A common concern in comparison studies like the current one is that those receiving the intervention—in this case, a faith-based prison program—are selected in a way that increases the likelihood of successful outcomes for the study group. One might argue that since the program is "Christ-centered," Christian prisoners might get preferential treatment in the selection process. Having observed the selection process, and having interviewed hundreds of prisoners eventually selected for the program, the research team saw no evidence to support such a conclusion.

A related concern is that the most devoutly religious prisoners in TDCJ would be the ones most likely to volunteer for the IFI program in the first place. Indeed, the argument goes, these individuals represent the cream of the correctional crop—those who have already found God or who have been spiritually transformed and rehabilitated before arriving at IFI. If this concern was valid, the logical extension of this criticism is quite interesting: namely, if such individuals fare better on parole, it is not due to the IFI intervention but rather the religious or spiritual change that took place before participation in this faith-based program. In either case, such a criticism implies that religious programs or experiences do reduce recidivism. The only problem is unraveling which spiritual intervention is responsible for the effect.

The best response to this concern is that the matched design utilized in this research provides three different comparison groups to the study group. As mentioned earlier, the matched groups look very much like the study group on key factors known to be associated with recidivism. Stated differently, the study group seems to resemble in important ways the matched comparison groups. It can still be argued, however, that these key predictive factors do not control for religious commitment or spirituality. Indeed, inmates volunteering for the program may well be more religious than the matched group, but this would be an invalid criticism of the third comparison group that also volunteered for the program or the fourth comparison group of those who were paroled early.

The research team interviewed many correctional officers, correctional administrators, and prison chaplains throughout TDCJ to learn what they thought about the inmates who would seek to participate in the IFI program. In general, there was skepticism, even among chaplains, about the motivation for participation in the IFI program. Many correctional workers were suspicious of prisoners volunteering for the program and believed they were simply trying to con the system and earn an early release on parole.

Interestingly, while chaplains believe there are those prisoners who are quite sincere in their religious or spiritual commitments, and that some of these may well find their way into the program, they were more

likely to respond in ways that validated the response of correctional officers. A number of chaplains in TDCJ told us that some of the worst cons
in the state would certainly be applying for the program—indicating
that such inmates are quick to try every program available in hopes of
impressing prison personnel as well as the parole board, and that IFI
would simply be the latest gimmick. In fact, one senior chaplain predicted that if the IFI program succeeded with the kind of inmates it
would attract (i.e., cons interested in manipulating the system), it would
no doubt be effective with any inmate from the TDCJ. However, motivation for participation is always the Achilles heel of comparison group
designs. The bottom line is that motivation is present and we do not
know which direction, if any, the bias might take.

Graduating from the IFI Program

In the current study, more than sheer length in the IFI program, we
were particularly interested in comparing those individuals who had
completed the program with those who had not. IFI made the decision
that after having completed the three phases of the program, a member
is eligible to officially "graduate" from the program. Technically speaking, to qualify as a graduate of IFI a participant must complete sixteen
months in the IFI program at the Carol Vance Unit,[11] complete six or
more months in aftercare, hold a job and have been an active member
in church for the previous three months prior to graduation, and verify
that he has satisfactorily completed the aftercare requirements.[12] It is
very common for researchers to compare recidivism rates for program
completers and noncompleters. However, IFI's requirements necessary
for being classified a graduate are quite restrictive. When compared to
nongraduates, IFI graduates are clearly the beneficiaries of preferential
treatment, on average, for three to six months postrelease. We revisit this
problem in the findings section, as well as the likelihood that defining
graduates in such a restrictive manner carries the potential for under-
reporting the actual recidivism rate.

Recidivism studies are based strictly on dates of the specified tracking
period; they are not based on the length of program participation. For
example, a number of the 177 IFI participants were only in the prison
program for a matter of days, some for several weeks, and others went

beyond twenty months. This does not indicate that recidivism studies are uninterested in the length of program participation. It simply means that a lack of participation, no matter how minor, is not a factor for excluding such subjects from the evaluation group under study. In fact, we examine whether length in the IFI program relates to rates of recidivism.

MEASURING RECIDIVISM

Two commonly used recidivism measures are included in the current study. The first recidivism measure, arrest, is a broader, less restrictive measure of recidivism. It is quite possible, for example, for an individual to be arrested and receive no other sanction, or a series of sanctions other than incarceration. The second measure of recidivism utilized in the current study is incarceration. It is a more restrictive measure of recidivism and is the most often utilized measure of recidivism. Incarceration in the current study is based on the percentage of offenders returning to prison or state jail within two years of release due to a conviction for a new offense or revocation for violating conditions of parole.

MONITORING THE ROLE OF MENTORING

IFI was designed to incorporate aftercare as an essential part of program completion. After six months in the IFI program, in general, participants were matched with a church-based mentor from the Houston area. IFI staff believed mentors would play a critical role in the long-term success of program participants. It was hoped that the mentoring relationship that was developed while the offender was still in prison would continue during the difficult months following release from prison. Mentors are supposed to help with as many aspects of prisoner reentry as possible. For example, mentors are encouraged to accompany IFI members when they make regular visits to their parole officer. Mentors are also asked to help with transportation, job referrals, and a host of other issues affecting prisoner reentry. Mentors tend to discuss almost anything the IFI participant wants to discuss. From family matters, to employment and housing, to various struggles they confront during the week, to spiritual issues, mentors and IFI members feel quite comfortable discussing any issue, problem, or obstacle. As stated earlier, however, the matching of mentors did not always happen on time or at all, since a significant number of prisoners were paroled early and before a mentor could be assigned. Surveys of parole officers were conducted in 1999 and 2001, to determine the level of contact between mentors and parole officers and the level of contact between mentors and IFI participants.[13]

Prisoner Reentry Initiative Sites

	Name of Group	Location	Population Served	Organization Type	Number of Faith Partners
1.	Primavera Foundation	Tucson, AZ	400 participants	Community-Based	1
2.	AZ Women's Education & Employment	Phoenix, AZ	400 male and female ex-offenders released in Maricopa County, AZ	Community-Based	8
3.	Metro United Method-ist Urban Ministries	San Diego, CA	200 adult ex-offenders	Faith-Based	50+ faith-based groups (including 48 churches)
4.	Allen Temple Housing & Economic Development Corporation	Oakland, CA	200 adult ex-prisoners	Faith-Based	1
5.	Mexican American Alcoholism Program Inc.	Sacra-mento, CA	200 participants	Community-Based	1—mentoring
6.	Fresno Career Development Center	Fresno, CA	200 clients	Community-Based	20
7.	Empowerment Program	Denver, CO	200 recently released nonviolent ex-offenders	Community-Based	6

8.	Community Partners in Action	Hartford, CT	200 adult ex-offenders; main target men 25-40	Community-Based	None known
9.	OIC of Broward County	Fort Lauderdale, FL	220 nonviolent ex-offenders	Community-Based	1 (this FBO pulls from 15 different faith entities), OIC also works with 10 more faith groups
10.	Directors Council	Des Moines, IA	210 nonviolent ex-offenders released in the prior 6 months	Community-Based	2—mentoring
11.	Safer Foundation	Chicago, IL	300 formerly incarcerated individuals	Community-Based	6
12.	Church United for Community Development	Baton Rouge, LA	200 participants	Faith-Based and Community-Based	Many
13.	Odyssey House LA	New Orleans, LA	200 adult ex-offenders	Community-Based	2—mentoring
14.	Span Inc.	Boston, MA	200 nonviolent ex-offenders	Community-Based	4
15.	Episcopal Community Services of Maryland	Baltimore, MD	300 ex-offenders ages 21–40 with a history of drug/alcohol addiction	Faith-Based	1
16.	Oakland Livingston Human Service Agency	Pontiac, MI	200 new parolees	Community-Based	2-mentoring
17.	St. Patrick Center	St. Louis, MO	200 ex-prisoners over age 18; nonviolent, non-sex-related offenses	Faith-Based (Catholic Charities)	7

18.	Connections to Success	Kansas City, MO	200 adult ex-prisoners	Faith-Based	25–30
19.	Career Opportunity Development	Egg Harbor/ Atlantic City, NJ	From Atlantic County	Community-Based	1—mentoring
20.	The Doe Fund	Brooklyn, NY	200 primarily from Queensboro Prison	Community-Based	Unsuccessful in partnering w/FBOs; but utilize many faith-based mentors
21.	Goodwill Industries of Greater NY and Northern NJ	Astoria, NY; Newark, NJ	204 nonviolent offenders	Community-Based	None
22.	Urban Youth Alliance International	Bronx, NY	400 returning prisoners from Rikers Island Jail ages 18–24	Faith-Based	1
23.	Talbert House	Cincinnati, OH	200 ex-prisoners	Community-Based	3
24.	S.E. Works	Portland, OR	200 participants	Community-Based	No mention of faith-based partners
25.	Connection Training Services	Philadelphia, PA	208 recently released ex-offenders each year	Community-Based	2
26.	WABC Central City Comprehensive Community Center	Houston, TX	Ex-offenders in Harris County, TX	Faith-Based	4
27.	Goodwill Industries of San Antonio	San Antonio, TX	400 returning offenders	Community-Based	2
28.	Urban League Greater Dallas & North Central TX	Dallas, TX	400 participants	Community-Based	10

| 29. | People of Color Against AIDS Network | Seattle, WA | 200 nonviolent ex-offenders and subgroup of violent offenders of color | Community-Based | 10 |
| 30. | Word of Hope Ministries | Milwaukee, WI | 200 formerly incarcerated individuals | Faith-Based | 1 |

Notes

Chapter 1—The Last Acceptable Prejudice

1. Byron R. Johnson and Sung Joon Jang. "Crime and Religion: Assessing the Role of the Faith Factor," *Contemporary Issues in Criminological Theory and Research: The Role of Social Institutions,* ed. Richard Rosenfeld, Kenna Quinet, and Crystal Garcia. (Belmont, CA: Wadsworth, 2010). Papers from the American Society of Criminology 2010 Conference.

2. For an intriguing commentary on the weight of my work as well as that of John DiIulio in influencing public policy, see Paul Knepper, "Faith, Public Policy, and the Limits of Social Science," *Criminology and Public Policy* 2 (2003): 331–51. See also the essay in response to Knepper's commentary: Francis T. Cullen and Jody L. Sundt, "Reaffirming Evidence-Based Corrections," *Criminology and Public Policy* 2 (2003): 353–58.

3. "Justice System Direct and Intergovernmental Expenditures," *Sourcebook of Criminal Justice Statistics Online,* Table 1.1.2006, http://www.albany.edu/sourcebook/pdf/t112006.pdf.

4. Mark A. Cohen, *The Costs of Crime and Justice* (New York: Routledge, 2005).

5. James Austin, "Using Early Release to Relieve Prison Crowding: A Dilemma in Public Policy," *Crime and Delinquency* 32 (1986): 404–502.

6. T. R. Miller, M. A. Cohen, and B. Wiersema, "Victims Costs and Consequences: A New Look," National Institute of Justice Research Report, 1996, NCJ-155282, http://www.ncjrs.org/pdffiles/victcost.pdf.

7. Robert D. Putnam suggests that churches are enormous repositories of goodwill and that houses of worship build and sustain more social capital—and social capital of more varied forms—than any other type of institution in America. See Robert D. Putnam et al., *Better Together: Report of the Saguaro Seminar* (Cambridge, MA: Harvard University, John F. Kennedy School of Government, 2001).

Chapter 2—Preachers Partner with Police to Reduce Gang Violence

1. Paul F. Evans, "Cops, Crime and Clergy: Boston's Commish on How the New Alliance between Police and Preachers Works," *Newsweek,* June 1, 1998.

2. Jenny Berrien and Christopher Winship, "Should We Have Faith in the Churches? The TenPoint Coalition's Effect on Boston's Youth Violence," in *Guns, Crime, and*

Punishment in America, ed. Bernard E. Harcourt (New York: New York University Press, 2003), 249–76.

3. Rev. Brown is the executive director of the TenPoint Coalition as of this writing.

4. Interviews with Rev. Brown occurred in August and September 2010.

5. Mission statement of the TenPoint Coalition, www.bostontenpoint.org. See also Christopher Winship, "End of a Miracle? Crime, Faith, and Partnership in the 1990s," in *Long March Ahead: The Public Influences of African American Churches*, vol. 2, ed. R. Drew Smith (Durham, NC: Duke University Press, 2004), 170–92.

6. Mission statement of the TenPoint Coalition.

7. "God vs. Gangs: What's the Hottest Idea in Crime Fighting? The Power of Religion," *Newsweek*, June 1, 1998; Berrien and Winship, "Should We Have Faith in the Churches?" 231.

8. Mission statement of the TenPoint Coalition.

9. Berrien and Winship, "Should We Have Faith in the Churches?" 235.

10. Ibid.

11. Data provided by the Boston Police Department.

12. See descriptions of the programs offered through the TenPoint Coalition, www.bostontenpoint.org.

13. Anthony A. Braga, David M. Kennedy, Elin J. Waring, and Anne M. Piel, "Problem-Oriented Policing, Deterrence, and Youth Violence: An Evaluation of Boston's Operation Ceasefire," *Journal of Research in Crime and Delinquency* 38 (2001): 195–225; David M. Kennedy, *Deterrence and Crime Prevention: Reconsidering the Prospect of Sanction* (New York: Routledge, 2009).

14. Berrien and Winship, "Should We Have Faith in the Churches?" 232.

15. See David Kennedy, "Pulling Levers: Chronic Offenders, High-Crime Settings, and a Theory of Prevention," *Valparaiso University Law Review* 31 (1997): 449.

16. See David M. Kennedy, Anthony A. Braga, Anne M. Piehl, and Elin J. Waring, "Reducing Gun Violence: The Boston Gun Project's Operation Ceasefire," U.S. Department of Justice, National Institute of Justice, Washington, DC, September 2001, NCJ 188741; Anthony A. Braga and Glenn L. Pierce, "Disrupting Illegal Firearms Markets in Boston: The Effects of Operation Ceasefire on the Supply of New Handguns to Criminals," *Criminology and Public Policy* 4 (2005): 717–48.

17. Wesley G. Skogan, Susan M. Hartnett, Natalie Bump, and Jill Dubois, "Evaluation of Ceasefire-Chicago," National Institute of Justice, Office of Justice Programs, Department of Justice, Washington, DC, 2008.

18. Lawrence W. Sherman, Denise Gottfredson, Doris MacKenzie, John Eck, Peter Reuter, and Shawn Bushway, "Preventing Crime: What Works, What Doesn't, What's Promising," A Report to the United States Congress, 1997.

19. Ibid., 9.

20. Vincent Phillip Munoz, "Supreme Court Hostility toward Religious Expression in the Public Square," Testimony before Senate Subcommittee on the Constitution, Civil Rights, and Property Rights, June 8, 2004.

21. "Unlevel Playing Field: Barriers to Participation by Faith-Based and Community Organizations in Federal Social Service Programs," White House Office of Faith-Based and Community Initiatives, Washington, DC, August 2001.

22. Ibid., 25.

CHAPTER 3—CHILDREN OF PRISONERS

1. Lauren Glaze and Laura M. Maruschak, "Parents in Prison and Their Minor Children," a special report from the Bureau of Justice Statistics, Department of Justice, Washington, DC, 2008; Christopher Mumola, "Incarcerated Parents and Their Children," Bureau of Justice Statistics, Special Report, Washington, DC, 2000, NCJ 182335. At year-end 2008, federal and state prisons held over 1.6 million inmates (1,610,446) under their jurisdiction (*State and Federal Prisoners and Prison Facilities,* Bureau of Justice Statistics, Department of Justice, Washington, DC, http://bjs.ojp.usdoj.gov/index.cfm?ty=tp&tid=13).

2. "Juvenile Residential Facility Census, 2002: Selected Findings," Bulletin, OJJDP National Report Series, June 2006, NCJ 211080.

3. The overwhelming number of prisoners exiting prison has caused a national prisoner reentry crisis. Policy makers are searching for strategies for how best to handle the reentry crisis. Chapter 10 is dedicated to a discussion of the role of the faith factor in effectively addressing the prisoner reentry crisis.

4. From 2000 to 2008 the number of jail inmates rose from 621,149 to 785,556, and declined to 767,620 in 2009. "Local Jail Inmates and Jail Facilities," Bureau of Justice Statistics, Department of Justice, Washington, DC, http://bjs.ojp.usdoj.gov/index.cfm?ty=tp&tid=12.

5. Joan Petersilia, "When Prisoners Return to the Community: Political, Economic, and Social Consequences," U.S. Department of Justice, Office of Justice Programs, National Institute of Justice, Washington, DC, 2000, NCJ 184253; Petersilia, *When Prisoners Come Home: Parole and Prisoner Reentry* (New York: Oxford University Press, 2003).

6. Jeremy Travis, Amy J. Solomon, Michelle Waul, *From Prison to Home: The Dimensions and Consequences of Prisoner Reentry* (Washington, DC: Urban Institute, 2001 [NCJ 190429]); Jeremy Travis, "But They All Come Back: Rethinking Prisoners Reentry," U.S. Department of Justice, Office of Justice Programs, National Institute of Justice, Washington, DC, 2000, NCJ 181413.

7. Joan Petersilia, "Parole and Prisoner Reentry in the United States," *Perspectives* 24 (2000): 32–46 [NCJ 184143].

8. Ingrid A. Binswanger, Marc F. Stern, Richard A. Deyo, Patrick J. Heagerty, Allen Cheadle, Joann G. Elmore, and Thomas D. Koepsell, "Release from Prison—A High Risk of Death for Former Inmates," *New England Journal of Medicine* 356 (2007): 536.

9. Elizabeth I. Johnson and Jane Waldfogel, "Children of Incarcerated Parents: Cumulative Risk and Children's Living Arrangements," JCPR Working Paper #306, Joint Center for Poverty Research, Northwestern University/University of Chicago, Chicago, 2002, http://www.jcpr.org/wp/wpprofile.cfm?id=364.

10. Glaze and Maruschak, "Parents in Prison and Their Minor Children."

11. See Frank Furstenberg, "Family Change and the Welfare of Children: What Do We Know and What Can We Do about It?" in *Gender and Family Change in Industrialized Countries,* ed. Karen O. Mason and A. M. Jensen (Oxford: Clarendon Press, 1995), 245–57; Barry Krisberg, *The Plight of Children Whose Parents Are in Prison* (Oakland, CA: National Council on Crime and Delinquency, 2001).

12. Denise Johnston, "Effects of Parental Incarceration," in *Children of Incarcerated Parents,* ed. Katherine Gabel and Denise Johnston (New York: Lexington Books, 1995).

13. John Hagan and Ronit Dinovitzer, "Collateral Consequences of Imprisonment for Children, Communities and Prisoners," in *Crime and Justice*, vol. 26, ed. Michael Tonry and Joan Petersilia (Chicago: University of Chicago Press, 1999), 121–62.

14. Child Welfare League of America, Federal Resource Center for Children of Prisoners; see http://www.cwla.org/.

15. Krisberg, *Plight of Children Whose Parents Are in Prison.*

16. William H. Sack and Jack Seidler, "Should Children Visit Their Parents in Prison?" *Law and Human Behavior* 2 (1978): 261–66; Sack, "Children of Imprisoned Fathers," *Psychiatry* 40 (1977): 163–74; and Sack, Seidler, and Susan Thomas, "The Children of Imprisoned Parents: A Psychosocial Exploration," *American Journal of Prothopsychiatry* 46 (1976): 618–28.

17. Travis A. Fritsch and John D. Burkhead, "Behavioral Reactions of Children to Parental Absence Due to Imprisonment," *Family Relations* 30 (1981): 83–88; Brenda G. McGowan and K. L. Blumenthal, *Why Punish the Children? A Study of Children of Women Prisoners* (Hackensack, NJ: National Council on Crime and Delinquency, 1978).

18. Elijah Anderson, *Code of the Street: Decency, Violence and the Moral Life of the Inner City* (New York: W. W. Norton, 1999); C. Mumola, "Incarcerated Parents and Their Children," U.S. Department of Justice, Office of Justice Programs, Bureau of Justice Statistics, Washington, DC, 2000, NCJ 182335

19. See Katherine Gabel and Denise Johnston, eds., *Children of Incarcerated Parents* (New York: Lexington Books, 1995); Women's Prison Association, *Breaking the Cycle of Despair: Children of Incarcerated Mothers* (New York: Author, 1995).

20. Joseph Murray and David Farrington, "Evidence-Based Programs for Children of Prisoners," reaction essay, *Criminology and Public Policy* 5 (2007): 721–36.

21. See William Damon, *The Path to Purpose: How Young People Find Their Calling in Life* (New York: Free Press, 2008); Damon, *Noble Purpose* (Radnor, PA: Templeton Press, 2003); Damon, *The Youth Charter: How Communities Can Work Together to Raise Standards for All Our Children* (New York: Free Press, 1997); Damon, *The Moral Child: Nurturing Children's Natural Moral Growth* (New York: Free Press, 1990).

22. Damon, *Path to Purpose.*

23. Damon, *Moral Child.*

24. Joseph P. Tierney, Jen Baldwin Grossman, and Nancy L. Resch, *Making a Difference: An Impact Study of Big Brothers and Big Sisters* (Philadelphia: Public/Private Ventures, 1995).

25. David L. DuBois, B. E. Holloway, J. C. Valentine, and H. Cooper, "Effectiveness of Mentoring Programs for Youth: A Meta-Analytic Review," *American Journal of Community Psychology* 30 (2002): 157–97.

26. Jean B. Grossman and Jean E. Rhodes, "The Test of Time: Predictors and Effects of Duration in Youth Mentoring Programs," *American Journal of Community Psychology* 30 (2002): 199–206.

27. Timothy Cavell, David DuBois, Michael Karcher, Thomas Keller, and Jean Rhodes, "Strengthening Mentoring Opportunities for At-Risk Youth," Policy Brief, University of Illinois, Chicago, 2009.

28. DuBois et al., "Effectiveness of Mentoring Programs for Youth."

29. Cavell et al., "Strengthening Mentoring Opportunities for At-Risk Youth."

30. David L. DuBois and Michael A. Karcher, eds., *Handbook of Youth Mentoring* (Thousand Oaks, CA: Sage, 2005).

31. The possibilities of this particular collaboration as well as other research initiatives would play a key role in my decision to leave Vanderbilt University and accept the offer to come to the University of Pennsylvania and partner with DiIulio, as well as connecting with new colleagues at Public/Private Ventures.

32. Located in North Philadelphia, Greater Exodus Baptist Church and Pastor Herbert Lusk, a former Philadelphia Eagles running back, would become one of the key churches to participate in the project.

33. Public/Private Ventures has a long and successful history of leading major demonstration and evaluation projects. To learn more about P/PV's track record in leading projects such as Amachi or to review some of their publications, go to http://www.ppv.org/ppv/index.asp.

34. See Linda Jucovy, *Amachi: Mentoring Children of Prisoners in Philadelphia* (Philadelphia: Public/Private Ventures and the Center for Research on Religion and Urban Civil Society, University of Pennsylvania, 2003); see also Tracy A. Hartmann, *Moving beyond the Walls: Faith and Justice Partnerships Working with High-Risk Youth* (Philadelphia: Public/Private Ventures, 2003).

35. The Church Volunteer Coordinator (CVC) often had previous experience with youth in the congregation. Among other duties, CVCs stayed in touch with mentors on a weekly basis to monitor progress regarding the mentoring relationship. Participating congregations received an annual stipend of fifteen hundred dollars, as well as five thousand dollars to support the part-time CVC position.

36. Ram A. Cnaan and Stephanie C. Boddie, "Philadelphia Census of Congregations and Their Involvement in Social Service Delivery," *Social Service Review* 75 (2001): 559–70.

37. DuBois and Karcher, *Handbook of Youth Mentoring*; Jean B. Grossman and Jean E. Rhodes, "The Test of Time: Predictors and Effects of Duration in Youth Mentoring Programs," *American Journal of Community Psychology* 30 (2002): 199–206; Tierney et al., *Making a Difference.*

38. Lillian T. Eby, Tammy D. Allen, Sarah C. Evans, Thomas Ng, and David L. DuBois, "Does Mentoring Matter? A Multidisciplinary Meta-Analysis Comparing Mentored and Non-Mentored Individuals," *Journal of Vocational Behavior* 72 (2008): 254–67; Cavell et al., "Strengthening Mentoring Opportunities for At-Risk Youth."

39. Jucovy, *Amachi.*

40. Strikingly, 82 percent of Amachi mentors were African American and an additional 8 percent were Latina. In addition, 34 percent were African American males—a significant percentage. For most mentoring programs, this is the most difficult group of volunteers to attract, and one that programs are most interested in recruiting so they can be paired with African American male children who might otherwise be growing up without a supportive male adult of the same race who is a consistent presence in their lives.

41. Jucovy, *Amachi.*

42. See the link to Amachi at P/PV's website, http://www.ppv.org/ppv/initiative.asp?section_id=22&initiative_id=51.

43. W. Wilson Goode Sr. and Thomas J. Smith, *Building from the Ground Up: Creating Effective Programs to Mentor Children of Prisoners (The Amachi Model)* (Philadelphia: Public/Private Ventures, 2005).

CHAPTER 4—THE CENTER FOR NEIGHBORHOOD ENTERPRISE AND THE VIOLENCE-FREE ZONE

1. Robert Woodson Sr., *The Triumphs of Joseph: How Today's Community Healers Are Reviving Our Streets and Neighborhoods* (New York: Free Press, 1998), 76.
2. Following the only loss of his political career, former House Speaker Tip O'Neill would coin the expression, "All politics is local," pinning the loss on his failure to consider the voters in his very own backyard. The expression would become O'Neill's most well-known quote and a classic reminder to those running for office not to overlook the importance of local constituents.
3. This chapter draws heavily from several of my research collaborations with William Wubbenhorst on the Violence-Free Zone in Milwaukee, Wisconsin, and Richmond, Virginia.
4. This data also included results from an annual student climate survey in Milwaukee that elicits student views on the degree of safety, order, and adherence to rules in their current school.
5. I am fully aware that randomized research designs provide a much more rigorous and preferred approach when it comes to evaluating the merits of various program interventions. Unfortunately, major-impact studies employing such stringent rigor are rare due to significant costs, time, and resources necessary to complete them. The current research, however, is useful in providing early insights into the functioning and results of the VFZ in Milwaukee and Richmond public schools. This research represents a first step in pursuit of a longitudinal and randomized impact study (i.e., random assignment of students into experimental and control groups) of the VFZ.
6. Excluding charter schools.
7. In January 2008 the Milwaukee Public School System added a seventh school, Madison, and in September 2009 an eighth, Bradley Tech, both of which were assigned to LCC for management of the VFZ.
8. The 15 percent increase in violent incidents is calculated by comparing the 5,261 violent incidents in AY 2006–2007, to the 6,054 violent incidents in AY 2008–2009 at Milwaukee Public Schools. Further, the 19 percent increase in the number of nonviolent incidents is based on 56,804 cases for AY 2006–2007, and 67,718 nonviolent incidents in AY 2008–2009 at Milwaukee Public Schools.
9. The 11 percent decrease in the number of violent incidents is based on 2,330 cases for AY 2006–2007, and 2,065 nonviolent incidents in AY 2008–2009 at Milwaukee Public Schools. The 21 percent decrease in the number of nonviolent incidents is based on 34,223 cases for AY 2006–2007, and 26,870 nonviolent incidents in AY 2008–2009 at Milwaukee Public Schools.
10. Teaching days are calculated by the number of students times the number of school days attended.

CHAPTER 5—A SYSTEMATIC REVIEW OF THE LITERATURE

1. There are some English proverbs that are worded similarly: Idle hands are the devil's workshop; Idle hands are the devil's tools; Idle brains are the devil's workhouses; An idle brain is the devil's workshop; If the Devil finds a Man idle, he'll set him at work; The devil finds work (or mischief) for idle hands to do.
2. Travis Hirschi and Rodney Stark, "Hellfire and Delinquency," *Social Problems* 17 (1969): 202–13.

3. S. Burkett and M. White, "Hellfire and Delinquency: Another Look," *Journal for the Scientific Study of Religion* 13, no. 4 (1974): 455–62.

4. See S. L. Albrecht, B. A. Chadwick, and D. Alcorn, "Religiosity and Deviance: Application of an Attitude-Behavior Contingent Consistency Model," *Journal for the Scientific Study of Religion* 16 (1977): 263–74; P. Higgins and G. Albrecht, "Hellfire and Delinquency Revisited," *Social Forces* 55, no. 4 (1977): 952–58; G. Jensen and M. Erickson, "The Religious Factor and Delinquency: Another Look at the Hellfire Hypothesis," in *The Religious Dimension*, ed. Robert Wuthnow (New York: Academic Press, 1979), 157–77.

5. R. Stark, L. Kent, and D. P. Doyle, "Religion and Delinquency: The Ecology of a Lost Relationship," *Journal of Research in Crime and Delinquency* 19 (1982): 4–24.

6. R. Stark, "Religion as Context: Hellfire and Delinquency One More Time," *Sociology of Religion* 57 (1996): 163–73; Stark et al., "Religion and Delinquency."

7. Richard B. Freeman, "Who Escapes? The Relation of Churchgoing and Other Background Factors to the Socioeconomic Performance of Black Male Youths from Inner-City Tracts," in *The Black Youth Employment Crisis*, ed. R. B. Freeman and H. J. Holzer (Chicago: University of Chicago Press, 1986), 353–376.

8. Decades of research confirm that inner-city black youth (especially males) represent one of the groups most at risk for participation in delinquent and criminal activity.

9. B. R. Johnson, D. B. Larson, S. D. Li, and S. J. Jang, "Escaping from the Crime of Inner Cities: Church Attendance and Religious Salience among Disadvantaged Youth," *Justice Quarterly* 17 (2000): 377–91.

10. B. R. Johnson and M. V. Siegel, "The Great Escape: How Religion Alters the Delinquent Behavior of High-Risk Adolescents," ISR Report, Institute for Studies of Religion, Baylor University, 2008, http://www.isreligion.org/pdf/ISR_Great_Escape.pdf.

11. Ibid.

12. "The Role of African American Churches in Reducing Crime among Black Youth," ISR Report, Institute for Studies of Religion, Baylor University, 2001.

13. T. D. Evans, F. Cullen, V. Burton, R. G. Dunaway, G. Payne, and S. Kethineni, "Religion, Social Bonds, and Delinquency," *Deviant Behavior* 17 (1996): 43–70.

14. C. J. Baier and B. E. Wright, "'If You Love Me, Keep My Commandments': A Meta-Analysis of the Effect of Religion on Crime," *Journal of Research in Crime and Delinquency* 38 (2001): 3–21; B. R. Johnson, S. D. Li, D. B. Larson, and M. E. McCullough, "Religion and Delinquency: A Systematic Review of the Literature," *Journal of Contemporary Criminal Justice* 16 (2000): 32–52; B. R. Johnson, R. B. Thompkins, and D. Webb, "Objective Hope—Assessing the Effectiveness of Faith-Based Organizations: A Review of the Literature," ISR Report, Institute for Studies of Religion, Baylor University, 2002, www.isreligion.org/pdf/ISR_Objective_Hope.pdf.

15. Johnson et al., "Religion and Delinquency."

16. Baier and Wright. "'If You Love Me.'"

17. Johnson et al., "Objective Hope."

18. We acknowledge that the current systematic review does not carry the same weight as a meta-analysis, where effect sizes for individual studies are considered in the overall assessment of research literature under consideration. While meta-analysis is a more rigorous and transparent (i.e., standardized) method than traditional narrative synthesis or systematic reviews, its utility for summarizing past research is limited for nonexperimental, correlational studies, which make up a majority of the criminological research. We will be publishing a separate meta-analysis of this same research literature in 2011.

19. This systematic review was recently published as part of the Presidential Paper Series presented at the annual meeting of the American Society of Criminology, in November 2010. Byron R. Johnson and Sung Joon Jang, "Crime and Religion: Assessing the Role of the Faith Factor," in *Contemporary Issues in Criminological Theory and Research: The Role of Social Institutions*, ed. Richard Rosenfeld, Kenna Quinet, and Crystal Garcia (Belmont, CA: Wadsworth, 2010).

20. This meta-analysis would entail a statistical procedure for standardizing and evaluating the relative impact of select variables on other variables. Meta-analysis, while a highly valued research tool, remains relatively rare simply because this type of research takes so much time to complete.

21. Gregory S. Paul, "Cross-National Correlations of Quantifiable Societal Health with Popular Religiosity and Secularism in the Prosperous Democracies," *Journal of Religion and Society* 7 (1995): 1–17.

Chapter 6—Can a Faith-Based Prison Reduce Recidivism

1. Robert Martinson, "What Works? Questions and Answers about Prison Reform," *Public Interest* 35 (1974): 22–35.

2. Lawrence W. Sherman, Denise Gottfredson, Doris MacKenzie, John Eck, Peter Reuter, and Shawn Bushway, "Preventing Crime: An Overview," in "Preventing Crime: What Works, What Doesn't, What's Promising," a report to the U.S. Congress, 1997.

3. See, for example, Steve Aos, Polly Phipps, Robert Barnoski, and Roxanne Lieb, *The Comparative Costs and Benefits of Programs to Reduce Crime* (Seattle: Washington State Institute for Public Policy, 2001); Francis T. Cullen, "Rehabilitation and Treatment Programs," in *Crime: Public Policies for Crime Control*, ed. James Q. Wilson and Joan Petersilia (Oakland, CA: Institute for Contemporary Studies, 2002), 253–91; Gerald Gaes, Timothy J. Flanagan, Laurence L. Motiuk, and Lynn Stewart, "Adult Correctional Treatment," in *Prisons*, ed. Michael Tonry and Joan Petersilia (Chicago: University of Chicago Press, 1999), 361–426; Sarah Lawrence, Daniel Mears, Glenn Dublin, and Jeremy Travis, *The Practice and Promise of Prison Programming* (Washington, DC: Urban Institute, 2002); Doris L. MacKenzie and Laura J. Hickman, *What Works in Corrections? An Examination of the Effectiveness of the Type of Rehabilitation Programs Offered by Washington State Department of Corrections* (College Park: University of Maryland, 1998).

4. See Joan Petersilia, *When Prisoners Come Home: Parole and Prisoner Reentry* (Oxford: Oxford University Press, 2003), 177.

5. PF is the largest organized prison ministry in the United States. According to Prison Fellowship's most recent Annual Report, the ministry is supported by the efforts of over three hundred thousand volunteers. Some two hundred thousand prisoners per month participate in either Bible studies or seminars led by PF-trained volunteers in over 1,300 of the country's 1,850 state and federal correctional facilities (see *God at Work in Prison Fellowship: Annual Report Fiscal Year 2001–2002*, Prison Fellowship Ministries, 44180 Riverside Parkway, Lansdowne, VA 20176, www.prisonfellowship.org).

6. Prison Fellowship identifies itself as a not-for-profit, volunteer-reliant ministry whose mission is to "exhort, equip, and assist the Church in its ministry to prisoners,

ex-prisoners, victims, and their families, and to promote biblical standards of justice in the criminal justice system."

7. Norval Morris and David J. Rothman, *The Oxford History of the Prison: The Practice of Punishment in Western Society* (New York: Oxford University Press, 1998).

8. Byron R. Johnson, David B. Larson, and Timothy G. Pitts, "Religious Programs, Institutional Adjustment, and Recidivism among Former Inmates in Prison Fellowship Programs," *Justice Quarterly* 14 (1997): 145–66.

9. Byron R. Johnson, "Religious Programs and Recidivism among Former Inmates in Prison Fellowship Programs: A Long-Term Follow-Up Study," *Justice Quarterly* 21 (2004): 329–54.

10. From the TDCJ Feasibility Study for monitoring and tracking participants in IFI.

11. Several existing programs, as well as new programs, were subsequently identified as meeting this legislative goal: In-Prison Therapeutic Community, Pre-Release Therapeutic Community, Pre-Release Substance Abuse Treatment, and the Sex Offender Treatment Program.

12. Prison Fellowship was awarded the contract after responding to a TDCJ competitive grant solicitation.

13. *Finding Common Ground: 29 Recommendations of the Working Group on Human Needs and Faith-Based and Community Initiatives*, Search for Common Ground: Washington, DC, 2002.

14. See www.ifiprison.org.

15. Technically, IFI was actually launched in January 1997 at the Jester II Unit, but was officially launched in April with the first cohort of prisoners. The prison was renamed the Carol Vance Unit in 1999.

16. Initially, only offenders from Harris County were considered, and then surrounding counties were added in order to increase the potential pool size. In order to further increase the pool of potential applicants to the program, as of 2002, prisoners eventually returning to the Dallas–Fort Worth area have been added to the IFI selection process. This has increased significantly the number of participants currently in IFI, though it has no bearing on the current study sample.

17. The Texas Department of Criminal Justice and Prison Fellowship later agreed to increase the IFI population at the Vance Unit. As of April 2003, the IFI program held over two hundred prisoners, and currently houses more than three hundred prisoners.

18. For example, Prison Fellowship's costs to operate IFI in fiscal year 2000–2001 alone were $1.45 million.

19. These resources deal with the basics of Christianity and progressing to more advanced concepts and understandings of Christianity and spiritual growth.

20. This decision was not uniformly supported by either IFI institutional staff at the prison or those workers in aftercare.

21. The primary focus of the CJPC evaluation would be to examine if these programs, including IFI, were able to reduce recidivism. The CJPC was an official Texas agency independent of TDCJ or other criminal justice agencies and existed from 1983 to 2003. The CJPC evaluation of the IFI program can be accessed at http://web.archive.org/web/20030705113355/http://cjpc.state.tx.us/reports/adltrehab/IFIInitiative.pdf.

22. Because of my track record in publishing scholarly research examining the impact of religion and spiritual commitment in relation to delinquency, criminality, prisoner

adjustment, and recidivism, PF approached me and I subsequently agreed to conduct a second independent evaluation of IFI.

23. The information in this chapter largely draws upon the following report originally released by the Center for Research on Religion and Urban Civil Society, University of Pennsylvania, in 2003 and rereleased by Baylor University in 2006: Byron R. Johnson with David B. Larson, "The InnerChange Freedom Initiative: A Preliminary Evaluation of a Faith-Based Prison Program," Research Report, Institute for Studies of Religion, Baylor University, 2003/2006.

24. According to Mike Eisenberg, author of the evaluation conducted by the Criminal Justice Policy Council, programs implemented in correctional settings typically require two or three years to address start-up problems and institutionalize the program into day-to-day operations. IFI certainly experienced a number of significant start-up problems during the first several years of its existence. Interestingly, exactly those IFI participants, the initial members who had to deal with the problems associated with a new program, make up the study group in this research. Stated differently, IFI was not evaluated on those prisoners who went through the program after all the program problems and shortcomings were remedied; rather IFI is being assessed on the first offenders to participate in and leave from the program.

25. A fourth area in need of reform, changing prison release and revocation practices, is a reform presently beyond IFI's authority.

26. John Braithwaite, *Crime, Shame, and Reintegration* (New York: Cambridge University Press, 1989).

Chapter 7—Can a Faith-Based Prison Rehabilitate Inmates?

1. "Biblically based" refers to the idea that all program components can logically be based on scripture.

2. Shadd Maruna, *Making Good: How Ex-Convicts Reform and Rebuild Their Lives* (Washington, DC: American Psychological Association, 2001).

3. In order to protect the identity of mentors, volunteers, staff, and prisoners, pseudonyms are used in the dialogue.

4. See David Wexler, "Therapeutic Jurisprudence: An Overview," 2002, http://www.law.arizona.edu/depts/upr-intj/intj-0.html.

5. See also the description of "differential anticipation" in the classic work of Daniel Glaser, *The Effectiveness of a Prison and Parole System* (Indianapolis: Bobbs-Merrill, 1969).

6. See Donald Clemmer, *Prison Community* (Fort Worth, TX: Harcourt Brace College Publishers, 1987).

7. John Laub and Robert J. Sampson, "Understanding Desistance from Crime," in *Crime and Justice*, ed. M. Tonry and Norval Morris (Chicago: University of Chicago Press, 2001), 1–70.

8. Gresham M. Sykes and David Matza, "Techniques of Neutralization: A Theory of Delinquency," *American Sociological Review* 22 (1957): 664–70.

9. All inmates in the TDCJ system are transported to Huntsville and go through this prison when officially released on parole.

CHAPTER 8—JAILHOUSE RELIGION, SPIRITUAL TRANSFORMATION, AND LONG-TERM CHANGE

1. Charles "Tex" Watson, *Will You Die for Me? The Man Who Killed for Charles Manson Tells His Own Story* (Grand Rapids: Fleming H. Revell Company, 1978).
2. William E. Counselman, chaplaincy services coordinator for the Florida Department of Corrections, Tallahassee, Florida, August 1, 1984.
3. Film documentary, *Faith in the Big House* (Interlock Media, 2004), http://www.interlockmedia.com/productions/fitbh/fitbh.html.
4. Written by David Wilkerson, and published in 1963, the book has sold more than 15 million copies.
5. Cruz would publish a book, *Run Baby Run*, in 1968, documenting his story of coming to New York and being a gang leader and his subsequent conversion to Christianity through the ministry of David Wilkerson.
6. *The Cross and the Switchblade* would eventually become a motion picture in 1970, starring Pat Boone as David Wilkerson and Erik Estrada as Nicky Cruz.
7. More information on Champions for Life is available at www.billglasscfl.org.
8. A more detailed description of the reentry process as well as aftercare for ex-prisoners and the role of the faith factor are discussed in chapter 9.
9. Established in 1958, Teen Challenge provides youth, adults, and families with a comprehensive Christian faith-based solution to life-controlling drug and alcohol problems in order to become productive members of society. By applying biblical principles, Teen Challenge endeavors to help people become mentally sound, emotionally balanced, socially adjusted, physically well, and spiritually alive; www.teenchallengeusa.com.
10. See, for example, John Lofland, and Rodney Stark, "Becoming a World-Saver: A Theory of Conversion to a Deviant Perspective," *American Sociological Review* 30 (1965): 862–75.
11. Todd Clear and Melvina Sumter, "Prisoners, Prison, and Religion: Religion and Adjustment to Prison," *Journal of Offender Rehabilitation* 35 (2002): 127–59.
12. Byron R. Johnson, "Religiosity and Institutional Deviance: The Impact of Religious Variables upon Inmate Adjustment," *Criminal Justice Review* 12 (1987): 21–30; Johnson, David B. Larson, and Timothy G. Pitts, "Religious Programs, Institutional Adjustment, and Recidivism among Former Inmates in Prison Fellowship Programs," *Justice Quarterly* 14 (1997): 145–66; Johnson, "Religious Programs and Recidivism among Former Inmates in Prison Fellowship Programs: A Long-Term Follow-Up Study," *Justice Quarterly* 21 (2004): 329–54; Johnson with David B. Larson, "The InnerChange Freedom Initiative: A Preliminary Evaluation of a Faith-Based Prison Program," Research Report, Institute for Studies of Religion, Baylor University, 2003/2006; Melvina Sumter, "Religiousness and Post-Release Community Adjustment," doctoral dissertation, Florida State University, 2000; Amy Solomon, C. G. Roman, and M. Waul, "Summary of Focus Group with Ex-Prisoners in the District: Ingredients for Successful Reintegration," Urban Institute, Washington, DC, 2001.
13. Byron R. Johnson, "Hellfire and Corrections: A Quantitative Study of Florida Prison Inmates," PhD dissertation, Florida State University, 1984.
14. Incidentally, this study was the one that presented problems for folks from Champions for Life.

15. Watson, *Will You Die for Me?* From chapter 16 of the online book: http://www.aboundinglove.org/sensational/wydfm/wydfm-018.php.

16. Including Waly Bacre Ndiaye (former U.N. commissioner on summary and arbitrary executions), the World Council of Churches, Pope John Paul II, former Italian prime minister Romano Prodi, Newt Gingrich, Pat Robertson, and Ron Carlson, the brother of Tucker's murder victim Debbie Thornton.

17. Following the *Furman vs. George* Supreme Court case, there were no executions in Florida between May 1964 and May 1979.

18. In 1998 I traveled to visit a prison in Quito, Ecuador, where the conditions were even worse than those at Changi Prison.

19. A former British state, Singapore was influenced by British customs in many different ways, including the hanging of those receiving the death penalty.

20. Rev. Henry Khoo died in 2008 at the age of seventy-six. He ministered to prisoners as a chaplain for thirty-eight years.

21. Oswald Chambers, *My Utmost for His Highest* (Uhrichsville, OH: Barbour and Company, 1963), 210.

22. Sheldon Glueck and Eleanor Glueck, *Unraveling Juvenile Delinquency* (New York: Commonwealth Fund, 1950).

23. Robert J. Sampson and John H. Laub, "Crime and Deviance over the Life Course: The Salience of Adult Social Bonds," *American Sociological Review* 55 (1995): 609–27.

24. Robert J. Sampson and John H. Laub, *Crime in the Making: Pathways and Turning Points through Life* (Cambridge, MA: Harvard University Press, 1993).

25. See, for example, Julie Horney, Wayne D. Osgood, and H. Marshall-Ineke, "Criminal Careers in the Short-Term: Intra-Individual Variability in Crime and Its Relation to Local Life Circumstances," *American Sociological Review* 60 (1995): 655–73; Doris L. MacKenzie, K. Browning, H. Priu, S. Skroban, and D. Smith, "Probationer Compliance with Conditions of Supervision," unpublished report, National Institute of Justice, U.S. Department of Justice, Washington, DC, 1998; MacKenzie and Spencer D. Li, "The Impact of Formal and Informal Social Controls on the Criminal Activities of Probationers," *Journal of Research in Crime and Delinquency* 39 (2002): 243–76.

26. Doris L. MacKenzie, *What Works in Corrections: Reducing the Criminal Activities of Offenders and Delinquents* (New York: Cambridge University Press, 2006).

27. Peggy Giordano, Stephen A. Cernkovich, and Jennifer L. Rudolph, "Gender, Crime, and Desistance: Toward a Theory of Cognitive Transformation," *American Journal of Sociology* 107 (2002): 990–1064.

28. Peggy C. Giordano, Monica A. Longmore, Ryan D. Schroeder, and Patrick M. Seffrin, "A Life-Course Perspective on Spirituality and Desistance from Crime," *Criminology* 46 (2008): 99–132.

29. See also Shadd Maruna, *Making Good: How Ex-Offenders Reform and Reclaim Their Lives* (Washington, DC: American Psychological Association, 2001); Charles M. Terry, *The Fellas: Overcoming Prison and Addiction* (Belmont, CA: Wadsworth, 2003); Karen Heimer and Ross L. Matsueda, "A Symbolic Interactionist Theory of Motivation and Deviance: Interpreting Psychological Research," in *Motivation and Delinquency*, ed. D. Wayne Osgood (Lincoln: University of Nebraska Press, 1997), 223–276.

30. Maruna, *Making Good*.

31. Victim-Offender Mediation Programs (VOMP), also known as Victim-Offender Reconciliation Programs (VORP), is a restorative justice approach that brings

offenders face-to-face with the victims of their crimes with the assistance of a trained mediator, usually a community volunteer. Crime is personalized as offenders learn the human consequences of their actions, and victims (whom the criminal justice system may ignore) have the opportunity to speak their minds and their feelings to the one who most ought to hear them, contributing to the healing process of the victim. Offenders take meaningful responsibility for their actions by mediating a restitution agreement with the victim, to restore the victims' losses in whatever ways that may be possible. Restitution may be monetary or symbolic; it may consist of work for the victim, community service, or anything else that creates a sense of justice between the victim and the offender. For more information on victim-offender reconciliation go to http://vorp.com/.

32. To make it even more of a long shot, sex offenders and inmates convicted of murder were no longer accepted into the program shortly after Flowers entered the Inner-Change Freedom Initiative.

33. Conversations on July 26 and 28, 2010.

Chapter 9—Why Religion Matters

1. See also Harold Koenig, David B. Larson, and Michael E. McCullough, *Handbook of Religion and Health* (Oxford: Oxford University Press, 2001); and Byron R. Johnson, "Objective Hope—Assessing the Effectiveness of Faith-Based Organizations: A Review of the Literature," ISR Report, Institute for Studies of Religion, Baylor University, 2002. In addition to crime and delinquency, these systematic reviews of the research literature document the protective role of religion in depression, suicide, mortality, promiscuous sex, alcohol abuse, and drug use/abuse.

2. Gary A. Tobin and Aryeh Weinberg, *Profiles of the American University*, vol. 1, *Political Beliefs and Behavior of College Faculty* (San Francisco: Institute for Jewish and Community Research, 2006); Tobin and Weinberg, *Profiles of the American University*, vol. 2, *Political Beliefs and Behavior of College Faculty* (San Francisco: Institute for Jewish and Community Research, 2007).

3. A completely separate category would represent scholars who keep their faith private because they believe it is inappropriate for one's faith to be anything but private. In other words, keeping their faith private is a preference.

4. The election of Bush signaled that the role of religion, the "armies of compassion," and faith-based organizations would be a prominent feature of his administration. NIJ recognized it knew little about the subject and certainly had not been funders of research assessing the link between faith-based approaches and crime reduction.

5. In this particular article I found that increasing religious practices were a deterrent to future criminal activities.

6. C. Baier and B. Wright, "'If You Love Me, Keep My Commandments': A Meta-Analysis of the Effects of Religion on Crime," *Journal of Research in Crime and Delinquency* 38 (2001): 3–21. Baier and Wright reviewed a total of sixty published studies and found that (1) religious beliefs and behaviors exert a moderate deterrent effect on individuals' criminal behavior, and (2) conceptual and methodological approaches account for some of the inconsistencies in the research literature. Byron R. Johnson with Ralph Brett Tompkins and Derek Webb, "Objective Hope Assessing the Effectiveness of Faith-Based Organizations: A Review of the Literature," ISR Report, Institute for Studies of Religion, Baylor University, 2006. In a second review,

Johnson and colleagues reviewed 151 studies that examined the relationship between religiosity and drug use (n=54) or alcohol use (n=97) and abuse. The vast majority of these studies demonstrate that participation in religious activities is associated with less of a tendency to use or abuse drugs (87 percent) or alcohol (94 percent). These findings hold regardless of the population under study (i.e., children, adolescents, and adult populations), or whether the research was conducted prospectively or retrospectively. In this same study, Johnson reviewed 46 published studies that examined the religiosity-delinquency relationship. Seventy-eight percent of these studies report that reductions in delinquency and criminal acts are associated with higher levels of religious activity and involvements.

7. See, for example, Richard B. Freeman, "Who Escapes? The Relation of Churchgoing and Other Background Factors to the Socioeconomic Performance of Black Male Youths from Inner-city Poverty Tracts," in *The Black Youth Employment Crisis*, ed. R. B. Freeman and H. J. Holzer (Chicago: University of Chicago Press, 1986), 353–376; Byron R. Johnson, David B. Larson, Sung Joon Jang, and Spencer Li, "Who Escapes the Crime of Inner Cities: Church Attendance and Religious Salience among Disadvantaged Youth," *Justice Quarterly* 17 (2006): 701–15.

8. Sung Joon Jang and Byron R. Johnson, "Neighborhood Disorder, Individual Religiosity, and Adolescent Drug Use: A Test of Multilevel Hypotheses," *Criminology* 39 (2001): 501–35.

9. T. David Evans, Francis Cullen, V. Burton, R. G. Dunaway, G. Payne, and S. Kethineni, "Religion, Social Bonds, and Delinquency," *Deviant Behavior* 17 (1996): 43–70.

10. Byron R. Johnson, Sung Joon Jang, David B. Larson, and Spencer Li, "Does Adolescent Religious Commitment Matter? A Reexamination of the effects of Religiosity on Delinquency," *Journal of Research in Crime and Delinquency* 38 (2001): 22–44.

11. B. Johnson, D. Larson, S. J. Jang, and S. Li, "The 'Invisible Institution' and Black Youth Crime: The Church as an Agency of Local Social Control," *Journal of Youth and Adolescence* 29 (2000): 479–98; Johnson et al., "Who Escapes the Crime of Inner Cities?"

12. J. M. Wallace and T. A. Forman, "Religion's Role in Promoting Health and Reducing the Risk among American Youth," *Health Education and Behavior* 25 (1998): 721–41.

13. Evans et al., "Religion, Social Bonds, and Delinquency"; David T. Evans, Francis T. Cullen, R. Gregory Dunaway, and Velmer S. Burton, "Religion and Crime Reexamined: The Impact of Religion, Secular Controls, and Social Ecology on Adult Criminality," *Criminology* 33 (1995): 195–224; Mark Regnerus, "Linked Lives, Faith, and Behavior: Intergenerational Religious Influence on Adolescent Delinquency," *Journal for the Scientific Study of Religion* 42, no. 2 (2003): 189–203; John M. Wallace and Tyrone A. Forman, "Religion's Role in Promoting Health and Reducing the Risk among American Youth," *Health Education and Behavior* 25 (1998): 721–41.

14. Byron R. Johnson and Sung Joon Jang "Crime and Religion: Assessing the Role of the Faith Factor," in Contemporary Issues in Criminological Theory and Research: The Role of Social Institutions, ed. Richard Rosenfeld, Kenna Quinet, and Crystal Garcia. (Belmont, CA: Wadsworth, 2010); Byron R. Johnson, "The Role of Religious Institutions in Responding to Crime and Delinquency," in *The Oxford Handbook of the Sociology of Religion*, ed. Peter B. Clarke (Oxford: Oxford University Press, 2009), 857–75.

15. Robert D. Putnam et al., *Better Together: Report of the Saguaro Seminar* (Cambridge, MA: Harvard University, John F. Kennedy School of Government, 2001).

16. In fact, this is the subject of Putnam's new book: Robert D. Putnam and David Campbell, *American Grace: How Religion Divides and Unites Us* (New York: Simon and Schuster, 2010).

17. Chaeyoon Lim and Robert D. Putnam, "Praying Alone Is No Fun: Religion, Social Networks, and Subjective Well-Being," paper presented at the Legatum Institute, London, England, 2009.

18. Ibid.

19. Marvin D. Krohn and Terence P. Thornberry, "Network Theory: A Model for Understanding Drug Abuse among African-American and Hispanic Youth," in *Drug Abuse among Minority Youth: Advances in Research and Methodology*, ed. Mario R. De La Rosa and Juan-Luis Recio Adrados (NIDA Research Monograph 130; Washington, DC: U.S. Department of Health and Human Services, 1993).

20. Walter Reckless, Simon Dinitz, and Ellen Murray, "Self-Concept as an Insulator against Delinquency," *American Sociological Review* 21 (1956): 744–56.

21. Sung Joon Jang and Byron R. Johnson, "Neighborhood Disorder, Individual Religiosity, and Adolescent Drug Use: A Test of Multilevel Hypotheses," *Criminology* 39 (2001): 501–35; Jang, Christopher Bader, and Johnson, "The Cumulative Advantage of Religiosity in Preventing Drug Use," *Journal of Drug Issues* 38, no. 3 (2008): 771–98.

22. Byron R. Johnson, Sung Joon Jang, David B. Larson, and Spencer D. Li, "Does Adolescent Religious Commitment Matter? A Reexamination of the Effects of Religiosity on Delinquency," *Journal of Research in Crime and Delinquency* 38 (2001): 22–44.

23. Regnerus, "Linked Lives, Faith, and Behavior"; Richard J. Petts, "Family and Religious Characteristics' Influence on Delinquency Trajectories from Adolescence to Young Adulthood," *American Sociological Review* 74 (2009): 465–83.

24. Freeman, "Who Escapes?"; Johnson et al., "Who Escapes the Crime of Inner Cities?"

25. Jang and Johnson, "Neighborhood Disorder."

26. Michelle J. Pearce, Stephanie M. Jones, Mary E. Schwab-Stone, and Vladislav Ruchkin, "The Protective Effects of Religiousness and Parent Involvement on the Development of Conduct Problems among Youth Exposed to Violence," *Child Development* 74 (2003): 1682–96.

27. Robert Crosnoe, Kristan Glasgow Erickson, and Stanford M. Dornbusch, "Protective Functions of Family Relationships and School Factors on the Deviant Behavior of Adolescent Boys and Girls: Reducing the Impact of Risky Friendships," *Youth and Society* 33 (2002): 515–44; Richard Jessor, Jill Van Den Bos, Judith Vanderryn, Frances M. Costa, and M. Turbin, "Protective Factors in Adolescent Problem Behavior: Moderator Effects and Developmental Change," *Developmental Psychology* 31 (1995): 923–33; Alan W. Stacy, Michael D. Newcomb, and Peter M. Bentler, "Interactive and Higher-Order Effects of Social Influences on Drug Use," *Journal of Health and Social Behavior* 33 (1992): 226–41; Thomas A. Wills, Donato Vaccaro, and Grace McNamara, "The Role of Life Events, Family Support, and Competence in Adolescent Substance Use: A Test of Vulnerability and Protective Factors," *American Journal of Community Psychology* 20 (1992): 349–74.

28. Johnson et al., "Who Escapes the Crime of Inner Cities?"

29. Johnson et al., "'Invisible Institution' and Black Youth Crime"; "The Role of African American Churches in Reducing Crime among Black Youth," ISR Report, Institute for Studies of Religion, Baylor University, 2001.

30. David T. Evans, Francis T. Cullen, R. Gregory Dunaway, and Velmer S. Burton,

"Religion and Crime Reexamined: The Impact of Religion, Secular Controls, and Social Ecology on Adult Criminality," *Criminology* 33 (1995): 195–224.

31. Robert J. Sampson and John H. Laub, "A Life-Course View of the Development of Crime," *ANNALS: The American Academy of Political and Social Science* 602 (2005): 12–45; Richard J. Petts, "Trajectories of Religious Participation from Adolescence to Young Adulthood," *Journal for the Scientific Study of Religion* 48 (2009): 552–71.

32. Jeanette Hercik, *Rediscovering Compassion: An Evaluation of Kairos Horizon Communities in Prison* (Fairfax, VA: Caliber Associates, 2005).

33. Byron R. Johnson, "Religious Program and Recidivism among Former Inmates in Prison Fellowship Programs: A Long-Term Follow-Up Study," *Justice Quarterly* 21 (2004): 329–54; Byron R. Johnson, David B. Larson, and Timothy Pitts, "Religious Programming, Institutional Adjustment and Recidivism among Former Inmates in Prison Fellowship Programs," *Justice Quarterly* 14 (1997): 145–66.

34. Byron R. Johnson, "The InnerChange Freedom Initiative: A Preliminary Evaluation of a Faith-Based Prison Program," ISR Report, Institute for Studies of Religion, Baylor University, 2003.

35. Based on a Catholic model, the faith-based prison went by the name Humaita.

36. Byron R. Johnson, "Assessing the Impact of Religious Programs and Prison Industry on Recidivism: An Exploratory Study," *Journal of Corrections* 28 (2002): 7–11.

37. See Travis Hirschi, *Causes of Delinquency* (Berkeley: University of California Press, 1969). Social control theory is not unique in its theoretical relevance for the role of religion in reducing or preventing crime and delinquency. Studying and emphasizing factors that essentially keep people from breaking the law, control theorists reason, ultimately advances our understanding of how to pursue crime prevention. It is easy to see how religion could play a "bonding" role between each of the four elements at the heart of social control theory: attachments, commitments, involvements, and beliefs.

38. Freeman, "Who Escapes?"; Johnson et al., "Who Escapes the Crime of Inner Cities?"

39. D. G. Blazer and E. Palmore, "Religion and Aging in a Longitudinal Panel," *Gerontologist* 16 (1976): 82–85; M. J. Graney, "Happiness and Social Participation in Aging," *Journal of Gerontology* 30 (1975): 701–6; K. S. Markides, "Aging, Religiosity, and Adjustment: A Longitudinal Analysis," *Journal of Gerontology* 38 (1983): 621–25; Marc A. Musick, "Religion and Subjective Health among Black and White Elders," *Journal of Health and Social Behavior* 37 (1996): 221–37; A. P. Tix and P. A. Frazier, "The Use of Religious Coping during Stressful Life Events: Main Effects, Moderation, and Medication," *Journal of Consulting and Clinical Psychology* 66 (1997): 411–22; F. K. Willits and D. M. Crider, "Religion and Well-Being: Men and Women in the Middle Years," *Review of Religious Research* 29 (1988): 281–94.

40. Sheena Sethi and Martin E. P. Seligman, "The Hope of Fundamentalists," *Psychological Science* 5 (1993): 58.

41. Christopher Ellison and Linda K. George, "Religious Involvement, Social Ties, and Social Support in a Southeastern Community," *Journal for the Scientific Study of Religion* 33 (1994): 46–61; D. E. Bradley, "Religious Involvement and Social Resources: Evidence from the Data Set 'Americans' Changing Lives,'" *Journal for the Scientific Study of Religion* 34 (1995): 259–67; Harold G. Koenig, D. Hays, D. Larson, L. George, H. Cohen, K. McCullough, K. Meador, and D. Blazer, "Does Religious Attendance Prolong Survival? A Six-Year Follow-up Study of 3,968 Older Adults," *Journal of Gerontology* 54 (1999): 370–76.

42. Mark D. Regnerus, "Shaping Schooling Success: Religious Socialization and Educational Outcomes in Metropolitan Public Schools," *Journal for the Scientific Study of Religion* 39 (2000): 363–70; Mark D. Regnerus, "Making the Grade: The Influence of Religion upon the Academic Performance of Youth in Disadvantaged Communities. Research Report," Institute for Studies of Religion. Baylor University, 2008; William Jeynes, "Religion, Intact Families, and the Achievement Gap," *Interdisciplinary Journal of Research on Religion* 3 (2007): 1–22.

43. Arthur C. Brooks, *Who Really Cares: The Surprising Truth about Compassionate Conservatism: America's Charity Divide—Who Gives, Who Doesn't, and Why It Matters* (New York: Basic Books, 2006).

44. Koenig et al., *Handbook of Religion and Health*.

45. Johnson, "Role of Religious Institutions in Responding to Crime and Delinquency."

46. Byron R. Johnson, "A Tale of Two Religious Effects: Evidence for the Protective and Prosocial Impact of Organic Religion," in *Authoritative Communities: The Scientific Case for Nurturing the Whole Child*, ed. Kathleen Kline (New York: Springer Press, 2007), 187–226.

Chapter 10—Prisoner Reentry and Aftercare

1. President George W. Bush, State of the Union Address, January 20, 2004.

2. From 319,598 to 1,540,805, and the parole population has increased by 374 percent (from 220,438 to 824,365) (U.S. Department of Justice, Bureau of Justice Statistics, 2008).

3. Jeremy Travis, *But They All Come Back: Facing the Challenges of Prisoner Reentry* (Washington, DC: Urban Institute Press, 2005).

4. Joan Petersilia, *When Prisoners Come Home: Parole and Prisoner Reentry* (New York: Oxford University Press, 2003).

5. P. A. Langan and D. J. Levin, "Recidivism of Prisoners Released in 1994," Bureau of Justice Statistics, U.S. Department of Justice, Washington, DC, 2002 (NCJ 193427).

6. "Parole, Desistance from Crime, and Community Integration," Committee on Community Supervision and Desistance from Crime, National Research Council, 2007.

7. Ingrid A. Binswanger, Marc F. Stern, Richard A. Deyo, Patrick J. Heagerty, Allen Cheadle, Joann G. Elmore, and Thomas D. Koepsell, "Release from Prison — A High Risk of Death for Former Inmates," *New England Journal of Medicine* 356 (2007): 157–65.

8. See, for example, R. McGowen, "The Well-Ordered Prison: England, 1780–1865," in *The Oxford History of the Prison: The Practice of Punishment in Western Society*, ed. Norval Morris and David J. Rothman (New York: Oxford University Press, 1995): ,71-99; E. M. Peters, "Prison before the Prison: The Ancient and Medieval Worlds," in *The Oxford History of the Prison: The Practice of Punishment in Western Society*, ed. Norval Morris and David J. Rothman (New York: Oxford University Press, 1995), 3-43.

9. Data based on face-to-face interviews with 13,986 inmates in 1991 and published by the Bureau of Justice Statistics. Similar surveys were conducted in 1974, 1979, and 1986.

10. This discussion draws from two of my recent papers: "Innovations in Effective Compassion: Compendium on Research, Outcomes, and Evaluation of Faith-Based and Community Initiatives," Office of the Secretary for Planning and Evaluation, U.S.

Department of Health and Human Services, June 2008; "The Faith Factor and Prisoner Reentry," *Interdisciplinary Journal of Research on Religion* 4 (2009): 1–21.

11. On the basis of a multivariate matched sampling method, seven variables most strongly predicted members of the PF groups: age, race, religious denomination, county of residence, military discharge, minimum sentence, and security classification.

12. B. Johnson, D. B. Larson, and T. Pitts, "Religious Programming, Institutional Adjustment, and Recidivism among Former Inmates in Prison Fellowship Programs," *Justice Quarterly* 14 (1997): 145–66.

13. B. Johnson, "Religious Program and Recidivism among Former Inmates in Prison Fellowship Programs: A Long-Term Follow-Up Study," *Justice Quarterly* 21 (2004): 329–54.

14. See T. Clear and M. Sumter, "Prisoner, Prison, and Religion: Religion and Adjustment to Prison," *Journal of Offender Rehabilitation* 35 (2002): 127–59; B. Johnson, *The InnerChange Freedom Initiative: A Preliminary Evaluation of a Faith-Based Prison Program*, ISR Report, Institute for Studies of Religion, Baylor University, 2003; Johnson, "Religious Program and Recidivism."

15. See Clear and Sumter, "Prisoner, Prison, and Religion"; J. M. Hercik, *Rediscovering Compassion: An Evaluation of Kairos Horizon Communities in Prison* (Fairfax, VA: Caliber Associates, 2005).

16. The comparison group was matched with IFI participants based on the following characteristics: race, age, offense type, and salient factor risk score (a correctional assessment tool commonly used in most prisons to help predict the level of risk that prisoners pose to correctional authorities).

17. The subculture of prison inmates has been an ongoing topic of sociological and criminological inquiry. Donald Clemmer coined the term "prisonization," whereby inmates become socialized into prison culture. An assumption of prisonization is that inmates internalize prison culture and their subsequent behavior is a reflection of this internalization.

18. Executive Order 13199 created the White House Office of Faith-Based and Community Initiatives on January 29, 2001.

19. Executive Order 13198 created five Centers for Faith-Based and Community Initiatives on January 29, 2001; Executive Order 13280 created two Centers for Faith-Based and Community Initiatives on December 12, 2002; Executive Order 13279 requires equal protection for faith-based and community organizations as of December 12, 2002; Executive Order 13342 created three new Centers for Faith-Based and Community Initiatives at the Departments of Commerce and Veterans Affairs and the Small Business Administration on June 1, 2004; and Executive Order 13397 created a new Center for Faith-Based and Community Initiatives at the Department of Homeland Security on March 7, 2006.

20. "Unlevel Playing Field: Barriers to Participation by Faith-Based and Community Organizations in Federal Social Service Programs," White House of Faith-Based and Community Initiatives, Washington, DC, August 2001.

21. J. Travis and C. Visher, eds., *Prisoner Reentry and Crime in America* (Cambridge: Cambridge University Press, 2005), 255–56.

22. The Recidivism Reduction and Second Chance Act authorizes $165 million annually to support mentoring programs, substance abuse treatment, literacy classes, job training, and other assistance intended to help ex-offenders pursue productive,

crime-free lives after their sentences are up. The bill authorized grant funding for fiscal years 2009 and 2010, for state and local governments to launch or continue programs to improve ex-offenders' return to society. It also allocated competitive grants to faith-based and community nonprofits to offer programs that link ex-offenders with mentors or that help them seek and keep jobs. The bill included elements of the Bush administration's Prisoner Re-Entry Initiative (PRI), launched in 2004, which connects ex-offenders with religious and secular nonprofits for mentoring and other programs intended to help them make a successful transition to community life.

23. The eleven sites include: City of Memphis Second Chance Ex-Felon Program (Memphis, TN); Allen Temple Housing and Economic Development Corporation (Oakland, CA); East of the River Clergy, Police and Community Partnership (Washington, DC); Exodus Transitional Community (East Harlem, NY); Holy Cathedral/ Word of Hope Ministries (Milwaukee, WI); Operation New Hope (Jacksonville, FL); SAFER Foundation (Chicago, IL); Search for Common Ground (Philadelphia, PA); Union Rescue Mission (Los Angeles, CA); Wheeler Avenue Baptist Church and the InnerChange Freedom Initiative (Houston, TX); America Works Detroit (Detroit, MI).

24. Participant eligibility for Ready4Work was determined based on three factors: (1) age of the ex-offender, (2) presenting offense, and (3) length of time pre- or postrelease. Ex-prisoners between the ages of eighteen and thirty-four who had most recently been incarcerated for a nonviolent felony offense and were no more than ninety days pre- or postrelease were eligible to enroll in the program.

25. C. Farley and S. Hackman, "Ready4Work in Brief—Interim Outcomes Are In: Recidivism at Half the National Average," P/PV in Brief, Public/Private Ventures, Philadelphia, PA, 2006.

26. Ibid.

27. C. Farley and W. McClanahan, "Ready4Work In Brief—Update on Outcomes; Reentry May Be Critical for States, Cities," P/PV in Brief, Public/Private Ventures, Philadelphia, PA, 2007, 2.

28. W. McClanahan, "P/PV Preview: Mentoring Ex-Prisoners in the Ready4Work Reentry Initiative," Public/Private Ventures, Philadelphia, PA, 2007.

29. See, for example, Rodney Stark, *For the Glory of God: How Monotheism Led to Reformations, Science, Witch-Hunts, and the End of Slavery* (Princeton, NJ: Princeton University Press, 2003).

30. See, for example, Gary A. Tobin, Aryeh K. Weinberg, and Jenna Ferer, *The Uncivil University* (San Francisco: Institute for Jewish and Community Research, 2005); Tobin and Weinberg, *Political Beliefs and Behavior of College Faculty*, vol. 1 (San Francisco: Institute for Jewish and Community Research, 2006); and Tobin and Weinberg, *Political Beliefs and Behavior of College Faculty*, vol. 2 (San Francisco: Institute for Jewish and Community Research, 2007).

31. See, for example, M. Musick and J. Wilson, *Volunteers: A Social Profile* (Bloomington: Indiana University Press, 2007), 308–10; B. Cornwell and J. A. Harrison, "Labor Unions and Voluntary Association Membership," *American Sociological Review* 69 (2004): 751–67.

32. See Big Brothers and Big Sisters of America (www.bbbsa.org).

33. Amachi: People of Faith Mentoring Children of Promise (www.amachimentoring. org).

34. Musick and Wilson, *Volunteers*.

35. See American Church Lists, www.americanchurchlists.com.

36. See S. Clain and C. E. Zech, "A Household Production Analysis of Religious and Charitable Activity," *American Journal of Economics and Sociology* 58 (1999): 923–46; Cornwell and Harrison, "Labor Unions and Voluntary Association Membership."

37. "Giving and Volunteering in the United States 2001: Findings from A National Survey," Independent Sector, Washington, DC; Arthur C. Brooks, *Who Really Cares: The Surprising Truth about Compassionate Conservatism: America's Charity Divide— Who Gives, Who Doesn't, and Why It Matters* (New York: Basic Books, 2006).

38. R. D. Putnam et al., *Better Together: Report of the Saguaro Seminar* (Cambridge, MA: Harvard University, John F. Kennedy School of Government, 2001).

39. Mark Early, president of Prison Fellowship Ministries, White House event on prisoner reentry in 2007.

40. See www.Out4Life.com or www.prisonfellowship.org.

41. Amachi Texas, a joint initiative between the Office of the Governor, the Texas Department of Criminal Justice, Texas Workforce Commission, OneStar Foundation, and Big Brothers Big Sisters of Texas, was launched in 2005. The program helps children of prisoners by working in communities throughout the state of Texas via mentoring relationships. The Amachi Texas initiative is currently the subject of a three-year evaluation that incorporates a randomized controlled study.

42. F. Cullen, "Rehabilitation and Treatment Programs," in *Crime: Public Policies for Crime Control*, ed. James Q. Wilson and Joan Petersilia (Oakland, CA: ICS Press, 2002), 253–89.

CHAPTER 11—NOT BY FAITH ALONE

1. http://www.Out4Life.com.

2. Byron R. Johnson and William Wubbenhorst, "Can Ex-Prisoners Stay Out for Life? A Case Study Assessing the Effectiveness of Out4Life," Institute for Studies of Religion, Baylor University, 2011.

3. See, for example, Byron R. Johnson, R. Brett Thompkins, and Derek Webb, "Objective Hope—Assessing the Effectiveness of Faith-Based Organizations: A Review of the Literature," ISR Report, Institute for Studies of Religion, Baylor University, www.isreligion.org/pdf/ISR_Objective_Hope.pdf); Harold G. Koenig, Michael E. McCullough, and David B. Larson, *Handbook of Religion and Health* (New York: Oxford University Press, 2001).

4. Marc A. Musick and John Wilson, *Volunteers: A Social Profile* (Indianapolis: Indiana University Press, 2008); Robert D. Putnam and David E. Campbell, *American Grace: How Religion Divides and Unites Us* (New York: Simon and Schuster, 2010); Arthur C. Brooks, *Who Really Cares: The Surprising Truth about Compassionate Conservatism: America's Charity Divide—Who Gives, Who Doesn't, and Why It Matters* (New York: Basic Books, 2006).

5. William H. Jeynes, "The Effects of Religious Commitment on the Academic Achievement of Black and Hispanic Children," *Urban Education* 34 (1999): 458–79; Jeynes, "Religion, Intact Families, and the Achievement Gap," *Interdisciplinary Journal of Research on Religion* 3 (2007): 1–22; Jeynes, *Religion, Education, and Academic Success* (Greenwich, CT: Information Age Press, 2003); Jeynes, "The Effects of Black and Hispanic Twelfth Graders Living in Intact Families and Being Religious on Their Academic Achievement," *Urban Education* 38 (2003): 35–57; Mark D. Regnerus,

"Shaping Schooling Success: Religious Socialization and Educational Outcomes in Urban Public Schools," *Journal for the Scientific Study of Religion* 39 (2000): 363–70; Regnerus, "Making the Grade: The Influence of Religion upon the Academic Performance of Youth in Disadvantaged Communities," Institute for Studies of Religion, Baylor University, 2008, http://www.isreligion.org/pdf/ISR_Making_Grade.pdf.

6. Decades of survey data consistently confirm that Americans are highly religious, and these levels of religious commitment have remained remarkably stable over time. Many scholars have refuted the secularization theory. For more on levels of American religious commitment, see Rodney Stark, *What Americans Really Believe: New Findings from the Baylor Surveys of Religion* (Waco, TX: Baylor University Press, 2008).

7. Bradley R. E. Wright, *Christians Are Hate-Filled Hypocrites . . . and Other Lies You've Been Told: A Sociologist Shatters Myths from the Secular and Christian Media* (Minneapolis: Bethany House, 2010).

8. Numerous publications and national surveys for more than seven decades confirm that Americans tend to be highly religious. See, for example, *American Piety in the 21st Century: New Insights to the Depth and Complexity of Religion in the US*, with Christopher Bader, Kevin Dougherty, Paul Froese, Byron Johnson, Carson Mencken, Jerry Park, and Rodney Stark, Institute for Studies of Religion, Baylor University, 2006, http://www.isreligion.org/research/surveysofreligion/americanpiety/.

9. See Matthew 26:11.

10. The opposite oversight tends to be true among many secular observers. They understand the need for a host of social supports, but they fail to consider the role of religious belief or spiritual transformation as part of an integrated strategy.

11. Rasmussen Reports, "Americans Still Regard Congress as Least Respected Profession," August 5, 2010.

12. For a review of studies focusing only on the influence of religion and faith-based institutions to prevent crime and delinquency, see B. Johnson, D. Larson, S. Jang, and S. Li, "Who Escapes the Crime of Inner Cities: Church Attendance and Religious Salience among Disadvantaged Youth," *Justice Quarterly* 17 (2000): 701–15; Johnson, Li, Larson, and M. McCullough, "Religion and Delinquency: A Systematic Review of the Literature," *Journal of Contemporary Criminal Justice* 16 (2000): 32–52; Johnson, Larson, S. Jang, and Li, "The 'Invisible Institution' and Black Youth Crime: The Church as an Agency of Local Social Control," *Journal of Youth and Adolescence* 29 (2000): 479–98; Jang and Johnson, "Neighborhood Disorder, Individual Religiosity, and Adolescent Drug Use: A Test of Multilevel Hypotheses," *Criminology* 39 (2001): 501–35; Johnson, "A Tale of Two Effects: Evidence for the Protective and Prosocial Impact of Religious Practice on Youth," in "Hardwired to Connect: Social, Moral, and Spiritual Foundations of Child Well-Being," Commission on Children At-Risk, Dartmouth College, 2002; Johnson, "Assessing the Impact of Religious Programs on Prisoners: An Eight-Year Recidivism Study," *Justice Quarterly* 21 (2004): 329–54; Johnson "Rethinking Prisoner Reentry," in "Innovations in Effective Compassion: Compendium on Research, Outcomes, and Evaluation of Faith-Based and Community Initiatives," Office of the Secretary for Planning and Evaluation, U.S. Department of Health and Human Services, 2008; Johnson, "The Role of the Faith Factor in Reducing Crime and Delinquency," in Johnson, ed., "Not by Faith or Government Alone: Rethinking the Role of Faith-Based Organizations," ISR Special Research Report, Institute for Studies of Religion, Baylor University, 2008.

13. Vincent Phillip Munoz, "Supreme Court Hostility toward Religious Expression in the Public Square," testimony before Senate Subcommittee on the Constitution, Civil Rights, and Property Rights, June 8, 2004; see also "Unlevel Playing Field: Barriers to Participation by Faith-Based and Community Organizations in Federal Social Service Programs," White House of Faith-Based and Community Initiatives, Washington, DC, August 2001.

14. Meredith I. Honig, "The New Middle Management: Intermediary Organizations in Education Policy Implementation," *Educational Evaluation and Policy Analysis* 26 (2004): 65–87.

15. Byron Johnson and Neil Websdale, "Faith and Community Technical Support: Final Report," Office on Violence Against Women, United States Department of Justice, Office of Justice Programs, Rural Domestic Violence and Child Victimization Grant Program Special Initiative: Faith-Based and Community Organization Pilot Program, 2007 (Grant Number 2006-WR-AX-K001).

16. McKinsey and Company, "Effective Capacity Building in Nonprofit Organizations," Venture Philanthropy Partners, 2001, 27–32.

17. B. Fink and A. Branch, "Promising Practices for Improving the Capacity of Faith- and Community-Based Organization," Branch Associates Inc. and Abt Associates Inc., 2005.

18. The United Way is a national network of more than thirteen hundred locally governed organizations that work to create lasting positive changes in communities.

19. For additional examples of federally funded intermediaries see the Latino Coalition for Faith and Community Initiatives (funded by the Department of Labor), Faith and Community Technical Support (funded by the Office on Violence Against Women), and the Compassion Capital Fund (http://www.acf.hhs.gov/programs/ccf).

20. Byron R. Johnson and William Wubbenhorst, "The Role of Intermediaries in Workforce Development: A Case Study," Institute for Studies of Religion, Baylor University, 2011.

Appendix B—IFI Selection Criteria

1. In order to increase the pool size, this criterion was eventually changed to eighteen to thirty months from release or mandatory supervision or parole.

2. There is now an IFI program located at a female prison in Wrightsville, Arkansas.

3. See the following publication for additional information on the selection process developed in 1997: Michael Eisenberg and Brittani Trusty, "Overview of the Inner-Change Freedom Initiative: The Faith-Based Prison Program within the Texas Department of Criminal Justice," Criminal Justice Policy Council, Austin, Texas, 2002.

4. To further increase the pool of potential offenders to choose from, counties adjacent to Harris also became eligible for consideration.

5. "Classification Plan," Institutional Division, Texas Department of Criminal Justice, 1998.

6. Conversely, violation of prison rules or other inappropriate behavior can lead to increases in one's security or custody classification.

7. Minimum-out refers to "a designator used to identify minimum custody offenders

who have not been approved to work with minimal supervision outside the security perimeter" ("Classification Plan").

8. The loss of random assignment, while a methodological setback to the evaluation team, did not cause concern for those tasked with completing the CJPC evaluation, as they routinely use matched group designs in their evaluations of TDCJ programs.

9. While comparison groups are widely used and commonly accepted in evaluation research, a program's impact on participants can only be measured accurately if one knows what would have happened to the participants had they not enrolled in the program. For a more thorough explanation, see Jean Grossman and Joseph P. Tierney, "The Fallibility of Comparison Groups," *Evaluation Review* 5 (1993): 556–71.

10. Salient factor risk score is a correctional assessment tool commonly used in most prisons to help predict the level of risk that prisoners pose to correctional authorities.

11. Initially IFI required eighteen months in the prison program, and then reduced that number to sixteen months. However, if one completes fewer months and then essentially makes up the difference in Phase III (Aftercare), the Aftercare staff can still choose to graduate the person.

12. Such verification tends to be established with either the IFI member's parole officer, mentor, or IFI staff.

13. This survey was undertaken by TDCJ and the Parole Division.

Index